SQL ESSENTIALS

Gary Randolph

Purdue University

Jeffrey Griffin

Purdue University

Franklin, Beedle & Associates, Incorporated ○ 8536 SW St. Helens Drive, Suite D

Wilsonville, Oregon 97070 ○ 503-682-7668 ○ www.fbeedle.com

To my wife, Mary Ann, and my family for encouraging and supporting me. To my students and colleagues for an environment where I am challenged to learn skills and figure out how to pass them on.

—*G.R.*

To my wife, Mary Ellen, and our daughters, Kelly, Kadra, and Kelsey, for the love and support they offered during this project. Thanks to the many colleagues and students for their valuable feedback.

—*J.G.*

President and Publisher	Jim Leisy (jimleisy@fbeedle.com)
Production	Tom Sumner
	Jeni Lee
	Dean Lake
Cover	Neo Nova
Marketing	Christine Collier
Order Processing	Krista Brown

Printed in the U.S.A.

Library of Congress Cataloging-in-Publication Data

Randolph, Gary (Gary B.)
SQL essentials / Gary Randolph, Jeffrey Griffin.
p. cm.
ISBN 1-59028-029-6
1. SQL (Computer program language) 2. Database management. I. Griffin, Jeffrey, 1960- II. Title.

QA76.73.S67R395 2004
005.75'65--dc22

2004047195

Contents

7 Data Manipulation 163

8 Data Definition Language 185

9 Database Security 218

Preface

This textbook was designed to be used as a supplemental book in a database theory course where more coverage of SQL topics is needed. It is also well suited for a course covering just SQL with a few design concepts during a typical 15-week semester, so for this situation we have included a small appendix covering the principles of database design. This book assumes that the students have no prior knowledge of SQL.

What This Book Is and Is Not

SQL Essentials provides practical information about SQL for readers of all levels—from novice to advanced. This book is not a complete reference for SQL, and it does not cover database theory.

The book shows comparisons between Oracle, Microsoft SQL Server, Microsoft Access, and MySQL. Throughout we stick as close to ANSI (American National Standards Institute)-SQL as possible and note differences among the various database management system (DBMS) products. We use database-specific code only when necessary to accomplish common tasks. As will be evident as you read the book, you can probably never write SQL that is 100-percent portable among different DBMS products. But it is our experience that the further you stray from ANSI-SQL, the more portability you lose.

What Is SQL?

Structured Query Language (SQL) is a language used to create relational databases and manipulate the data in them. It is pronounced either by its letters (Ess-Que-Ell) or as a word (See-quel), depending with whom you talk. This book provides the reader with the fundamental concepts to become competent in the basics of relational database management systems. Although SQL has been around for more than 20 years, its importance has never been greater. In recent years with the dramatic increase in the use of DBMSs in Web-based and personal computer applications, SQL is no longer just being used by database administrators and application programmers.

Database management systems such as Oracle, Sybase, Microsoft SQL Server, MySQL, IBM DB2, Microsoft Access, Lotus Approach, and many others all support SQL. Indeed, over 100 database management products, running on everything from PCs to mainframes, support SQL. Most systems also have their own visual Query by Example (QBE) interface. But while QBE varies widely among database systems, SQL is an ANSI standard and varies only slightly. Also, some kinds of queries cannot be done in QBE on many database systems.

SQL is an open standard database language, supported by ANSI. SQL has become the language of choice for designing, querying, and updating relational databases. It is the premier tool for viewing information from a relational database. It doesn't just give you a data dump, but provides sophisticated tools to summarize, consolidate, and calculate from the data. Using table relationships, data can be combined from multiple tables in a number of ways. With a properly designed database, SQL can answer practically any question about the data.

Why We Wrote This Book

This book is largely a product of our frustration in being unable to find an "academic" textbook from which to teach a course on Database Concepts that provided enough coverage of SQL and compared various SQL standards and dialects.

How To Use This Book

Conventions Used in This Book

This book uses several conventions in an effort to highlight important points.

Bold-Italic Boldface italic type is used to indicate chapter key terms and SQL key words.

Tip These sections point out important information, "tricks," handy hints, and easier or alternative methods.

Note These sections point out important information about SQL implementations.

SQL syntax is shown with vertical bars (|) separating options. So, for instance, the syntax shown as:

```
SELECT Field | Field, Field, Field | * FROM Table
```

Indicates that a single field could be used, or multiple fields separated by commas, or an asterisk. In some cases only the most common options are shown in the interest of clarity.

How This Book Is Organized

Chapter 1 **Introduction to Relational Databases and SQL**
This chapter defines the basic terms of relational databases and the various kinds of datatypes available in popular database-management systems. The chapter also discusses the history and significance of SQL, the universal language for reading and writing data from relational databases.

Chapter 2 **Basic Single-Table Select Statements**
This chapter outlines the basic foundational commands of SQL. It details all the ways to use SQL to report information from a single table other than using aggregates (found in Chapter 3), subqueries (Chapter 3), and vendor-specific extensions to SQL (Chapter 5). The chapter will explain the syntax of each SQL command and provide several examples. The chapter will also discuss how to handle values in each of our four target database systems.

Chapter 3 **Aggregate Calculations and Subqueries**
So far we have examined all the basic ways to query information from a single table, but there are many more powerful query tools in SQL. In this chapter we will examine two more. One uses aggregate functions to assemble rows of data into totals, counts, and other calculations. The other sets a query inside a query. This is called a subquery, and it provides tremendous extensions to the power of SQL.

Chapter 4 **Joining Tables**
This chapter will discuss the concepts and techniques for creating multi-table queries, including joining two subqueries in the FROM clause. SQL can pull information from any number of tables, but for two tables to be used in a query, they must share a common field. The process of creating a multi-table query involves joining tables through their primary key-foreign key relationships. Not all tables have to share the same field, but each table must share a field with at least one other table to form a "relationship chain." There are different ways to join tables, and the syntax varies among database systems.

Chapter 5 **Database-Specific Statements and Functions**
Each database vendor has tweaked and added to SQL for its particular system. Sometimes this has been to add much-needed functionality. Sometimes this has been to make its implementation of SQL more consistent with other products

offered by the vendor or simply to differentiate the database system from competitors. Wise SQL programmers know when they are using ANSI-SQL and when they are using database-specific SQL. It makes a difference should you ever have to move your back-end data to a different system. This chapter will discuss how each of our four target database systems handles concatenation and other kinds of text manipulation, date manipulation, null manipulation, and datatype conversion. The chapter will also discuss features specific to only one database system, such as Access IIF and Oracle Decode.

Chapter 6 **Advanced Queries**

This chapter discusses both advanced SQL syntax and advanced ways to use SQL. Many of these techniques are things you will seldom or rarely do, but it seems that a need is always popping up for one or another of these techniques, so this is good knowledge to have. Specifically, the chapter will focus on the UNION keyword, the INTERSECT and MINUS capabilities of Oracle, and advanced uses of subqueries.

Chapter 7 **Data Manipulation**

SQL is not just for reading information from a database. SQL can also add, edit, and delete records. In this chapter we will learn the powerful INSERT, DELETE, and UPDATE commands. These can operate with specified values or with data read from other tables. The chapter will also discuss the concept of transactions, which let you group individual commands and require they be completed or not completed as a group. The chapter will demonstrate the use of Commit and Rollback for controlling transactions and provide a brief look at procedural programming to SQL Server and Oracle to issue Commits and Rollbacks based on errors. Finally, this chapter will discuss the issues of concurrency, data locking, and the problem of deadlock.

Chapter 8 **Data Definition Language**

In this chapter we will explore the Data Definition Language (DDL) commands of SQL. We will learn how to use SQL to create and alter tables. The chapter will also discuss the related concepts of constraints, indexes, and views. With these tools, the database developer can control the data entered to the database, increase performance, simplify things for the end user and front-end developer, and guard security. We will also introduce the concepts of stored procedures and triggers and discuss their use in a database system. Finally, we will discuss using scripts to assist the database developer to port SQL code from one database installation to another.

Chapter 9 **Database Security**

This chapter will explore the principles and implementation of security in a database. Security is important to keep hackers out of your database and to protect the privacy of your customers and employees. Users should have all the privileges to the database that they need to do their jobs, and nothing beyond that. We will discuss security concepts of users, roles, privileges, and database objects. Then we will see how those concepts can be applied in each of our four target databases. This will include how to create users and roles, how to grant and revoke privileges, and how to perform necessary housekeeping chores, such as changing passwords and dropping old users. Finally, we will discuss password and role strategy.

Appendix A: **The Lyric Music Database**
Appendix B: **Datatypes**
Appendix C: **Principles of Database Design**
Appendix D: **SQL Syntax Quick Reference**
Appendix E: **SQL Reserved Words**

For the Instructor

Instructors who adopt this book are eligible to receive support materials that aid in teaching their course. A comprehensive package of supporting materials is available. The supplements for *SQL Essentials* include the following items:

- Answers to all end-of-chapter review questions
- Possible solutions to the end-of-chapter exercises
- Simple PowerPoint slides for each chapter
- A test bank that covers all of the chapters in this book. The test bank contains questions in multiple-choice and true/false formats.

For the student, a CD ROM disc is included with this book. It contains the Lyric database used throughout the book in various formats.

Acknowledgments

As another project comes to an end, it's time to reflect on what has brought this project to a successful close. Thanks to our colleagues in the Computer Technology Department at Purdue University for their support during this project. We also appreciate the valuable suggestions from the book's reviewer, Steve Conger at Seattle Central Community College; thank you for your time.

Thanks to the many fine people at Franklin, Beedle & Associates: Jim Leisy for keeping this project on track and his strong support of this project, Tom Sumner, and Dean Lake for their editing and production work, and Christine Collier and Krista Brown for all their hard work.

—Gary Randolph
Associate Professor of Computer Technology
Purdue University

—Jeffrey Griffin
Associate Professor of Computer Technology
Purdue University

1 Introduction to Relational Databases and SQL

Chapter Overview

This chapter defines the basic terms of relational databases and the various kinds of datatypes available in popular database-management systems. The chapter also discusses the history and significance of Structured Query Language (SQL), the universal language for reading and writing data from relational databases.

Chapter Objectives

In this chapter, we will:

- Study the terms and concepts of relational databases
- Study the basic concepts of datatypes
- Learn about the history and importance of SQL as a database language
- Learn how to issue SQL commands using common database engines

Database Concepts

Relational databases have been around for 30 years, but they were not the original kind of database, nor are they the newest kind of database. XML and object-oriented data structures have evolved in recent years. But relational databases are still by far the most popular kind of database available and will be for some time to come.

Before we get into the details of using ***SQL (Structured Query Language)***, it is important to understand some of the history and terminology associated with relational databases. The first computerized database-management systems were very different from the relational database systems we see today in products such as Oracle, SQL Server, and MySQL. In the 1970s, two data models were commonly used: hierarchical and network.

Hierarchical Databases

The hierarchical model dates back to the early 1960s and is the oldest of the database models. The most popular hierarchical database management system was IBM's IMS, which is still in use today. In the hierarchical model, the data is structured in what is referred to as parent-child relationships. Visualize this relationship as an upside down tree. An example is shown below.

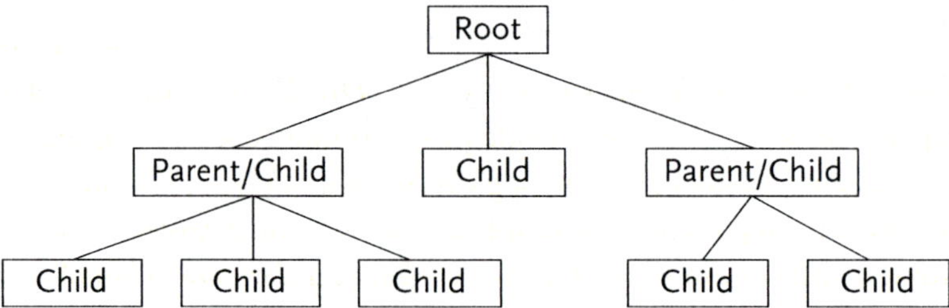

An important concept to understand about this model is that a child element can have only one parent, but a parent element can have many children. This relationship in database design terms is known as a one-to-many relationship. For example, one department can have many employees. If you are having problems visualizing this structure, use Windows Explorer to look at the file structure of your PC . You see a file structure organized in a hierarchical fashion. To access any part of this structure you must navigate your way through the tree structure until your destination is reached. The hierarchical model is not without its problems; a major drawback is data redundancy. This problem occurs because the hierarchical model handles the one-to-many relationship very well, but is unable to deal with a many-to-many relationship, causing data to be duplicated. For example, a hierarchical chart showing an employee who reports to more than one supervisor would require duplicating that employee's information.

Network Databases

The network model was developed in response to the problems encountered with the hierarchical model. Representing data using set theory instead of a hierarchy eliminates the major problem of redundancy. The network model is very similar to the hierarchical model, except in this structure a child element is allowed to have more than one parent, so the underlying concept behind the network model is that a child can have many parents and parents can have many children. This allows many-to-many relationships to be represented. For example, each student can take many courses and many students can take each course. Another difference between the two models is that the network model allows the structure to be navigated without having to start at the root element.

Both the hierarchical and the network models have limitations. One limitation is that their indexing scheme is tied to the sector scheme of the hard drive on which they reside, which creates a mess if ever moved. Furthermore, it is difficult to query data from multiple tables.

Querying a database to retrieve data involves creating a program to navigate the database structure to retrieve the requested data. These programs use procedural or proprietary languages that require a great deal of knowledge and skill. Describing these two models in any more detail is beyond the scope of this book.

Relational Database Concepts

In 1970 an IBM researcher, ***Dr. E. F. Codd***, came up with a better way—the relational data model. In this model, the database management system (***DBMS***) itself keeps track of all table relationships independent of hardware or outside programming languages. In the relational model, the user only needs to understand the logical structure of data, not how it is physically stored. In this model data is represented in simple two-dimensional ***tables*** (relations), which consist of rows (tuples) and columns (attributes). A ***relational database*** is simply a collection of tables.

As we discuss these relational concepts, we will use a portion of the Lyric Music database shown here. A full description of the Lyric Music database can be found in Appendix A.

Artists

ArtistID	ArtistName	City	Region	Country	WebAddress	EntryDate	LeadSource
1	The Neurotics	Peterson	NC	USA	www.theneurotics.com	5/14/2003	Directmail
2	Louis Holiday	Clinton	IL	USA		6/3/2003	Directmail
3	Word	Anderson	IN	USA		6/8/2003	Email
5	Sonata	Alexandria	VA	USA	www.classical.com/sonata	6/8/2003	Ad
10	The Bullets	Alverez	TX	USA		8/10/2003	Email
14	Jose MacArthur	Santa Rosa	CA	USA	www.josemacarthur.com	8/17/2003	Ad
15	Confused	Tybee Island	GA	USA		9/14/2003	Directmail
17	The Kicks	New Rochelle	NY	USA		12/3/2003	Ad
16	Today	London	ONT	Canada	www.today.com	10/7/2003	Email
18	21 West Elm	Alabama	VT	USA	www.21westelm.com	2/5/2003	Ad
11	Highlander	Columbus	OH	USA		8/10/2002	Email

Titles

TitleID	ArtistID	Title	StudioID	UPC	Genre
1	1	Meet the Neurotics	1	2727366627	alternative
3	15	Smell the Glove	2	1283772282	metal
4	10	Time Flies	3	1882344222	alternative
5	1	Neurotic Sequel	1	2828830202	alternative
6	5	Sonatas	2	3999320021	classical
7	2	Louis at the Keys	3	3838227111	jazz

Table

The basic unit of a relational database is the table. You can think of a table as rows and columns of information, as in a spreadsheet. A relational database is a collection of at least one—and generally, several—tables. Each table tracks data about something different: employees, products for sale, orders, etc. In the Lyric Music database, we have tables for artists and titles, among other tables.

The "relational" part of relational databases is how these multiple tables relate to each other, allowing a user to pull information from a combination of tables. For instance, in the Lyric Music database a relationship exists between artists (the Artists table) and titles (the CD Titles table). Using the ArtistID field in Titles, one could look up the artist's name and other information for each CD title.

Record/Row

A record holds all the information about one item or subject. Conceptually, if you collected business cards from 50 people, all 50 cards would represent a table and the information on any one business card would represent one record. In a database table, each row is a record. In the same way, the seven rows in the Titles table represent seven different CD titles available through Lyric Music. Some database experts prefer to just use the word row, since record sometimes has other connotations outside of relational databases.

Field/Column

A field holds one piece of information about an item or subject. Since a field is a column in a database table, some database experts prefer to just use the word *column*. In the Artists table there are fields for City, WebAddress, LeadSource, etc. In a relational database, the relationships are maintained by having matching fields in two tables. For instance, the Artists table and the Titles table share the ArtistID field, thus allowing the two tables to be linked and data to be pulled from the two tables together.

Datatype

Every field in a database table is assigned a ***datatype***, which describes the kind of data that can be stored in the field. You need to be familiar with datatypes because how you handle the data in SQL depends a lot upon the datatype.

Generic Datatype	Access	SQL Server	Oracle	MySQL	Description
Text or Char	Text Memo	Char VarChar NChar NVarChar	Char NChar VarChar2 Long CLob	Char VarChar TinyText Text MediumText LongText Set	Holds alphanumeric data (letters and numbers). Used for all fields that will hold at least one letter. Also, generally used for numeric fields that don't involve calculations, such as phone number and postal code. Some variations of these datatypes hold either 8-bit or 16-bit numbers, pad with spaces or not, or have other characteristics.
Numeric	Byte Integer Long Integer Single Double Decimal	TinyInt SmallInt BigInt Integer Decimal	Byte SmallInt Integer Number Float Real	TinyInt SmallInt MediumInt Int BigInt Float Real	Holds numeric data. Some variations of these datatypes hold larger or smaller numbers and either whole numbers or fractions.
Currency	Currency	SmallMoney Money	Money	Decimal	Used for money fields.
Date	DateTime	SmallDateTime DateTime	Date	Date Time DateTime	Holds date and/or time data.
Boolean or True/False	Yes/No	Bit	Bit	TinyInt Enum	Holds only two values: On/Off, True/False, Yes/No. This datatype often stands behind checkboxes. Generally, Yes/No fields are stored with a 0 for No/False and a 1 for Yes/True (-1 in the case of Microsoft Access). See the mp3 and RealAud fields of the Tracks table for an example.
Special	OLE Object Hyperlink	Image Binary	Blob Raw Long Raw	TinyBlob Blob MediumBlob LongBlob	Used to hold graphics, sounds, hyperlinks, and other special kinds of data.

Datatypes vary depending on the database system you are working in. Below are generic datatypes that are found in most database systems and the equivalent specific datatypes in each of four popular database systems. This list is not exhaustive, as datatypes vary from one version of a database system to another. For more information see Appendix B.

Primary Key

A primary key is a field (or possibly multiple fields used together) that uniquely identifies each record in the table from every other record in the table. In our Artists table it is ArtistID. Each artist has an ArtistID that is different from every other artist in the table. In our Tracks table, the primary key is composed of TitleID and TrackNum. TitleID is not unique because a given title will have multiple tracks. TrackNum is not unique because every title will have a track 1, track 2, etc. But the combination of TitleID and TrackNum is unique for every record.

Primary keys are essential in a relational database. Suppose you are working by the hour at some job. Your hours have to be recorded somehow. It may be with a pencil entry in a logbook. It may be with a mechanical punch clock. It may be with a magnetic employee card that you swipe through a reader. But no matter how the hours are recorded, getting paid the correct amount depends on the fact that your hours will not be confused with someone else's hours. Your hours must be recorded with some identifier that attributes them to you and to no one else. That is a primary key.

Foreign Key

Earlier we discussed how tables in relational databases relate to each other through matching fields. The primary key of one of the tables is almost always involved in the relationship. The field in the other table on the other end of that relationship is called the ***foreign key***. The term simply refers to the fact that this field is key to relating to a foreign (or other) table. In the Lyric Music database there is a relationship between artists and titles. The ArtistID field is the primary key in the Artists table. Therefore, the ArtistID field in the Titles table is a foreign key. It relates the Titles table to the primary key in the Artists table.

Most table relationships can be described as one-to-many. In a one-to-many relationship, a single record in the first table can be related to many records in the second table. However, each record in the second table relates to only one record in the first table. For instance, ArtistID 1, The Neurotics, has just one record in the Artists table (it can have only one record since ArtistID is the primary key in that table). But there are two records in the Titles table for ArtistID1 (the foreign key), Meet the Neurotics and Neurotic Sequel. So artists and titles have a one-to-many relationship. The table on the "one" side of the relationship is also called the "parent" table, while the table on the "many" side of the relationship is called the "child" table. A parent can have many children. In addition to one-to-many relationship, tables can have one-to-one relationships. But these are much less common.

Query/View

A *query* is used to display information from a database. Queries can be designed using either Query By Example (QBE), which is a GUI interface for query building, or Structured Query Language (SQL), which is a query language. Of the two, SQL is the more universal and more powerful tool. The end of this chapter will discuss SQL in detail.

Queries can report any columns from a table, any set of rows from a table, and even information from multiple tables using table relationships. Queries can summarize and calculate information. In addition to selecting information for display, queries can also insert, update, and delete data.

In some databases you can save queries for reuse. In high-end databases, a saved query is called a view. The creation of views or queries is a very powerful tool in Internet programming. A view can transform a very complicated multi-table query into something very simple, which in turn makes the programming code much simpler.

Stored Procedure

A stored procedure is a high-end database tool that adds programming power right into the database. Database administrators will often create stored procedures to handle inserts, edits, and updates of records. The front-end programmer, then, only needs to call the stored procedure to accomplish these functions. It makes the programming code simpler and helps protect the database from problems caused by program bugs.

Overview of SQL

What is SQL?

SQL, or Structured Query Language, is a language used to create relational databases and manipulate data in them. It is pronounced either by its letters (Ess-Que-Ell) or as a word (See-quel), depending on whom you talk to.

SQL is an open standard database language, supported by ANSI (American National Standards Institute). SQL has become the language of choice for designing, querying, and updating relational databases. Oracle, Sybase, Microsoft SQL Server, MySQL, IBM DB2, Microsoft Access, and Lotus Approach, and many others all support SQL. Indeed over 100 database management products, running on everything from PCs to mainframes, support SQL. Most systems also have their own visual Query by Example (QBE) interface. But while QBE varies widely among database systems, SQL is an ANSI standard and varies only slightly. Also, some kinds of queries cannot be done in QBE on many database systems.

For both database administrators and programmers, knowledge of SQL is essential and transportable. SQL is often used in client-server programming, web programming, and many other environments.

What Does SQL Do?

First, SQL is the premier tool for viewing information from a relational database. It doesn't just give you a data dump. SQL gives you sophisticated tools to summarize, consolidate, and calculate from the data. Using table relationships, data can be combined from multiple tables in a number of ways. With a properly designed database, SQL can answer practically any question about the data.

Second, SQL provides commands to manipulate the data in a relational database. Records can be updated and added to or deleted from a table. Here is where SQL as a database language really shines. Procedural programming languages, such as BASIC, might require several lines of code to update a record in a database table. In addition, procedural programming languages would have to use some sort of looping structure to repeat this process on every record. SQL operates on an entire set of records all at the same time. SQL is like haiku for programmers; often a dozen words or fewer can delete or change thousands of records.

Finally, SQL is a complete data definition language (*DDL*). The database itself can be created along with all tables, fields, primary keys, and relationships. Add to that the record insert commands, and you can have a complete database and all its data expressed in programming code. This greatly enhances a database programmer's ability to work remotely or to port data enhancements among various installations.

The History of SQL

OK. Not everyone likes history, so this will be short. But to understand the present impact of SQL, it helps to understand how it came about.

Remember, the idea behind relational databases was that the database management system (DBMS) would itself keep track of all table relationships independent of hardware or outside programming languages. Thus a language to query data from multiple tables could be much more high level and easy to use. Dr. E.F. Codd, the IBM researcher described such a language, calling it Structured English QUEry Language (or SEQUEL). Later the name was shortened to just Structured Query Language (SQL).

Codd's ideas quickly caught on. Several companies began working on DBMSs to implement the relational concept. The first systems to hit the market in the late 1970s were Oracle, Relational Technology's Ingres, and IBM's System/R. All of them used a version of SQL to manipulate the data and database structures. With IBM's market dominance, SQL quickly caught on and IBM's version of SQL became the de facto standard.

The computer industry saw a need to bring all the versions of SQL together into a standard that everyone could adopt. The American National Standards Institute (ANSI), one of the major standards bodies in the United States representing 1,000 companies, organizations, and government agencies, headed up this effort. The first SQL standard (called SQL89) was released in 1989. The SQL specification has since been revised twice with SQL92 (in 1992) and SQL99 (in 1999).

One advantage of SQL being an open standard is that SQL programmers can transport their skill to any DBMS. Also, it allows specific databases to be ported to other DBMSs with only minor changes to the SQL code.

How Standard Is SQL?

Most DBMSs meet SQL89 standards, and many meet SQL92 standards. So to a large extent, SQL written for one DBMS will work in another DBMS with little or no changes. However, every DBMS vendor wants to differentiate its product on the market with more powerful features. In addition, the SQL standard does not define some things that programmers often want to do with data, thus leaving a gap in functionality that each vendor must fill. Finally, for whatever reason, DBMS vendors often digress from the SQL standard in both minor and major ways.

Every implementation of SQL is at least a little different. Throughout this book, we will stick as close to ANSI-SQL as possible and note differences among the various DBMS products. Chapter 5 lists many of the SQL extensions added by various vendors. Many of these are quite useful. In addition, many of the SQL extensions provide faster performance than ANSI-SQL because they are optimized for a particular DBMS.

However, programmers should approach DBMS-specific extensions to SQL with caution. Suppose you are writing a database-driven web application. You shop around for a web-hosting company and find one you like that offers SQL Server as the back-end database. A year later that web-hosting company goes out of business and you switch to a hosting company that does not offer SQL Server but does offer MySQL for database connectivity. The more you have relied upon SQL Server–specific functions in your code, the more work you are going to have to do to get your application running on the new host.

On the other hand, suppose your company purchases Oracle to use as the back-end database for a company intranet. It is likely they will keep Oracle as their database forever, so if you can wring more performance from your code by using Oracle-specific functions, it may very well be worth it.

This book will stick as closely as possible to ANSI standard SQL, using database specific code only when necessary to accomplish common tasks. As will be evident as you read the book, one can probably never write SQL that is 100 percent portable among different DBMS products.

But be aware that the further you stray from ANSI-SQL, the more portability you lose.

Importance of SQL Today and Tomorrow

While hierarchical and network database systems still exist and while new, non-relational data concepts (such as Extensible Markup Language, XML, and object-oriented programming, OOP) have arisen, the relational database is still king, and SQL is the language of choice for relational data. In fact, SQL is being enlarged to include XML. Microsoft's SQL Server 2000 includes extensions to SQL called SQLXML to create XML views of relational data. Oracle9i Release 2 has fully incorporated the W3C (World Wide Web Consortium) XML data model into its DBMS and provides access methods for navigating and querying XML. So there is every indication that relational databases and SQL will remain important tools in the future.

Database administrators and back-end developers use SQL as a stand-alone language to create and maintain databases. SQL is also used by front-end application programmers as a set of embedded commands for database connectivity. This is standard practice in both client-server programming and many kinds of web programming, including ASP, PHP, JSP, Java, and other environments. SQL is everywhere.

SQL is an important skill even for non-programmers. Many managers face the demands of querying a corporate database to get vital information. Though many kinds of user interfaces have been developed for that task, nearly all of them use either SQL concepts or SQL syntax.

How to Practice SQL Commands with this Book

You can't learn SQL without practicing SQL. So what software tools can you use to practice the SQL commands in this book? You have several options.

Microsoft Access

Microsoft Access is part of Microsoft Office. It is a competent database system for personal use and small workgroups of as many as 25 users. Access also works adequately as a database backend for low traffic database-driven web sites.

If you have Microsoft Access 97 or higher, you can enter SQL commands directly in Access. Copy lyric2k.mdb (Access 2000 or higher) or lyric97.mdb (Access 97) from the CD-ROM. You may need to un-check the file's read-only property. Launch it in Access, and convert it if necessary. Then do the following:

Access 97

- ❍ Click on Queries
- ❍ Click on New
- ❍ Click on Design View and OK
- ❍ In the Show Tables dialog, click Close
- ❍ Click on the SQL button in the toolbar

Access 2000+

- ❍ Click on Queries
- ❍ Double-click on "Create query in Design view"
- ❍ In the Show Tables dialog, click Close
- ❍ Click on the SQL button in the toolbar

Data description commands:

- ❍ In Access you do not use SQL commands to view the tables and table information. To view the tables, go to the Tables tab of the database window. To view the information on any table, highlight that table and click on the Design button.

SQL Server

SQL Server is Microsoft's high-end client-server database. To load the Lyric Music database into SQL Server, do the following:

- ❍ Launch the SQL Server Query Analyzer and log in using the master **sa** (system administrator) login or a login provided to you by your database administrator.
- ❍ From the menu select File | Open. With the book's CD-ROM in your CD-ROM drive, browse to your CD-ROM drive and select LyricSQLServer.sql.
- ❍ If you do not have rights to create a database, delete the first four lines of the script file that is loaded.
- ❍ From the menu select Query | Execute to run the script and create the Lyric Music database.

To practice your SQL, do the following:

- ❍ Launch the SQL Server Query Analyzer and login using the master **sa** login or a login provided to you by your database administrator.
- ❍ Type the SQL command in the upper pane.
- ❍ Run the SQL by selecting Query | Execute from the menu or by clicking the green triangle icon in the toolbar. The results will appear in the lower pane.

Data description commands:

- ❍ To list all user tables in your SQL Server database type: **select name from sysobjects where type = 'U'**
- ❍ To list all fields, data types, and related information for a particular table type: **exec sp_help *tablename*;**

MySQL

MySQL is a free client-server database that can be downloaded from http://www.mysql.com. MySQL is used in many websites, especially web sites hosted on Linux servers. However, it also runs under Windows. To load the Lyric Music database, do the following:

- Go to a command prompt (Start | All Programs | Accessories Command Prompt depending on your version of Windows).
- Once at a command prompt you will probably need to change to the directory in which your MySQL programs are installed. Under Windows that is normally done with: cd\mysql\bin
- Place the book's CD-ROM in your CD-ROM drive, then type: **mysql mysql < d:LyricMySQL.sql**. Replace the **d:** with the letter of your CD-ROM drive.

To practice your SQL, do the following:

- Launch MySQLManager (You will find this in the /mysql/bin folder. It would be a good idea to create a shortcut on your desktop or in your Start menu. This program is where you can enter SQL.)
- From the drop-down menu select Tools | SQL Query
- Click the yellow cylinder database icon to view a list of your databases. Select Lyric
- Click on the Query tab and type **Use** followed by the name of your Lyric Music database (i.e., **Use Lyric**).
- Click the green triangle run icon. The display will switch to the Results tab, but not show any results.
- Click back on the Query tab and type your SQL command. Use the green triangle run icon to view your results.

Data description commands:

- To list all user tables in your Oracle database type: **show tables**
- To list all fields and data types in a particular table type: **describe *tablename***

Oracle

Oracle is the most popular client-server database system in the current market. If you have access to an Oracle database, you can load the Lyric Music database with the following steps.

- Launch Oracle SQL Plus and log in using the master system user name or a login provided to you by your database administrator.
- Place the book's CD-ROM in your CD-ROM drive.
- At the SQL prompt type @ followed by the drive letter of your CD-ROM drive followed by a colon (:) and **LyricOracle.sql** (i.e. **d: LyricOracle.sql**)

To practice your SQL, do the following:

- Launch Oracle SQL Plus and login using the master system user name or a login provided to you by your database administrator.
- At the SQL prompt type your SQL command. You may use multiple lines for the command if you wish. At the end of the last line add a semi-colon (;) to execute the command.

Data description commands:

- To list all user tables in your Oracle database type: select table_name from user_tables;
- To list all fields and data types in a particular table type: describe *tablename*;

Chapter Summary

Though other kinds of data structures exist (including XML and object-oriented databases), relational databases are the backbone of most applications today. Relational databases keep data in various tables that relate to each other through primary key–foreign key relationships. A primary key is one field or a group of fields that uniquely identifies each row (or record) in a table. Each column (field) in a database table has a datatype that defines the type of data that can be stored in it. These datatypes vary from one database system to another, but fall into the general categories of text, numeric, currency, date, Boolean, and special datatypes.

Structured Query Language (SQL) is the language of choice for querying data from a relational database. In addition to being a sophisticated query language, SQL has commands to insert, update, and delete records and even to create a relational database completely from scratch. SQL is nearly universally implemented in relational database products. In addition, SQL is an ANSI standard, which means there is a high level of consistency in SQL between various database systems. Still, there are differences in each vendor's SQL implementation. Often, the database-specific extensions for SQL add needed features and welcomed speed. However, programmers who desire maximum portability will want to stick as close to ANSI standard SQL as possible.

Key Terms

ANSI (American National Standards Institute)
Dr. E.F. Codd
datatype
DBMS (database management system)
DDL (data definition language)field
foreign key
primary key
query
record
relational database
SQL (Structured Query Language)
stored procedure
table
view

Review Questions

1. How are relational databases an improvement over the databases that came before them?
2. What does a primary key do in a relational database table?
3. What does a foreign key do in a relational database table?
4. What does the term "one-to-many" mean in a relational database?
5. Why is it a good thing that SQL is an ANSI standard?
6. What kind of datatype would best be used to hold a street address such as "203 West 11th Street"?

Exercises

Using any of the SQL tools described above, issue the following SQL commands and answer the following questions:

1. SQL Command: Select * from Studios
   List the name of the fields (columns) in the Studios table. How many records (rows) are in the Studios table?
2. SQL Command: Select * from Titles
   What field (column) does the Titles table share with the Studios table? Judging from the data, in which table is it the primary key and in which is it the foreign key? How can you tell?
3. SQL Command: Select * from Artists
   List the names of each of the fields (columns) along with what is the likely generic datatype for each.
4. Use the appropriate data description command listed in the "How to Practice SQL Commands with This Book" section to view a list of the user tables. List their names.
5. Use the appropriate data description command listed in the "How to Practice SQL Commands with This Book" section to view information in the Artists table. What is the datatype of the ArtistID column?

6. Suppose we needed to add tables and fields to the Lyric Music database to sell CDs through e-commerce. Select the appropriate generic datatypes for each of the following new fields:
   Order Number
   Order Date
   Customer Name
   Customer Ship Address
   Customer Ship City
   Customer Ship State
   Customer Ship Zip
   Qty Ordered
   Shipping Charge

Additional References

A Brief History of SQL	**http://www.vbip.com/books/1861001800/chapter_1800_02.asp**
The Rise of Relational Databases	**http://www.nap.edu/readingroom/books/far/ch6.html**
A Brief History of Databases	**http://wwwinfo.cern.ch/db/aboutdbs/history/industry.html**
MySQL	**http://www.mysql.com/**

2

Basic Single-Table Select Statements

Chapter Overview

This chapter outlines the basic foundational commands of SQL. It details all the ways to use SQL to report information from a single table other than using aggregates (found in Chapter 3), subqueries (Chapter 3), and vendor-specific extensions to SQL (Chapter 5). This chapter will explain the syntax of each SQL command and provide several examples. The chapter will also discuss how to handle values in each of our four target database systems.

Chapter Objectives

In this chapter, we will:

- Study to reporting information from one, several, or all fields from a single table for a query
- Study how to sort the results of a query
- Study creating computed columns
- Study the various options for specifying which rows to include in the query

Selecting Data from Tables

In this chapter we will explore using *Select statements* in SQL to retrieve data from a database. These are called SELECT statements because they all begin with the keyword SELECT and because they select and display data that matches criteria specified by the user. The basic structure of an SQL statement to retrieve data from a table is quite simple:

```
SELECT columns
  FROM tablename
  WHERE condition
  ORDER BY columns
```

The simple SELECT statement consists of four clauses: SELECT, FROM, WHERE, and ORDER BY. The first two clauses of the SELECT statement are required; the last two are optional. The SELECT clause is the first clause in the statement and is followed by the name or names of columns you want to retrieve. The *FROM* clause should be followed by the name of the table where the column or columns can be found. The *WHERE* clause is used to restrict the rows that are returned in the result set based on some criteria. The *ORDER BY* keyword sorts the results in a particular order.

All the examples below use the Lyric Music database. You are encouraged to use any of the SQL tools described in Chapter 1 to issue these example SQL commands and experiment with commands of your own.

Select From

SELECT FROM is the most basic kind of SQL statement. It simply selects one or more fields from a table, displaying the values from all the rows. If you want to retrieve the values of a single column, follow the *SELECT* keyword with that column name. If you want to retrieve the values of multiple columns, follow the SELECT keyword with each column name separated by commas. If you want to retrieve all columns, follow the SELECT keyword with an asterisk (*).

<table>
<tr><th colspan="2">Select From</th></tr>
<tr><th colspan="2">Access, SQL Server, Oracle, MySQL</th></tr>
<tr><td>Syntax</td><td>SELECT Field | Field, Field, Field | * FROM Table</td></tr>
<tr><td rowspan="3">Examples</td><td>1. List the ArtistName of every Artist.
<code>Select ArtistName</code>
<code>From Artists</code></td></tr>
<tr><td>2. List the ArtistName, City, and Region of every Artist.
<code>Select ArtistName, City, Region</code>
<code>From Artists</code></td></tr>
<tr><td>3. List all the information of every Artist.
<code>Select *</code>
<code>From Artists</code></td></tr>
</table>

Let's examine the results from each of the above examples. There are a total of 11 rows in the Artists table (see Appendix A) and all three of these examples will produce 11 rows of output. First let's look at Example 1, which is a single-column select. This query selects only the ArtistName column from the table Artists.

```
Select ArtistName
From Artists

ArtistName
-----------
The Neurotics
Louis Holiday
Word
Sonata
The Bullets
Jose MacArthur
Confused
The Kicks
Today
21 West Elm
Highlander
```

Now let's look at Example 2, which is an example of a multicolumn select. This query selects three columns from the Artists table at the same time by placing the column names in the SELECT clause and separating them with commas.

```
Select ArtistName, City, Region
From Artists

ArtistName          City                       Region
-----------         -----------                -------
The Neurotics       Peterson                   NC
Louis Holiday       Clinton                    IL
Word                Anderson                   IN
Sonata              Alexandria                 VA
The Bullets         Alverez                    TX
Jose MacArthur      Santa Rosa                 CA
Confused            Tybee Island               GA
The Kicks           New Rochelle               NY
Today               London                     ONT
21 West Elm         Alamaba                    VT
Highlander          Columbus                   OH
```

Now for Example 3, which is an example of selecting all columns from the Artists table using the asterisk (*) to indicate that all the columns are to be retrieved.

```
Select *
From Artists

ArtistID     ArtistName     City           Region   Country   WebAddress
--------    ----------     ----           ------   ------    ----------
     1      The Neurotics  Peterson        NC      USA
     2      Louis Holiday  Clinton         IL      USA
     3      Word           Anderson        IN      USA
     5      Sonata         Alexandria      VA      USA
    10      The Bullets    Alverez         TX      USA
    14      Jose MacArthur Santa Rosa      CA      USA
    15      Confused       Tybee Island    GA      USA
    17      The Kicks      New Rochelle    NY      USA
    16      Today          London          ONT     Canada
    18      21 West Elm    Alamaba         VT      USA
    11      Highlander     Columbus        OH      USA
```

In the example output above not all columns are illustrated. The missing columns are EntryDate and LeadSource.

Note

In Oracle, every SQL statement must end with a semi-colon (;). The semi-colon acts as a "go" command. This may be true also in some MySQL front-ends, though not in MySQL Manager. The semi-colon can safely be omitted in many database systems, including Access and SQL Server. A little experimentation will tell you what works in your system. In this book, we will not include the semi-colon on every line. If you are using Oracle you will know to include it.

Note

SQL is generally not case sensitive for field names, table names, or SQL key words, though it can be with certain drivers and front-end programs. So unless you are using one of those special cases, you may type field and table names using any combination of upper and lowercase letters. Of course, you must spell key words, field names, and table names correctly.

Tip

If any of your field names or your table names contains a space, you must include the name in square brackets [ ]. You also need to use square brackets around fields or tables that have the same name as SQL key words, such as Order or Group. The best practice in data design is never to include a space in field or table names, and never to name a table or field the same as an SQL keyword. With good design, brackets are rarely needed. MySQL does not support tables or field names with embedded spaces.

Select Distinct

Use the *DISTINCT* keyword after SELECT to eliminate duplicates from the list of values being reported.

Select Distinct	
Access, SQL Server, Oracle, MySQL	
Syntax	SELECT DISTINCT Field | Field, Field, Field | * FROM Table

Examples (All)	1. List each city where a member lives, listing each only once.
	`Select Distinct Region`
	`From Members`

	2. List each combination of college and major in the student table, listing each combination only once.
	`Select Distinct City, Region`
	`From Members`

Let's examine the results from each of the above examples. There are a total of 23 rows in the Members table (see Appendix A). First let's look at Example 1.

```
Select Distinct Region
From Members

Region
------
CA
GA
IL
IN
```

```
NC
NY
OH
ONT
TX
VA
VT

(11 row(s) affected)
```

Notice that only 11 rows are returned. This is because there are only 11 unique regions among the 23 rows. Now let's look at Example 2.

```
Select Distinct City, Region
From Members

City                      Region
-----------------         ---------
Alamaba                   VT
Alexandria                VA
Allen                     VA
Alverez                   TX
Anderson                  IN
Clinton                   IL
Columbus                  OH
Fishers                   IN
London                    ONT
Lynchberg                 VA
McKensie                  ONT
New Rochelle              NY
Peterson                  NC
Pine                      VT
Reston                    VT
Santa Rosa                CA
Savannah                  GA
Tybee Island              GA

(18 row(s) affected)
```

There are 18 unique combinations of city and region. But that is still fewer than the total number of rows in the Members table because in some cases more than one member lives in the same city. SELECT DISTINCT returns unique combinations of the fields listed; the more fields you add in your SELECT DISTINCT clause, the more rows will be returned.

Calculated Columns

Columns in a query don't have to come directly from a table. Columns can be derived from calculations or even set text. The calculations use the names of columns and constants. The ***calculated columns*** can be assigned names by following the calculation with AS and what you want to use as the column name. The calculated column name following the AS keyword is called a column ***alias***. Actually, with Oracle, SQL Server, and MySQL, AS can be omitted. However, AS is required in Microsoft Access. For compatibility it is better to always use it.

The calculated columns can calculate from text and date fields as well as numeric fields. In this chapter we will deal exclusively with numeric calculations. Each database system has unique ways of dealing with deriving columns from date and text fields. See Chapter 5 for database-specific functions.

Calculated Columns	
Access, SQL Server, Oracle, MySQL	
Syntax	SELECT Expression AS column_name FROM Table

Examples (All)	1. List the Title and length in minutes of each.
	`TrackSelect TrackTitle, LengthSeconds/60 As LengthMinutes`
	`From Tracks`

	2. If the Base field reports the weekly base salary of each salesperson, report the Firstname, Lastname, and yearly base salary of each salesperson.
	`Select Firstname, Lastname, Base * 52 as YearlyBase`
	`From Salespeople`

SQL Server
MySQL
	3a. Report all ArtistIDs and WebAddresses in the Artists table, labeling the WebAddresses column 'Web Site'.
	`Select ArtistID, WebAddress As 'Web Site'`
	`From Artists`

Oracle
SQL Server
MySQL
	3b. Report all ArtistIDs and WebAddresses in the Artists table, labeling the WebAddresses column 'Web Site'.
	`Select ArtistID, WebAddress As "Web Site"`
	`From Artists`

Access
SQL Server
	3c. Report all ArtistIDs and WebAddresses in the Artists table, labeling the WebAddresses column 'Web Site'.
	`Select ArtistID, WebAddress As "Web Site"`
	`From Artists`

Note: SQL Server

If you are running Example 1 against Oracle, MySQL, or Access, you will notice that it reports numbers to the right of the decimal place for LengthMinutes. This makes sense since values in the LengthSeconds column are not all divisible by 60. However, if you run Example 1 against SQL Server, it returns only whole numbers for LengthMinutes. This is because LengthSeconds is stored in a field with a small integer datatype and all calculations from that field maintain that datatype. If you want to see the fractional minutes, you need to use an SQL Server function to cast or convert the calculated column to a different datatype. These will be explained in Chapter 5.

The AS keyword can be used for more than just calculated columns. It can be used to give any column an alias, whether that column is calculated or not. This can be useful in labeling columns so that they are more understandable. The AS keyword is straightforward as long as you use a one-word column alias. If you want to use two separate words as a column alias, you have to enclose it in either quotes or brackets. The various versions of Example 3 in the above table illustrate this. These may change with different versions of the DBMS. Experiment with your system to see what works.

Let's examine the results from each of the above examples. There are a total of 50 rows in the Tracks table (see Appendix A), so Example 1 will produce 50 rows of output. Example 2 uses the Salespeople table, which contains a total of five rows and will produce five rows of output. Example 3 uses the Artists table, which contains a total of 11 rows and will produce 11 rows of output. First let's look at Example 1, which performs a calculation and uses the AS keyword to assign a column alias for our calculated value.

```
Select TrackTitle, LengthSeconds/60 As LengthMinutes
From Tracks

TrackTitle                  LengthMinutes
-------------------------   -----------
Bob's Dream                 3.0833333333
Third's Folly               5.8666666666
My Wizard                   3.8833333333
Fat Cheeks                  5.8666666666
Hottie                      3.8833333333
Goodtime March              4.8833333333
TV Day                      5.0833333333
. . . .                    . . .
Wooden Man                  5.2333333333
```

```
UPS      1.6166666666
Empty    3.0333333333
Burrito        1.0833333333

(50 row(s) affected)
```

Now let's look at Example 2, which is an example of a multicolumn select with a calculated column using an alias.

```
Select Firstname, Lastname, Base * 52 as YearlyBase
From Salespeople

Firstname          Lastname          YearlyBase
----------------   ----------------  ----------
Bob                Bentley            $5,200.00
Lisa               Williams          $15,600.00
Clint              Sanchez            $5,200.00
Scott              Bull
Bryce              Sanders           $10,400.00
```

Now let's look at Example 3, which uses the AS keyword to label the output column with a different name.

```
Select ArtistID, WebAddress As [Web Site]
From Artists

ArtistID    Web Site
--------    ----------------------
       1    www.theneurotics.com
       2
       3
       5    www.classical.com/sonata
      10
      14    www.josemacarthur.com
      15
      17
      16    www.today.com
      18    www.21westelm.com
      11
```

Common Math Operators for Calculating Columns	
Access, SQL Server, Oracle, MySQL	
+	Addition
–	Subtraction
*	Multiplication
/	Division
\	Integer Division (Access)
Mod (Access) % (SQL Server) Mod (x,y) (Oracle) Mod (x,y) (MySQL)	Modulo-returns as a whole number the remainder of one number divided by another. For example, 13 Mod 5 (Access syntax) returns 3 because 5 goes into 13 two times with a remainder of 3.

Basic Where Clauses

The SQL we have seen so far will retrieve all the rows from whatever table is being queried. If you want to show only some of the rows, add a WHERE clause after the FROM clause to restrict the rows in the result set. The ***WHERE*** clause can compare a field to a value, a field to another field, or any calculated ***expression*** to a field, value, or calculated expression. Fields used in the WHERE clause do not have to be in the list of fields reported in the query.

Note

The WHERE clause must come after the FROM clause. The proper order for the SQL Keywords we have discussed so far is:

```
SELECT column, column | expression As column_name
  FROM tablename
  WHERE condition
```

Text and Numeric Where Clauses	
Access, SQL Server, Oracle, MySQL	
Syntax	SELECT Field | Field, Field, Field | * FROM Table Where Field | Expression comparison Value | Field | Expression

Examples (All)	1. List the Firstname and Lastname of every Member from Canada
	`Select Firstname, Lastname`
	`From Members`
	`Where Country = 'Canada'`

	2. List the Title and LengthSeconds of every Track that runs more than 240 seconds.
	`Select TrackTitle, LengthSeconds`
	`From Tracks`
	`Where LengthSeconds > 240`

	3. If the Base field reports the weekly base salary of each salesperson, report the Firstname, Lastname, and yearly base salary of each salesperson whose yearly base is less than $10,000.
	`Select Firstname, Lastname, Base * 52 as YearlyBase`
	`From Salespeople`
	`Where Base * 52 < 10000`

	4. List all fields from the Tracks table for any Track whose TrackNum is the same as its TitleID.
	`Select *`
	`From Tracks`
	`Where TrackNum = TitleID`

Note

Text values need to be enclosed in quotes (as shown in Example 1 above). Numeric values are not enclosed. Field names are also not enclosed except two-word field names that must be enclosed in square brackets [].

In some database systems (including Oracle), SQL is case sensitive in evaluating text values. But in other database systems (including SQL Server, MySQL, and Access), it is not. In Example 1, for SQL Server you could type canada or Canada or CANADA or CaNAdA. Oracle, on the other hand, is case sensitive in evaluating text values, though not in table or field names. Run a few tests with your database system, and you will soon find out if you need to be careful of this.

In constructing WHERE clauses, use the comparison operators below:

Basic Comparison Operators for Where Clauses

Comparison	Access	SQL Server	Oracle	MySQL
Equal to	=	=	=	=
Not equal to	<>	<> or !=	<> or !=	<> or !=
Less than (Earlier than)	<	<	<	<
Greater than (Later than)	>	>	>	>
Greater than or equal to	>=	>= or !<	<=	<=
Less than or equal to	<=	<= or !>	>=	>=

Let's examine the results from each of the text and numeric WHERE clause examples. Consider the following query from Example 1:

```
Select Firstname, Lastname
From Members
Where Country = 'Canada'
```

This query produces the following result set with two rows:

```
Firstname          Lastname
---------------    ----------
Brian              Ranier
Tony               Wong
```

In this first example the equal to operator (=) is used to retrieve only the rows that have a value of Canada in the country column. Consider the following query from Example 2:

```
Select TrackTitle, LengthSeconds
From Tracks
Where LengthSeconds>240
```

This query produces the following result set with 28 rows:

```
TrackTitle                    LengthSeconds
---------------------         ----------------
Third's Folly                 352
Fat Cheeks                    352
Goodtime March                293
TV Day                        305
. . . .                      . . .
Meeting You                   321
Improv 34                     441
Hey                           288
Wooden Man                    314
```

In the second example the greater than (>) operator is used to retrieve only those rows that have a track length greater than 240 seconds. Consider the following query from Example 3:

```
Select Firstname, Lastname, Base * 52 as YearlyBase
From Salespeople
Where Base * 52 < 10000
```

This query produces the following result set with two rows:

```
Firstname         Lastname          YearlyBase
--------------    --------------    -----------
Bob               Bentley            $5,200.00
Clint             Sanchez            $5,200.00
```

The query and results should look somewhat familiar to you; this query was used as one of the calculated column examples, but it returned five rows because it did not have a WHERE clause to limit the number of rows returned. In this third example the base column is used to calculate a value, and the less than (<) operator is used to determine if the calculated value is less than the literal value of 10000.

Date values are handled differently in different database systems. In Access date values need to be enclosed in pound signs (#). In our other target database systems, date values are enclosed in quotes, like text values. The various database systems also vary in what they accept as a valid date value format. SQL Server and Access are the most lenient, accepting practically any common date format and either two- or four-digit years.

Date Where Clauses	
Access, SQL Server, Oracle, MySQL	

Syntax	`SELECT Field | Field, Field, Field | *`
	`FROM Table`
	`Where Field | Expression comparison Value | Field | Expression`

Access	List the Firstname, Lastname, and Birthday of any member born on or after June 1, 1975.
	`Select Firstname, Lastname, Birthday`
	`From members`
	`Where Birthday >= #06-01-1975#`

SQL Server	List the Firstname, Lastname, and Birthday of any member born on or after June 1, 1975.
	`Select Firstname, Lastname, Birthday`
	`From Members`
	`Where Birthday >='06-01-1975'`

Oracle	List the Firstname, Lastname, and Birthday of any member born on or after June 1, 1975.
	`Select Firstname, Lastname, Birthday`
	`From Members`
	`Where Birthday >= '1975-06-01'`

MySQL	List the Firstname, Lastname, and Birthday of any member born on or after June 1, 1975.
	`Select Firstname, Lastname, Birthday`
	`From Members`
	`Where Birthday >='01-Jun-1975'`

WHERE clauses that use calculations based on dates may need to use database-specific functions. See Chapter 5 for examples.

Let's examine the results from the WHERE clause example using dates. Consider the following query:

```
Select Firstname, Lastname, Birthday
From members
Where Birthday >= #06-01-1975#
```

This query produces the following result set with four rows:

```
Firstname        Lastname         Birthday
---------------  ---------------  ---------
Jose             MacArthur        6/24/1978
Aiden            Franks           9/2/1983
Carol            Wanner           11/8/1978
Davis            Goodman          10/27/1980
```

Boolean Where Clauses	
Access, SQL Server, Oracle, MySQL	

Syntax	`SELECT Field | Field, Field, Field | *`
	`FROM Table`
	`Where Field | Expression comparison Value | Field | Expression`

Access	List the TrackTitles and RealAud fields for all Track records that do not have a Real Audio file.
	`Select TrackTitle, RealAud`
	`From Tracks`
	`Where RealAud = False`

SQL Server
Oracle
MySQL
	List the TrackTitles and RealAud fields for all Track records that do not have a Real Audio file.
	`Select TrackTitle, RealAud`
	`From Tracks`
	`Where RealAud = 0`

Boolean, or True/False, values also are handled differently among the various database systems. For Microsoft Access the best approach is to use the keywords True or False. These keywords should not be enclosed in quotation marks. Access is the only one of our target database systems that has a datatype taking the values of True or False. The others represent Boolean values with a numeric datatype that takes the values of 1 (for True) and 0 (for False).

Tip

Actually, the Microsoft Access True and False values also have numeric equivalents. But unlike the other database systems, Access uses -1 for True and 0 for False. So if you want to write SQL code that will work with any of our target database systems, you can use Field = 0 to test for False and Field <> 0 to test for True.

Like and Wildcards

LIKE is a special comparison operator that allows you to test text fields for a group of letters anywhere in the field value. LIKE is used with ***wildcards*** that stand for either a single character or any number of characters. While LIKE operates the same in all our target database systems, the wildcards vary. The various wildcard characters are shown below.

Like Wildcards				
	Access	SQL Server	Oracle	MySQL
Single character	?	_	_	_
Any number of characters	*	%	%	%

Note

Under certain circumstances, Access will respond to the wildcards used by the other database systems. One example is when an Active Server Page web programmer sends SQL to Access through an ADO connection.

In constructing a WHERE condition using LIKE, the syntax calls for the field name followed by LIKE followed by a value surrounded by quotation marks. Inside the quotes you place constant text and wildcards as needed. The position of the wildcard(s) to the literal text in your selection criteria determines where the text is searched for in the field. Let's examine that more closely by looking at results from each of the above examples:

```
Select TrackTitle
From Tracks
Where TrackTitle Like '%time%'

TrackTitle
-----------------------------
Goodtime March
Time In - In Time
Don't Care About Time

(3 row(s) affected)
```

In the example above, the wildcards on both sides of the literal "time" locates "time" anywhere in the field. Notice that "time" is located at the end of the field, at both the end and the beginning of the field, and in the word "Goodtime."

<table>
<tr><th colspan="2">Like</th></tr>
<tr><th colspan="2">Access, SQL Server, Oracle, MySQL</th></tr>
<tr><td>Syntax</td><td>SELECT Field | Field, Field, Field | *
FROM Table
Where Field Like '%search_text%' | 'search_text%' | '%search_text'</td></tr>
<tr><td>SQL Server
Oracle
MySQL</td><td>1a. List any track titles with the word 'time' anywhere in the title.
Select TrackTitle
From Tracks
Where TrackTitle Like '%time%'</td></tr>
<tr><td>Access</td><td>1b. List any track titles with the word 'time' anywhere in the title.
Select TrackTitle
From Tracks
Where TrackTitle Like '%time%'</td></tr>
<tr><td>SQL Server
Oracle
MySQL</td><td>2a. List the names of any artist whose artist name begins with the word 'the.'
Select Artistname
From Artists
Where Artistname Like 'the%'</td></tr>
<tr><td>Access</td><td>2a. List the names of any artist whose artist name begins with the word 'the.'
Select Artistname
From Artists
Where Artistname Like 'the*'</td></tr>
<tr><td>SQL Server
Oracle
MySQL</td><td>3a. List the web site URL of any studio with a .com domain.
Select WebAddress
From Studios
Where WebAddress Like '%.com'</td></tr>
<tr><td>Access</td><td>3a. List the web site URL of any studio with a .com domain.
Select WebAddress
From Studios
Where WebAddress Like '*.com'</td></tr>
<tr><td>SQL Server
Oracle
MySQL</td><td>4a. List the Titles and UPCs of every Title that has a UPC with 8 in the second digit.
Select Title, UPC
From Titles
Where UPC Like '_8%'</td></tr>
<tr><td>Access</td><td>4b. List the Titles and UPCs of every Title that has a UPC with 8 in the second digit.
Select Title, UPC
From Titles
Where UPC Like '?8*'</td></tr>
</table>

```
Select Artistname
From Artists
Where Artistname Like 'the%'

Artistname
-----------------------------------
The Neurotics
The Bullets
The Kicks

(3 row(s) affected)
```

The example uses one wildcard on the right of the literal "the." It locates all artist names that begin with "the."

```
Select WebAddress
From Studios
Where WebAddress Like '%.com'

WebAddress
--------------------
www.maketrax.com
www.lsrecords.com

(2 row(s) affected)
```

In the above example with one wildcard on the left of the literal ".com," all web addresses that end in ".com" will be located.

```
Select Title, UPC
From Titles
Where UPC Like '_8%'

Title                          UPC
---------------------------    --------
Time Flies                     1882344222
Neurotic Sequel                2828830202
Louis at the Keys              3838227111

(3 row(s) affected)
```

This example shows the use of both the single character wildcard and the multi-character wildcard. This criterion says that anything can be the first digit, an 8 must be the second digit, and any digit can reside in any of the remaining places.

Between

BETWEEN is a useful way to select a field whose value falls between two values. This is most often used with dates. However, BETWEEN also works with numeric and text values.

Between	
Access, SQL Server, Oracle, MySQL	
Syntax	`Syntax SELECT Field | Field, Field, Field | * FROM Table Where Field | Expression Between Value | Field And Value | Field`

Examples (All with date formatting differences)	1. List the Artist name and entry date for all artists with entry dates in August 2003.
	
	`Select ArtistName, EntryDate`
	`From Artists`
	`Where EntryDate Between '01-Aug-2003'`
	`And '31-Aug-2003'`

Examples (All)	2. List the title and length of all tracks with lengths between 240 and 305 seconds.
	
	`Select TrackTitle, LengthSeconds`
	`From Tracks`
	`Where LengthSeconds Between 240 And 305`

	3. List the names of all members with last names between A and M.
	
	`Select Lastname, Firstname`
	`From Members`
	`Where Lastname Between 'A' and 'Mzzz'`

Note

BETWEEN is inclusive of the two values. In Example 2, tracks with lengths of exactly 240 or 360 would be included in the results.

Tip

When using BETWEEN with text fields it is important to understand how text values are sorted. Text is sorted alphabetically with nulls coming before any character. Tom would come before Tommy since they match on all characters up to the length of the shorter text value. That is why Example 3 above uses 'mzzz' to get all last names A-M. If it used just 'm,' then no last name beginning with the letter 'm' would appear in the list.

Is Null

The *IS NULL* keywords test for empty field values.

Is Null	
Access, SQL Server, Oracle, MySQL	

Syntax	`SELECT Field | Field, Field, Field | *`
	`FROM Table`
	`Where Field is Null`

Examples (All)	1. List the artists without a web page.
	
	`Select Artistname`
	`From Artists`
	`Where WebAddress Is Null`

Note

Numeric fields either have a numeric value or are null (empty). Similarly, date fields either hold a valid date or are null. Text fields, on the other hand, can hold a text value, a null, or an empty text value. What is an empty text value? It is what would be found with the WHERE condition: **fieldname=''**. It is not uncommon for user applications to add records with empty text values. For instance, in an online e-commerce application, a user might leave blank the textbox for Apt Num. Depending on how the application was written, it might write the record with either a null value in the Apt Num field or an empty text value. IS NULL would find only the null records and not those with an empty text value. If you don't know how the records are saved and you want to query for either nulls or empty text values, see OR below.

In

Use *IN* to test if the value of a field matches any items in a list. The list is placed inside parentheses that follow the keyword IN. The individual items in the list are separated by commas. The individual items should also be enclosed in the appropriate characters if the field is non-numeric.

In addition to using IN with a manually typed list, the list can itself be a query. For this second use, see Chapter 3's discussion of subqueries.

In	
Access, SQL Server, Oracle, MySQL	

Syntax	`SELECT Field | Field, Field, Field | *`
	`FROM Table`
	`Where Field IN (value1,value2,value3)`

Examples (All)	1. List the names, cities, and regions of all members living in Indiana (IN), Illinois (IL), or Ohio (OH).
	
	`Select Lastname, Firstname, City, Region`
	`From Members`
	`Where Region IN ('IN','IL','OH')`

	2. List all tracks for Titles 5 and 6. `Select * From Tracks Where TitleID IN(5,6)`

Access, SQL Server, and Oracle (With date formatting differences)	3. List the names and entry dates of all artists with entry dates of either 08/10/2003 or 08/17/2003.
	
	`Select * From Artists`
	`Where EntryDate IN('2003-08-10','2003-08-17')`

From the above examples, you'll see that all four of our target databases work the same with text and numeric datatypes. Access, SQL Server, and Oracle can all use IN with date datatypes, though with different formatting. MySQL cannot use IN with date datatypes.

And & Or

Multiple selection criteria can be combined in two ways. If *AND* is placed between two selection criteria, they must both be true for a record to be selected. If ***OR*** is used, then the record will be selected if either of the selection criteria is true. Any number of ANDs and ORs can be combined and grouped using parentheses.

Let's examine these examples more closely:

```
Select Firstname, Lastname, Region, SalesID
From Members
Where Region='GA'
And SalesID=2
```

<table>
<tr><th colspan="2">And & Or</th></tr>
<tr><th colspan="2">Access, SQL Server, Oracle, MySQL</th></tr>
<tr><td>Syntax</td><td><pre>Syntax SELECT Field | Field, Field, Field | *
FROM Table
Where Field | Expression comparison Value | Field
And|Or Field | Expression comparison Value | Field</pre></td></tr>
<tr><td>Examples (All)</td><td>1. List the Firstname, Lastname, Region and SalesID of every Member from Georgia (GA) who worked with salesperson 2.<pre>Select Firstname, Lastname, Region, SalesID
From Members
Where Region='GA'
And SalesID=2</pre></td></tr>
<tr><td></td><td>2. List the Firstname, Lastname, Region and SalesID of every Member who is either from Georgia (GA) or who worked with salesperson 2.<pre>Select Firstname, Lastname, Region, SalesID
From Members
Where Region ='GA'
Or SalesID = 2</pre></td></tr>
<tr><td></td><td>3. List the Firstname, Lastname, Region and SalesID of every Member who worked with salesperson 2 and is either from Georgia (GA) or Texas (TX).<pre>Select Firstname, Lastname, Region, SalesID
From Members
Where (Region='GA' Or Region='TX')
And SalesID = 2</pre></td></tr>
</table>

```
Firstname              Lastname             Region          SalesID
---------------------- -------------------- --------------  -------
Michelle               Henderson            GA              2

(1 row(s) affected)
```

Notice that by using AND we only receive one row. There is only one record in which the region is GA and the SalesID is 2.

```
Select Firstname, Lastname, Region, SalesID
From Members
Where Region='GA'
Or SalesID = 2
```

```
Firstname                Lastname                 Region          SalesID
--------------------     -------------------      --------------  -------
Roberto                  Alvarez                  IN              2
Warren                   Boyer                    TX              2
Doug                     Finney                   GA              3
Terry                    Irving                   GA              3
Michelle                 Henderson                GA              2
William                  Morrow                   NY              2
Aiden                    Franks                   TX              2
Bryce                    Sanders                  NC              2
Tony                     Wong                     ONT             2
Louis                    Holliday                 IL              2
Vic                      Cleaver                  VT              2
Davis                    Goodman                  OH              2

(12 row(s) affected)
```

Notice what happens when the AND is changed to an OR. Any record that matches either of the criteria will be included, so we have records with any region as long as the SalesID is 2, and we have records with any SalesID as long as region is GA.

Tip

Remember that the more ANDs you use, the fewer records will be returned since each record has to satisfy all the criteria to be selected. But the more ORs you use, the more records will be returned since each record has to satisfy only one of the criteria to be selected.

```
Select Firstname, Lastname, Region, SalesID
From Members
Where (Region='GA' Or Region='TX')
And SalesID=2
```

```
Firstname                Lastname                 Region          SalesID
---------------------    ---------------------    --------------   ------
Warren                   Boyer                    TX              2
Michelle                 Henderson                GA              2
Aiden                    Franks                   TX              2

(3 row(s) affected)
```

See the interaction between the AND and OR along with the parentheses. The parentheses group together the two OR conditions so that a record will be selected if SalesID is 2 and if the region is either GA or TX.

Tip

You can string together any number of ANDs or any number of ORs without using parentheses, since they are all treated the same way. But when mixing ANDs and ORs you should always use parentheses to group the criteria.

Not

Use the keyword *NOT* before any selection criterion to select records that do not meet that selection criterion. In effect, this reverses the selection criterion. The placement of the NOT can be confusing. Using parentheses around the part of the criteria that you want the NOT to apply to can help eliminate confusion. In fact, the parentheses are absolutely required in MySQL.

Not	
Access, SQL Server, Oracle, MySQL	

Syntax	`SELECT Field | Field, Field, Field | *`
	`FROM Table`
	`Where NOT (Field comparison Value | Field)`

Examples (All)	1. List all titles whose genre is not alternative.
	`Select *`
	`From Titles`
	`Where Not (Genre='alternative')`

	2. List the Artistname and Webaddress of all artists who have a non-blank Webaddress.
	`Select Artistname, Webaddress`
	`From Artists`
	`Where Not (Webaddress Is Null)`

	3. List the title and length of tracks that run 120 seconds or less.
	`Select TrackTitle, LengthSeconds`
	`From Tracks`
	`Where Not (LengthSeconds > 120)`

Let's look closely at two other examples to see the interaction of NOT, AND, and parentheses:

```
Select Firstname, Region, Gender
From Members
Where Not (Region='VA')
And Gender='F'

Firstname                Region         Gender
------------------------ -------------  ---------
Mary                     IN             F
Michelle                 GA             F
Carol                    TX             F
Bonnie                   VT             F

(4 row(s) affected)
```

In the example above, the parentheses indicate that the NOT applies only to Region='VA'. So this will select anyone who is female and not from Virginia (VA).

```
Select Firstname, Region, Gender
From Members
Where Not (Region='VA' And Gender='F')

Firstname                Region         Gender
----------------------   --------       ----------
Roberto                  IN             M
Jose                     CA             M
Mary                     IN             F
Warren                   TX             M
Doug                     GA             M
Terry                    GA             M
Michelle                 GA             F
William                  NY             M
Frank                    NY             M
Aiden                    TX             M
Bryce                    NC             M
Carol                    TX             F
Brian                    ONT            M
Marcellin                VA             M
Kerry                    VA             M
Tony                     ONT            M
Bonnie                   VT             F
Louis                    IL             M
Bobby                    VT             M
Vic                      VT             M
Roberto                  OH             M
Davis                    OH             M
```

```
(22 row(s) affected)
```

In this example, the only thing that has been changed is the position of the final parentheses. Now the NOT applies to both tests. So it will select everyone except those who are female from Virginia.

Case

SQL provides two forms of a *CASE* statement to allow you to evaluate the value in one or more fields and return a column of other values. CASE works in SQL Server, Oracle, and MySQL. It does not work in Access, though Access has some database-specific functions that provide similar functionality. See Chapter 5 for details.

<table>
<tr><th colspan="2">Simple Case</th></tr>
<tr><th colspan="2">SQL Server, Oracle, MySQL</th></tr>
<tr><td>Syntax</td><td><pre>SELECT Field, Field,
CASE Field | Expression
  WHEN value THEN result
  WHEN value THEN result
  ELSE result
END As alias
FROM Table</pre></td></tr>
<tr><td rowspan="2">Examples (SQL Server, Oracle, MySQL)</td><td>1. List the first names of every member and a column that identifies sex as either man or woman.<pre>Select Firstname,
Case Gender
  When 'F' Then 'woman'
  When 'M' Then 'man'
End As Sex
From Members</pre></td></tr>
<tr><td>2. List the name, region, and an area identifier for each artist.<pre>Select Artistname,
Region,
Case Region
  When 'NC' Then 'South'
  When 'VA' Then 'South'
  When 'IL' Then 'Midwest'
  When 'VT' Then 'New England'
  Else 'Somewhere Else'
End As Area
From Artists</pre></td></tr>
</table>

Let's review the results of the second example above. Notice how the logic plays out:

```
Select Artistname, Region,
Case Region
  When 'NC' Then 'South'
  When 'VA' Then 'South'
  When 'IL' Then 'Midwest'
  When 'VT' Then 'New England'
  Else 'Somewhere Else'
End As Area
From Artists

Artistname                              Region         Area
-------------------------------------   -------------  ------
The Neurotics                           NC             South
Louis Holiday                           IL             Midwest
Word                                    IN             Somewhere
Else
Sonata                                  VA             South
The Bullets                             TX             Somewhere
Else
Jose MacArthur                          CA             Somewhere
Else
Confused                                GA             Somewhere
Else
The Kicks                               NY             Somewhere
Else
Today                                   ONT            Somewhere
Else
21 West Elm                             VT             New England
Highlander                              OH             Somewhere
Else

(11 row(s) affected)
```

The ***searched CASE*** provides more power by adding two variations. First, there is no single field or expression that follows the CASE statement. Second, the WHEN statements are not values but independent tests.

Searched Case	
SQL Server, Oracle, MySQL	

Syntax	`SELECT Field, Field,`
	`CASE`
	`  WHEN Field | Expression comparison Value |`
	`Field | Expression THEN result`
	`  WHEN Field | Expression comparison Value |`
	`Field | Expression THEN result`
	`ELSE result`
	`END As alias`
	`FROM Table`

Examples (SQL Server, Oracle, MySQL)	1. List the first two tracks of each title, identifying short 1st tracks and long 1st tracks.
	`Select TrackNum, TrackTitle, LengthSeconds,`
	`Case`
	`  When TrackNum=1 And LengthSeconds<240`
	`    Then 'Short 1st Track'`
	`  When TrackNum=1 And LengthSeconds>480`
	`    Then 'Long 1st Track'`
	`Else 'Another Track'`
	`End as Eval`
	`From Tracks`
	`Where TrackNum<3`

Let's look at the results from Example 1 above. Each WHEN statement has two tests. If a WHEN statement evaluates to True, then the corresponding result is displayed. If two WHEN statements evaluate to True, the result from the first one that is True will be used.

```
Select TrackNum, TrackTitle, LengthSeconds,
Case
  When TrackNum=1 And LengthSeconds<240 Then 'Short 1st Track'
  When TrackNum=1 And LengthSeconds>480 Then 'Long 1st Track'
  Else 'Another Track'
End as Eval
From Tracks
Where TrackNum<3
```

```
TrackNum TrackTitle                       LengthSeconds Eval
------  -------------------------------- -----------   ----------
1        Bob's Dream                      185           Short 1st
Track
2        My Wizard                        233           Another Track
1        Fat Cheeks                       352           Another Track
1        Hottie                           233           Short 1st
Track
2        Goodtime March                   293           Another Track
2        Rocky and Natasha                283           Another Track
1        Violin Sonata No. 1 in D Major   511           Long 1st Track
2        Violin Sonata No. 2 in A Major   438           Another Track
1        Song 1                           285           Another Track
2        Song 2                           272           Another Track
1        I Don't Know                     201           Short 1st
Track
2        What's the Day                   332           Another Track

(12 row(s) affected)
```

Order By

Use ORDER BY to sort the results in a particular order. You can sort by one field or by multiple fields separated by commas. By default, the rows are sorted in ascending order (0–9, A–Z). To sort in descending order, follow the field name with DESC.

Note

The ORDER BY clause must come after the WHERE clause. The proper order for the SQL keywords we have discussed so far is:

```
SELECT column, column | expression As column_name
  FROM tablename
  WHERE condition
  ORDER BY columns
```

<table>
<tr><th colspan="2">Order By</th></tr>
<tr><th colspan="2">Access, SQL Server, Oracle, MySQL</th></tr>
<tr><td>Syntax</td><td><code>SELECT Field | Field, Field, Field | *
FROM Table
ORDER BY Field, Field | Field DESC</code></td></tr>
<tr><td rowspan="3">Examples (All)</td><td>1. List all artist names in alphabetical order.
<code>Select Artistname
From Artists
Order By Artistname</code></td></tr>
<tr><td>2. List the track titles and lengths for title 5 in order by length with the longest first.
<code>Select TrackTitle, LengthSeconds
From Tracks
Where TitleID = 5
Order By LengthSeconds DESC</code></td></tr>
<tr><td>3. List the title and genre of each title grouped by genre and sorted within genre by title.
<code>Select Title, Genre
From Titles
Order By Genre, Title</code></td></tr>
</table>

Using multiple ORDER BY fields can be confusing, so let's look at the results from Example 3 above.

```
Select Title, Genre
From Titles
Order By Genre, Title

Title                                              Genre
-------------------------------------------------- --------------
Meet the Neurotics                                 alternative
Neurotic Sequel                                    alternative
Time Flies                                         alternative
Sonatas                                            classical
Louis at the Keys                                  jazz
Smell the Glove                                    metal

(6 row(s) affected)
```

When multiple ORDER BY fields are used, the rows are ordered first by the first field listed. The second field comes into play only as a "tie breaker"; in other words, when the values for the first ORDER BY field are equal. In the results above, the primary sorting is by genre, not by title. Where there is more than one title in a genre (as in the alternative titles), the titles are ordered alphabetically.

In all the above examples and discussion, we have used field values in the ORDER BY statement. But an expression could be used to order the rows just as well.

```
Select TrackNum, TrackTitle, LengthSeconds,
Case
  When TrackNum=1 And LengthSeconds<240 Then 'Short 1st Track'
  When TrackNum=1 And LengthSeconds>480 Then 'Long 1st Track'
  Else 'Another Track'
End as Eval
From Tracks
Where TrackNum < 3
Order By Case
  When TrackNum = 1 And LengthSeconds < 240 Then 'Short 1st Track'
  When TrackNum = 1 And LengthSeconds > 480 Then 'Long 1st Track'
  Else 'Another Track'
End

TrackNum TrackTitle                       LengthSeconds Eval
-------- -------------------------------- ------------- ------------
2        My Wizard                        233           Another Track
1        Fat Cheeks                       352           Another Track
2        Goodtime March                   293           Another Track
2        Rocky and Natasha                283           Another Track
2        Violin Sonata No. 2 in A Major   438           Another Track
1        Song 1                           285           Another Track
2        Song 2                           272           Another Track
2        What's the Day                   332           Another Track
1        Violin Sonata No. 1 in D Major   511           Long 1st
Track
1        Bob's Dream                      185           Short 1st
Track
1        Hottie                           233           Short 1st
Track
1        I Don't Know                     201           Short 1st
Track

(12 row(s) affected)
```

Chapter Summary

The basic tools of SQL are SELECT, FROM, WHERE, and ORDER BY. There is much more to learn about SQL, but these are the bread and butter tools of the language. SELECT can report one, several, or all fields from a table. SELECT can also calculate a column of values "on the fly." WHERE is used to limit the rows that are reported. It has many special operators including IN, LIKE, CASE, and BETWEEN. ORDER BY is used to arrange or sort the results.

Key Terms

alias	expression	OR
AND	FROM	ORDER BY
BETWEEN	IN	SELECT
calculated column	IS NULL	searched CASE
CASE	LIKE	WHERE
DISTINCT	NOT	Wildcards

Review Questions

1. What SQL keyword is used to sort the results in a particular order?
2. Why might someone use a column alias in an SQL command?
3. What wildcard is used for multiple characters in SQL Server, Oracle, and MySQL?
4. What are the two differences between a simple CASE and a searched CASE?
5. What does the SQL keyword DISTINCT do?
6. Is SQL case sensitive with regard to table and field names?
7. Is SQL case sensitive with regard to values entered in the WHERE clause?
8. What does the SQL keyword DESC do?
9. Which would result in more rows: two WHERE criteria separated by an AND or two WHERE criteria separated by an OR?
10. What would the following WHERE clause select: NOT (Country='USA' AND Gender='F')?

Exercises

Using any SQL tool, write SQL commands to do the following:

1. Report the first name, last name, and region of all members from Virginia (VA).
2. Report the Title, StudioID, and Genre of all titles sorted by StudioID and then by Genre.
3. Report the first name, last name, home phone, and gender of all members who have a home phone in area code 822 and are female.

4. Report the first name, last name, home phone, and gender of all members who either have a home phone in area code 822 or are female.
5. Report the first name and last name of each member along with a calculated daytime phone number. The daytime phone number should be the work number. But if the work number is null, use the home phone number.
6. Report all the information on tracks that do not have an MP3.
7. Report the first name, last name, and region of all members in Virginia (VA) or Georgia (GA). Use the IN keyword to accomplish this task.
8. You can tell if an artist has its own web domain if the web address ends in .com, .org, or .net (there are others, but we'll ignore them). List the artist name and web address of any artist with a web site that does not have its own web domain.
9. Report the artist name and entry date of any artist whose entry date is not in 2003.
10. List all artist names with the letter "s" anywhere in the name.

Additional References

W3Schools.com – SQL Tutorial	**http://www.w3schools.com/sql/default.asp**
1KeyData.com – SQL Tutorial	**http://www.1keydata.com/sql/sql.html**
Web Developers Notes – MySQL Tutorial	**http://www.webdevelopersnotes.com/tutorials/sql/index.php3**

3

Aggregate Calculations and Subqueries

Chapter Overview

So far we have examined all the basic ways to query information from a single table, but there are many more powerful query tools in SQL. In this chapter we will examine two more. One uses aggregate functions to assemble rows of data into totals, counts, and other calculations. The other sets a query inside a query. This is called a subquery, and it provides tremendous extensions to the power of SQL.

Chapter Objectives

In this chapter, we will:

- Learn what aggregate functions are
- Write SQL queries to summarize data into aggregate calculations
- Learn what a subquery is and where it can be used in SQL
- Learn how to use subqueries in the WHERE clause
- Use the ANY and ALL keywords with subqueries

Aggregate Functions

We have already seen how to create calculated columns in a query. *Aggregates* are also calculations, but in a very different way. A calculated column calculates based on the values of a single row at a time. An aggregate calculation summarizes values from entire groups of rows. The word *aggregate* is one we don't often use in everyday speech, but it simply means a summary calculation, such as a total or average. The standard aggregate functions are:

Standard Aggregate Functions	
Sum	To calculate totals
Avg	To calculate averages
Count	To count the number of records
Min	To report the minimum value
Max	To report the maximum value

Some database systems add other aggregates. For instance, Access adds standard deviation, variance, first, and last. But these are rarely used. A recent newsgroup search for Access's StDev function yielded just 288 messages compared to 132,000 messages for Sum, for example. We will confine our discussion to the standard aggregate functions above. Let's see how to use them.

Basic Aggregate Functions	
Access, SQL Server, Oracle, MySQL	
Syntax	SELECT Aggregate (Field | Expression) AS ColumnName FROM Table

Examples (All)	1. Report the total time in seconds of all tracks.
	`Select Sum(lengthseconds)`
	`From Tracks`

	2. Report the number of members in the members table.
	`Select Count(*) As NumMembers`
	`From Members`

	3. Report the average length in minutes of the tracks for TitleID 1.
	`Select Avg(lengthseconds)/60`
	`From Tracks`
	`Where TitleID = 1`

	4. Report the shortest and longest track lengths in seconds.
	`Select Min(lengthseconds) As Shortest,`
	`Max(lengthseconds) As Longest`
	`From Tracks`

As you see from the above examples, the function is typed with the field or expression in parentheses. You can follow the function with the keyword AS and an alias column name after the function. In many database systems an alias is optional, but it is always good practice.

We also see that the aggregate can be used as just part of an expression (Example 2), that a WHERE clause can limit the number of rows being aggregated (Example 2), and that multiple aggregate functions can be included together (Example 3).

Sum

The *SUM* aggregate function is pretty obvious. It adds up a column. Normally you will want to sum up a numeric column as shown above in example 1. Any null values in the column of numbers are ignored, which essentially treats them as zeros.

Can it sum up anything else? It depends on the database. If you try to sum up a text column, Access, SQL Server, and Oracle will give you an error while MySQL will return a zero. If you try to sum up a column of dates, Access and MySQL will return the sum of the dates' numeric equivalents, though that probably has no relevance in the real world. Summing a date column will return an error in SQL Server and Oracle. You can sum a column of Boolean (True/False) values in Access, MySQL, and Oracle. Since true values are stored as 1 (or -1 in Access) while false values are stored as 0, summing these values will, in effect, count of the number of true values. Summing a Boolean bit value in SQL Server will yield an error.

Avg

The *AVG* aggregate function will return an average of the values. This also is generally done on numbers. The same rules apply to averaging other datatypes as with summing the datatypes discussed above. It is worth noting that AVG will not treat null values as zero. It will completely ignore nulls. For instance, consider the data below from the Salesperson table:

```
Select Base
From Salesperson

Base
--------------
100.0000
300.0000
100.0000
NULL

(4 row(s) affected)
```

Now consider an average of this data.

```
Select Avg(Base)
From Salespeople

---------------------
166.6666

(1 row(s) affected)
```

If you do the math, you will see that it is the sum of the numbers (500) divided by 3, not divided by 4. The null has been left out of the average entirely. You will get this same result with each of our four target databases. What if you want to count the null value as a zero? You can do that by applying a CASE statement as shown below. This works in SQL Server, Oracle, and MySQL. Access does not support the CASE statement. However, if you need to do this in Access, you could use the Access-specific IIF function documented in Chapter 5.

```
Select
Avg(Case
  When Base is Null Then 0
  Else Base
End)
From Salespeople

---------------------
125.0000

(1 row(s) affected)
```

Note: SQL Server

If you run Example 3 from the 'Basic Aggregate Functions' table above (Select Avg (lengthseconds)/60 from Tracks Where TitleID=1) against SQL Server, it returns a whole number. This is because LengthSeconds is stored in a field with a small integer datatype, and all calculations from that field maintain that datatype. If you want to see the fractional minutes, you need to use an SQL Server function to cast or convert the calculated column to a different datatype. This will be explained in Chapter 5. Access, MySQL, and Oracle will return numbers to the right of the decimal place, even when averaging an integer value.

Count

The *COUNT* aggregate function simply counts the resulting values or rows. Without a WHERE clause, COUNT counts all the rows in the table. If you add a WHERE clause it will count the rows that are returned. You can use COUNT on any datatype.

The COUNT aggregate function can take as an argument either a field name or an asterisk (*). Using an asterisk will simply count the rows. Counting a field will count the number of non-null values in that field. The following two SQL statements illustrate this:

```
Select Count(*) As NumArtists
From Artists

NumArtists
-------------
11


Select Count(WebAddress) As NumArtistsWithWebPage
From Artists

NumArtistsWithWebPage
-------------
6
```

Tip

If you want to count all the rows in a query and not just those with non-null values, either use COUNT(*) or count the primary key column. The primary key cannot be null.

Min and Max

The *MIN* and *MAX* aggregate functions report the minimum and maximum values. In addition to being used with numeric datatypes, they can be also used with dates to report the earliest and latest dates and with text to report the lowest and highest alphabetically.

```
Select Min(Lastname) As Lowest, Max(Lastname) as Highest
From Members

Lowest                    Highest
-----------------------   -------------
Alvarez                   Wong
```

Notice in the SQL results above that unlike the other aggregates that return summary statistics, MIN and MAX return raw field values. Alvarez and Wong come from two separate rows in the table, but they are reported together in one row because one is the minimum and one is the maximum.

```
Select Min(Birthday) As Oldest, Max(Birthday) as Youngest
From Members

Oldest                Youngest
------------------    --------
1955-11-01            1983-09-02
```

From these results we can identify the birth dates of the youngest and oldest members. We cannot identify who those people are. To do that we will need to use a subquery, as we will see later in this chapter.

Group By

In all the examples above, the columns in a query are aggregate functions. When that is the case the query will report just one row showing the sum, average, count, minimum, or maximum for the entire set of records selected for the query. If additional non-aggregate fields are included in the SELECT clause, the query will report one row for each combination of the non-aggregate fields with the sum, average, etc. for each of those combinations. In other words, the query will group the rows by the non-aggregate fields and calculate the aggregate functions for each group.

When you include non-aggregate fields with aggregates, you must include a GROUP BY clause listing the non-aggregate fields. The more fields in the GROUP BY clause, the more rows will be reported. One row will be reported for each combination of the non-aggregate fields. The GROUP BY clause must come after the WHERE clause. The proper order for all the clauses we have learned so far is:

```
SELECT column, Aggregate(column | expression) As column_name
  FROM tablename
  WHERE condition
  GROUP BY column
  ORDER BY column
```

Group By	
Access, SQL Server, Oracle, MySQL	
Syntax	SELECT Field, Aggregate(Expression) AS Column_Name FROM Table Where Field | Expression comparison Value | Field Group By Field

Examples	1. Report the total time in seconds for each title.
	`Select TitleID, Sum(lengthseconds)`
	`From Tracks`
	`Group By TitleID`

	2. Report the number of members in each state.
	`Select Region, Count(*) As NumMembers`
	`From Members`
	`Group by Region`

	3. Report the number of members by state and gender.
	`Select Region, Gender, Count(*) AS NumMembers`
	`From Members`
	`Group by Region, Gender`

	4. Report the shortest and longest track lengths in seconds for each title.
	`Select TitleID, Min(lengthseconds) As Shortest,`
	`Max(lengthseconds) As Longest`
	`From Tracks`
	`Group By TitleID`

Note

In each of the above examples that the fields listed in the GROUP BY clause are all the non-aggregate fields in the SELECT clause. It must be done this way or the SQL statement will not run. They do not have to be listed in the same order, but they all must be there.

Having and Where with Aggregates

We have already seen that aggregate functions can use WHERE clauses. *HAVING* is similar to WHERE. But while WHERE restricts the results based on individual row values, HAVING restricts the results based on aggregated values. Another way of saying this is that WHERE can eliminate records from the results before the aggregates are calculated while HAVING eliminates entire groups of records from the results based on the aggregated calculations. Because HAVING works on aggregated rows, it always uses an aggregate function as its test.

The HAVING clause must come after the GROUP BY clause and before the ORDER BY clause. The proper order for SQL clauses is:

```
SELECT column, Aggregate(column | expression) As column_name
  FROM tablename
  WHERE condition
  GROUP BY column
  HAVING condition
  ORDER BY column
```

Having	
Access, SQL Server, Oracle, MySQL	
Syntax	SELECT Field, Aggregate(Expression) AS Column_Name FROM Table Where Field | Expression comparison Value | Field Group By Field Having Aggregate(Expression) comparison Value

Examples	1. Report the total time in minutes for any title whose total length in more than 40 minutes.
	`Select TitleID, Sum(lengthseconds)/60 As TotMin`
	`From Tracks`
	`Group By TitleID`
	`Having Sum(lengthseconds)/60>40`

Let's explore the differences in how WHERE and HAVING work.

```
Select TitleID, Avg(lengthseconds) As AvgLength
From Tracks
Group by TitleID

TitleID      AvgLength
----------   ----------
1            279
3            212
```

```
4            221
5            231
6            532
7            309
```

This first SQL statement reports the average length in seconds of the titles on each track.

```
Select TitleID, Avg(lengthseconds) As AvgLength
From Tracks
Where lengthseconds>240
Group by TitleID

TitleID      AvgLength
----------   ----------
1            327
3            294
4            352
5            282
6            532
7            325
```

Now we add a WHERE clause. This eliminates all records with a length of 240 seconds (4 minutes) or less, so these shorter tracks are not even included in the calculated average. Thus the reported averages are higher. Since the numbers changed for all titles, we can assume that all of them had tracks of 240 seconds or less.

```
Select TitleID, Avg(lengthseconds) As AvgLength
From Tracks
Group by TitleID
Having Avg(lengthseconds)>240

TitleID      AvgLength
----------   ----------
1            279
6            532
7            309
```

In the last SQL statement we change the WHERE clause to a HAVING clause. We also change the test from testing for rows that are greater than 240 seconds to testing for aggregated averages greater than 240 seconds. Notice that the reported average lengths return to what they were in our first SQL statement. That is because we are no longer eliminating any records from the calculation. However, the HAVING clause eliminates some of the aggregated rows from the final results.

Note

You might be tempted to write the above SQL using the column alias in the HAVING clause as shown below:

```
Select TitleID, Avg(lengthseconds) As AvgLength
From Tracks
Group by TitleID
Having AvgLength>240
```

That will work in MySQL. But in Access, Oracle, and SQL Server the column alias from the SELECT clause has no meaning in the HAVING clause. So except in MySQL, you must repeat the aggregate function in the HAVING clause.

Subqueries in the Where Clause

Queries can be used within queries. These are called ***subqueries***, and they can be used in the WHERE clause returning a value or list of values to test against, in the SELECT clause returning a single value to use as a column, or in the FROM clause as if it were a table. We will save FROM clause subqueries for Chapter 4 and SELECT clause subqueries for Chapter 6.

A subquery is actually a query that could be run independently. It is placed inside parentheses when used inside another query. Subqueries are supported to varying degrees in different database systems. MySQL versions 4.1 and higher support subqueries in the WHERE and FROM clauses. Access 2000 and higher supports WHERE clause subqueries and FROM clause sub-queries.

<table>
<tr><th colspan="2">Where Clause Subqueries</th></tr>
<tr><th colspan="2">Access, SQL Server, Oracle, MySQL</th></tr>
<tr><td>Syntax</td><td>SELECT Field | Field, Field, Field | *
FROM Table
WHERE Field | Expression comparison
(Select Field
FROM Table)</td></tr>
<tr><td>Examples</td><td>1. List the name of the oldest member.
Select Lastname, Firstname
From Members
Where Birthday = (Select Min(Birthday)
From Members)</td></tr>
<tr><td></td><td>2. List all track titles and lengths of all tracks whose length is longer than the average of all track lengths.
Select Tracktitle, Lengthseconds
From Tracks
Where Lengthseconds >(Select Avg(Lengthseconds)
From Tracks)</td></tr>
<tr><td></td><td>3. List the names of all artists who have recorded a title.
Select Artistname
From Artists
Where ArtistID IN(Select ArtistID
From Titles)</td></tr>
</table>

Let's play with each of the above examples. Example 1 uses a subquery similar to a query we saw earlier in the chapter. It reports the minimum (or earliest) birthday from the Members table. If we ran the subquery separately we would get:

```
Select Min(Birthday)
From Members

--------------------
1955-11-01
```

This tells us the earliest birthday, but it does not tell us whose birthday it is. Further, there is no way to get that additional information from a simple query using an aggregate function. If we added first name and last name to the above query, we would also have to GROUP BY those non-aggregate fields. That would then return one row for each person rather than just a single row reporting the earliest birthday. To find the name of the oldest member we have to use a subquery. The outer query in Example 1 lists the first and last name but adds a WHERE clause to report only the member whose birthday is the date returned by the subquery. In other words, the query matches the birthdays of all members to the birthday of the oldest member and reports only the match. What if two people were born on November 1, 1955? In that case, both would be reported. But that would be okay because both would equally be oldest.

```
Select Lastname, Firstname
From Members
Where Birthday = (Select Min(Birthday)
                  From Members)

Lastname                   Firstname
-------------------------- ----------
Wong                       Tony
```

Example 2 is very similar except that it uses greater than instead of equal. The subquery calculates the average length of all tracks. The outer query reports all tracks whose length exceeds that average.

```
Select Tracktitle, Lengthseconds
From Tracks
Where Lengthseconds >(Select Avg(Lengthseconds)
                      From Tracks)

Tracktitle                                               Lengthseconds

Third's Folly                                            352
Fat Cheeks                                               352
Goodtime March                                           293
TV Day                                                   305
Call Me an Idiot                                         315
25                                                       402
Palm                                                     322
Rocky and Natasha                                        283
Violin Sonata No. 1 in D Major                           511
Violin Sonata No. 2 in A Major                           438
Violin Sonata No. 4 in E Minor                           821
Piano Sonata No. 1                                       493
Clarinet Sonata in E Flat                                399
Song 1                                                   285
Song 3                                                   299
Song 7                                                   303
```

```
What's the Day                                  332
Sirius                                          287
Hamburger Blues                                 292
Road Trip                                       314
Meeting You                                     321
Improv 34                                       441
Hey                                             288
Wooden Man                                      314
```

Example three uses the IN keyword. In Chapter 2 we saw that IN could evaluate each row against a list of possible values. In this example the subquery provides the possible values. The subquery `(Select ArtistID from Titles)` lists all the ArtistIDs in the Titles table. The outer query then reports the names of all artists in that list.

```
Select Artistname
From Artists
Where ArtistID IN(Select ArtistID
                  From Titles)

Artistname
-------------------------------------
The Neurotics
Louis Holiday
Sonata
The Bullets
Confused
```

We can easily turn this last example around to report Artists who haven't recorded a title. This is a very useful way to find unmatched rows between two tables. However, we will see another way to do this using JOIN in Chapter 4, and that way is often faster.

```
Select Artistname
From Artists
Where ArtistID NOT IN(Select ArtistID
                      From Titles)

Artistname
--------------------------
Word
Jose MacArthur
The Kicks
Today
```

```
21 West Elm
Highlander
```

All & Any

ALL and *ANY* are the WHERE clause keywords used most often with subqueries. They could be used with a simple list of values, but you would be hard pressed to think of an example when you would want to. ALL and ANY are used like IN to compare a value to a list of values in a subquery. But while IN is essentially an equal to comparison, ALL and ANY can be used with less than or greater than comparisons. If the subquery is preceded by ANY, the comparison will be true if it satisfies any value produced by the subquery. If the subquery is preceded by ALL, the comparison will be true if it satisfies all values produced by the subquery.

Note

SQL also has a keyword ***SOME***. It is functionally equivalent to ANY. Feel free to test the ANY example below using SOME.

Any & All	
Access, SQL Server, Oracle, MySQL	
Syntax	SELECT Field | Field, Field, Field | * FROM Table Where Field | Expression comparison Any|All (Select Field FROM Table)

Examples	1. List the name, region, and birthday of every member who is older than all of the members in Georgia (GA).
	`Select Lastname, Firstname, Region, Birthday`
	`From Members`
	`Where Birthday < ALL(Select Birthday`
	`                    From Members`
	`                    Where Region = 'GA')`

	2. List the name, region, and birthday of every member who is older than any of the members in Georgia (GA).
	`Select Lastname, Firstname, Region, Birthday`
	`From Members`
	`Where Birthday < ANY(Select Birthday`
	`                    From Members`
	`                    Where Region = 'GA')`

Let's begin by looking at the subquery by itself:

```
Select Birthday
From Members
Where Region = 'GA'

Birthday
----------
1963-08-04
1959-06-22
1964-03-15
```

This gives us a list of three birthdays. Now in Example 1 we want to look at all members (not just those from Georgia) and report anyone who is older than all of these three. In effect, that means anyone who is older than the oldest of these three, the person born in 1959.

```
Select Lastname, Firstname, Region, Birthday
From Members
Where Birthday < ALL(Select Birthday
                     From Members
                     Where Region='GA')

Lastname             Firstname          Region     Birthday
-------------------- ------------------ ---------- ----------
Ranier               Brian              ONT        1957-10-19
Kale                 Caroline           VA         1956-05-30
Wong                 Tony               ONT        1955-11-01
Cleaver              Vic                VT         1957-02-10
```

By definition, no member from Georgia is older than the members from Georgia, so we don't see any Georgia members on the list. We only see people born prior to June 22, 1959. Now if we change the ALL to ANY we are looking for people older than anyone on our subquery list. In effect, that means anyone who is older than the youngest of these three, the person born in 1964.

```
Select Lastname, Firstname, Region, Birthday
From Members
Where Birthday < ANY(Select Birthday
                     From Members
                     Where Region='GA')
```

```
Lastname                Firstname          Region      Birthday
__________ _________   _____ ________
Finney                  Doug               GA          1963-08-04
Irving                  Terry              GA          1959-06-22
Payne                   Frank              NY          1960-01-17
Ranier                  Brian              ONT         1957-10-19
Lambert                 Marcellin          VA          1959-11-14
Kale                    Caroline           VA          1956-05-30
Fernandez               Kerry              VA          1962-01-16
Wong                    Tony               ONT         1955-11-01
Taft                    Bonnie             VT          1960-09-21
Cleaver                 Vic                VT          1957-02-10
```

Chapter Summary

In addition to selecting data from a table, SQL can perform aggregate functions that calculate totals, averages, and other summary information. The standard aggregate functions are SUM (totals), AVG (averages), COUNT (count), MIN (minimum), and MAX (maximum). If the SELECT clause is made up entirely of aggregate functions, only one row will be returned reporting summary statistics for the entire table. If non-aggregate columns are included in the SELECT clause, and if a GROUP BY clause is included listing each non-aggregate column, then the query will report summary statistics for each combination of the non-aggregate column values. Queries with aggregates can use a WHERE clause to select the rows that will be included in the aggregated numbers. You can also use a HAVING clause, which will select aggregated values to be included in the final results.

Another powerful feature of SQL is its ability to place a query inside a query. These subqueries can be used in the WHERE clause, the SELECT clause, and the FROM clause. This chapter examined the use of subqueries in the WHERE clause. The chapter also discussed the ALL and ANY keywords that are often used with subqueries.

Key Terms

aggregate
ALL
ANY
AVG
COUNT
HAVING
MAX
MIN
SOME
subquery
SUM

Review Questions

1. What is an aggregate function used for in SQL?
2. What is the purpose of the HAVING SQL keyword?
3. What is the difference between COUNT(*) and COUNT(field)?
4. How does the AVG aggregate treat null values?
5. What is the proper order of the SQL keywords FROM, GROUP BY, HAVING, ORDER BY, SELECT, and WHERE?
6. What is a subquery?
7. Name the three SQL clauses in which a subquery can appear.
8. To what extent are subqueries supported in Access, SQL Server, Oracle, and MySQL?
9. If two queries with subqueries were identical except that one used > ANY and the other used > ALL, which one should return more rows? Why?
10. What is the difference between ANY and SOME?

Exercises

Using any SQL tool, write SQL commands to do the following. Use an alias for every aggregated and calculated column. Note that MySQL cannot be used for subqueries.

1. Report the number of tracks for each TitleID.
2. Report the TitleID and number of tracks for any TitleID with fewer than nine tracks.
3. For each kind of LeadSource, report the number of artists who came into the system through that lead source, the earliest EntryDate, and the most recent EntryDate.
4. Report the last name of the member who would be reported first in alphabetical order.
5. List the number of track titles that begin with the letter S and the average length of these tracks in seconds.
6. List the track titles of all titles in the 'alternative' genre.
7. List the length of the longest RealAud track in the "metal" genre.
8. For any region that has more than one member with an e-mail address, list the region and the number of members with an e-mail address.
9. List all genres from the Genre table that are not represented in the Titles tables.
10. List track titles and lengths of tracks with a length longer than all tracks of the "metal" genre. *Hint:* This requires a subquery within a subquery.

Additional References

W3Schools.com – SQL Functions	**http://www.w3schools.com/sql/sql_functions.asp**
MySQL Reference Manual	**http://www.mysql.com/documentation/mysql/bychapter/**

Joining Tables

Chapter Overview

This chapter will discuss the concepts and techniques for creating multi-table queries, including joining two subqueries in the FROM clause. SQL can pull information from any number of tables, but for two tables to be used in a query, they must share a common field. The process of creating a multi-table query involves joining tables through their primary key-foreign key relationships. Not all tables have to share the same field, but each table must share a field with at least one other table to form a "relationship chain." There are different ways to join tables, and the syntax varies among database systems.

Chapter Objectives

In this chapter, we will:

- Study how SQL joins tables
- Study how to join tables using an Equi Join
- Study how to join tables using an Inner Join
- Study the difference between an Inner Join and an Outer Join
- Study how to join tables using an Outer Join
- Study how to join a table to itself with a Self Join
- Study how to join to subqueries in the FROM clause

How SQL Joins Tables

Consider the two tables below. We'll step away from Lyric Music for a moment just so we can use smaller sample tables.

Employee Table			
EmpID	**FirstName**	**LastName**	**DeptID**
1	Tim	Wallace	Actg
2	Jacob	Anderson	Mktg
3	Laura	Miller	Mktg
4	Del	Ryan	Admn

Department Table	
DeptID	**DeptName**
Actg	Accounting
Admn	Administration
Fin	Finance
Mktg	Marketing

The primary key of the Employee table is EmpID. The primary key of the Department table is DeptID. The DeptID field in the Employee table is a foreign key that allows us to ***JOIN*** the two tables. The foreign key is very important, because without it SQL would not know which rows in the one table to join to which rows in the other table.

In fact, when SQL joins two tables it is a two-step process. The first step is to join every row in the first table to every row in the second table in every possible combination, as illustrated below. This is called a ***Cartesian product***, named after the French mathematician and philosopher, Rene Decartes.

Cartesian Product					
EmpID	**FirstName**	**LastName**	**DeptID**	**DeptID**	**DeptName**
1	Tim	Wallace	Actg	Actg	Accounting
2	Jacob	Anderson	Mktg	Actg	Accounting
3	Laura	Miller	Mktg	Actg	Accounting
4	Del	Ryan	Admn	Actg	Accounting
1	Tim	Wallace	Actg	Admn	Administration
2	Jacob	Anderson	Mktg	Admn	Administration
3	Laura	Miller	Mktg	Admn	Administration
4	Del	Ryan	Admn	Admn	Administration
1	Tim	Wallace	Actg	Fin	Finance
2	Jacob	Anderson	Mktg	Fin	Finance
3	Laura	Miller	Mktg	Fin	Finance
4	Del	Ryan	Admn	Fin	Finance
1	Tim	Wallace	Actg	Mktg	Marketing
2	Jacob	Anderson	Mktg	Mktg	Marketing
3	Laura	Miller	Mktg	Mktg	Marketing
4	Del	Ryan	Admn	Mktg	Marketing

Of course, with a Cartesian product, most of the joined rows do not match on the primary key-foreign key relationship. The shading above indicates the few rows that do match. The second step of SQL's joining process is to throw out the non-matching rows, yielding the joined recordset shown below.

Employee Table			
EmpID	**FirstName**	**LastName**	**DeptID**
1	Tim	Wallace	Actg
2	Jacob	Anderson	Mktg
3	Laura	Miller	Mktg
4	Del	Ryan	Admn

With this joined recordset you could report the name of each employee along with the name of the department the employee works in. With a joined recordset you can use columns from either of the joined tables in the SELECT clause, the WHERE clause, the ORDER BY clause, aggregate functions, calculated columns, and more. Joining tables is where SQL gains tremendous power in reporting virtually any kind of information.

These two steps in SQL's joining process (joining the two tables into a Cartesian product and then eliminating the non-matching rows) indicate the two tasks before the SQL programmer: Tell SQL which tables to join, and tell SQL which two fields to match. There are various options for specifying these two things, but these two things must always be done.

Equi Join

One way to write a join is to list the two tables in the FROM clause separated by commas and specify the table relationship in the WHERE clause. This is called an ***Equi Join***, and it is the original Join syntax for SQL, so most database systems support it, including all four of our target databases.

Let's look at the first example.

```
Select Title, TrackTitle
From Titles, Tracks
Where Titles.TitleID = Tracks.TitleID
And StudioID = 2

Title                           TrackTitle
--------------------------      -------------------
Smell the Glove                 Fat Cheeks
```

<table>
<tr><th colspan="2">Equi Join</th></tr>
<tr><th colspan="2">Access, SQL Server, Oracle, MySQL</th></tr>
<tr><td>Syntax</td><td><pre>SELECT Field | Field, Field, Field | *
FROM Table1, Table2
WHERE Table1.Field = Table2.Field</pre></td></tr>
<tr><td>Examples</td><td>1. List the CD title and the title of all tracks recorded in StudioID 2.<pre>Select Title, TrackTitle
From Titles, Tracks
Where Titles.TitleID=Tracks.TitleID And StudioID=2</pre></td></tr>
<tr><td></td><td>2. List the names of members from Georgia (GA) and their salespeople.<pre>Select Members.Lastname, Members.FirstName,
Salespeople.Lastname,Salespeople.Firstname
From Members, Salespeople
Where Members.SalesID= Salespeople.SalesID And
  Region='GA'</pre></td></tr>
<tr><td></td><td>3. List the names of all artists who have recorded a title and the number of titles they have.<pre>Select Artistname, Count(Titles.ArtistID)
  As NumTitles
From Artists, Titles
Where Artists.ArtistID = Titles.ArtistID
Group By Artistname</pre></td></tr>
<tr><td></td><td>4. List the names of members in The Bullets.<pre>Select Members.Lastname, Members.FirstName
From Members, XRefArtistsMembers, Artists
Where Members.MemberID = XRefArtistsMembers.MemberID
And Artists.ArtistID = XRefArtistsMembers.ArtistID
And Artistname = 'The Bullets'</pre></td></tr>
</table>

```
Smell the Glove              Rocky and Natasha
Smell the Glove              Dweeb
Smell the Glove              Funky Town
Smell the Glove              Shoes
Smell the Glove              Time In - In Time
Smell the Glove              Wooden Man
Smell the Glove              UPS
Smell the Glove              Empty
Smell the Glove              Burrito
Sonatas                      Violin Sonata No. 1 in D Major
```

```
Sonatas                      Violin Sonata No. 2 in A Major
Sonatas                      Violin Sonata No. 4 in E Minor
Sonatas                      Piano Sonata No. 1
Sonatas                      Clarinet Sonata in E Flat
```

Notice how the fields that are reported come from two different tables. This illustrates the power of joining tables. Also notice that the only rows reported are those where the primary key and foreign key match.

In the WHERE clause the primary key-foreign key relationship is expressed using the syntax Table1.Field = Table2.Field. This dot notation (table.field) is required anytime your Cartesian product contains more than one column with the same name. It specifies which table you are referring to. This is almost always needed in specifying the table relationship, since primary keys and foreign keys are generally named the same. It may also be needed in the SELECT clause as illustrated by Example 2.

```
Select Members.Lastname, Members.FirstName,
Salespeople.Lastname,Salespeople.Firstname
From Members, Salespeople
Where Members.SalesID = Salespeople.SalesID
And Region='GA'
```

Example 3 above shows that you can use aggregates and GROUP BY with a Join. In fact, once you have joined the tables, you can do practically anything with them that you can do with a single table.

Example 4 joins three tables. Here you can begin to see the limitations of the Equi Join syntax. As more tables are added, the WHERE clause gets more and more messy. If you try to combine that with a complex WHERE clause for selecting records, you can end up with something that is hard to write and hard to read. As we'll see later, other forms of the Join syntax separate the relationship specifications from the regular WHERE clause.

```
Select Members.Lastname, Members.FirstName
From Members, XRefArtistsMembers, Artists
Where Members.MemberID = XRefArtistsMembers.MemberID
And Artists.ArtistID = XRefArtistsMembers.ArtistID
And Artistname = 'The Bullets'
```

Another potential problem with the Equi Join syntax is that with all the tables listed in one place and the relationships specifications in another place, it would be easy to forget one of the relationship specifications. What would happen if you did that? You would end up with a Cartesian product of results. With 23 members, 11 artists, and 23 records in XRefArtistsMembers, that would yield a Cartesian product of 23 x 11 x 23 = 5,819 rows! If you ever return many, many more rows of results than you expected, it is probably because you left out a relationship specification. Other forms of the join syntax put the relationship specification nearer the table specification, making it less likely to forget.

Inner Join

An *INNER JOIN* produces the exact same results as an Equi Join. The only difference is in the syntax. Some SQL programmers prefer the Equi Join syntax while others prefer the Inner Join syntax. Also, not all database systems support the Inner Join syntax. Of our four target databases, Oracle prior to version 9 did not support INNER JOIN. However, Oracle 9i and all our other target databases support this syntax.

There are three differences in the syntax. First, the tables are listed with the keywords INNER JOIN between them rather than commas. Second, the relationship specification is moved out of the WHERE clause and placed in an ON clause, freeing the WHERE clause for traditional WHERE conditions. Finally, if more than two tables are joined, they are handled one join at a time with the ON specifying the relationship immediately following the Join of those two tables.

The examples below are the same examples used for Equi Join so that you can see the difference.

<table>
<tr><th colspan="2">Inner Join</th></tr>
<tr><th colspan="2">Access, SQL Server, Oracle 9i, MySQL</th></tr>
<tr><td>Syntax</td><td><pre>SELECT Field | Field, Field, Field | *
FROM Table1 INNER JOIN Table2 On Table1.Field =
Table2.Field</pre></td></tr>
<tr><td>Examples</td><td>1. List the CD title and the title of all tracks recorded in StudioID 2.<pre>Select Title, TrackTitle
From Titles Inner Join Tracks
On Titles.TitleID=Tracks.TitleID
Where StudioID=2</pre></td></tr>
<tr><td></td><td>2. List the names of members from Georgia (GA) and their salespeople.<pre>Select Members.Lastname, Members.FirstName,
Salespeople.Lastname,Salespeople.Firstname
From Members Inner Join Salespeople
On Members.SalesID= Salespeople.SalesID
Where Region='GA'</pre></td></tr>
<tr><td></td><td>3. List the names of all artists who have recorded a title and the number of titles they have.<pre>Select Artistname, Count(Titles.ArtistID) As NumTitles
From Artists Inner Join Titles
On Artists.ArtistID = Titles.ArtistID
Group By Artistname</pre></td></tr>
<tr><td>Oracle 9i, SQL Server, MySQL</td><td>4a. List the names of members in The Bullets.<pre>Select Members.Lastname, Members.FirstName
From Members Inner Join XrefArtistsMembers
On Members.MemberID = XRefArtistsMembers.MemberID
Inner Join Artists
On Artists.ArtistID = XRefArtistsMembers.ArtistID
Where Artistname = 'The Bullets'</pre></td></tr>
<tr><td>Access, Oracle 9i, SQL Server, MySQL</td><td>4b. List the names of members in The Bullets.<pre>Select Members.Lastname, Members.FirstName
From (Members Inner Join XrefArtistsMembers
On Members.MemberID = XRefArtistsMembers.MemberID)
Inner Join Artists
On Artists.ArtistID = XRefArtistsMembers.ArtistID
Where Artistname = 'The Bullets'</pre></td></tr>
</table>

Example 4 is listed with two versions of the syntax. In Access if you join more than two tables, the joins must be separated by parentheses. If you join more than three tables, you need to nest the parentheses. This can get a little confusing. Of our four target databases, these parentheses are required only by Access, though all of them support it.

Tip

Example 3 above does the same thing as Example 3 for WHERE Clause Subqueries in Chapter 3. The example in Chapter 3 used a subquery with IN. This example uses a Join. So which approach should you use? Generally, the Join is the better approach. Joins generally run faster than IN statements.

Using Table Aliases

We saw in previous chapters how to assign aliases to columns. We can also assign aliases to tables, significantly reducing typing. A ***table alias*** can also make the code shorter and thus easier to read. However, if you select a counter-intuitive alias, you can make the code more difficult to read.

To use an alias, in the FROM clause simply follow the real table name with a space and the alias you want to use. Optionally, you can place the word AS between the real table name and the alias, just as you do with column aliases. In none of our four target databases is an AS required for table aliases, so it will not be used here. In the rest of the query, you must refer to the table by its alias. This works with either Equi Joins, Inner Joins, or (as we will see) Outer Joins.

Note

If an alias is used, the table name cannot be used in the rest of the query. With some database systems, the alias is case sensitive. Why don't we discuss which ones? A complete list cannot be given. There are many front-end programs for MySQL, each with subtle differences. There are also differences between versions of the same database system. So experiment and you'll soon find out.

<table>
<tr><th colspan="2">Table Aliases</th></tr>
<tr><th colspan="2">Access, SQL Server, Oracle, MySQL</th></tr>
<tr><td>Syntax</td><td><pre>SELECT Field | Field, Field, Field | *
FROM Table1 Alias1
Inner Join Table2 Alias 2
On Alias1.Field = Alias2.Field
SELECT Field | Field, Field, Field | *
FROM Table1 Alias1, Table2 Alias2
Where Alias1.Field = Alias2.Field</pre></td></tr>
<tr><td rowspan="2">Examples</td><td>1. List the names of members from Georgia (GA) and their salespeople.<pre>Select M.Lastname, M.FirstName,
  S.Lastname,S.Firstname
From Members M, Salespeople S
Where M.SalesID= S.SalesID And Region='GA'</pre></td></tr>
<tr><td>2. List the names of members in The Bullets.<pre>Select M.Lastname, M.FirstName
From (Members M Inner Join XrefArtistsMembers X
On M.MemberID = X.MemberID)
Inner Join Artists AOn A.ArtistID = X.ArtistID
Where Artistname = 'The Bullets'</pre></td></tr>
</table>

Outer Join

When you do an INNER JOIN, SQL compares all the records of the tables being joined and essentially matches up the rows based on the shared fields. What about rows that don't match? For instance, consider the 11 rows in the Artists table compared to the six rows in the Titles table. Several artists don't have recorded titles. So if we join the Artists table and the Titles table, the unmatched rows will be thrown out.

Outer Joins are a way to make SQL show you unmatched rows. Technically, there are two kinds of Outer Joins: ***Left Joins*** and ***Right Joins***. But they are just mirror images of each other. Left Joins report all of the records of the first (left) of two tables, plus matching records in the second (right) table. Right Joins report all of the records of the second (right) of two tables plus matching records in the first (left) table.

There are three forms of the syntax. The first form is nearly identical to the syntax of Inner Joins. Both tables are listed in the FROM clause with the words LEFT JOIN or RIGHT JOIN between them. The second table name is followed with the word ON and a statement showing the shared field or fields.

The second syntax form is to list the tables in the FROM clause—separated by commas—and then include in the WHERE clause a statement showing the shared field or fields. In this second syntax form, the direction of the join is indicated by a symbol in the WHERE clause, which varies between database systems. The syntax shown is for Oracle. A plus sign (+) is placed on the side of the table that lacks information. Use `Table1.Field=Table2.Field (+)` to view all records from Table1 along with matching records from Table2. Use `Table1.Field (+)=Table2.Field` to view all records from Table2 along with matching records from Table1. This second syntax form will be documented only for Oracle. It is the required form for Oracle prior to version 9. Our other target database systems (as well as Oracle 9i) can use the first syntax form.

The third syntax form is an alternative only for SQL Server. It is the only syntax supported in some early versions of SQL Server and still works in SQL Server 2000. You will notice that it is a similar to but yet different from the older Oracle syntax. The relationship specification uses *= to indicate a LEFT JOIN and =* to indicate a RIGHT JOIN.

<table>
<tr><th colspan="2">Outer Join (first syntax form)</th></tr>
<tr><th colspan="2">Access, SQL Server, Oracle 9i, MySQL</th></tr>
<tr><td>Syntax</td><td><pre>SELECT Field | Field, Field, Field | *
FROM Table1 LEFT|RIGHT JOIN Table2
On Table1.Field = Table2.Field</pre></td></tr>
<tr><td rowspan="3">Examples</td><td>1. List the names of all artists and the titles (if any) that they have recorded.<pre>Select Artistname, Title
From Artists A Left Join Titles T
ON A.ArtistID = T.ArtistID</pre></td></tr>
<tr><td>2. List the names of all salespeople and a count of the number of members they work with.<pre>Select S.Lastname, S.FirstName, Count(M.SalesID)
  As NumMembers
From Salespeople S Left Join Members M
On S.SalesID=M.SalesID
Group By S.Lastname, S.FirstName</pre></td></tr>
<tr><td>3. List every genre from the Genre table and a count of the number of recorded tracks in that genre, if any.<pre>Select G.Genre, Count(Tracknum) As NumTracks
From Genre G Left Join Titles TI
On G.Genre = TI.Genre
Left Join Tracks TR
On TI.TitleID = TR.TitleID
Group By G.Genre</pre></td></tr>
</table>

<table>
<tr><th colspan="2">Outer Joins (second syntax form)</th></tr>
<tr><th colspan="2">Oracle (all versions)</th></tr>
<tr><td>Syntax</td><td><pre>SELECT Field | Field, Field, Field | *
FROM Table1, Table2
WHERE Table1.Field = Table2.Field (+)</pre></td></tr>
<tr><td rowspan="3">Examples</td><td>1. List the names of all artists and the titles (if any) that they have recorded.<pre>Select Artistname, Title
From Artists A, Titles T
Where A.ArtistID=T.ArtistID (+)</pre></td></tr>
<tr><td>2. List the names of all salespeople and a count of the number of members they work with.<pre>Select S.Lastname, S.FirstName, Count(M.SalesID)
As NumMembers
From Salespeople S, Members M
Where S.SalesID=M.SalesID (+)
Group By S.Lastname, S.FirstName</pre></td></tr>
<tr><td>3. List every genre from the Genre table and a count of the number of recorded tracks in that genre, if any.<pre>Select G.Genre, Count(Tracknum) As NumTracks
From Genre G, Titles TI, Tracks TR
Where G.Genre = TI.Genre (+)
And TI.TitleID = TR.TitleID (+)
Group By G.Genre</pre></td></tr>
</table>

<table>
<tr><th colspan="2">Outer Joins (third syntax form)</th></tr>
<tr><th colspan="2">SQL Server</th></tr>
<tr><td>Syntax</td><td><pre>SELECT Field | Field, Field, Field | *
FROM Table1, Table2
Where Table1.Field *= | =* Table2.Field</pre></td></tr>
<tr><td>Examples</td><td>1. List the names of all artists and the titles (if any) that they have recorded.<pre>Select Artistname, Title
From Artists A, Titles T
Where A.ArtistID*=T.ArtistID</pre></td></tr>
<tr><td></td><td>2. List the names of all salespeople and a count of the number of members they work with.<pre>Select S.Lastname, S.FirstName, Count(M.SalesID)
As NumMembers
From Salespeople S, Members M
Where S.SalesID*=M.SalesID
Group By S.Lastname, S.FirstName</pre></td></tr>
</table>

Example 3 shows a joining of three tables. When doing outer joins with more than two tables, the sequence of the joins can make significant difference. In fact, with Microsoft Access you must use parentheses to pair up the joins, and even then not all combinations will even run. SQL Server and MySQL are more flexible in this regard. When doing OUTER JOINs with more than two tables, always review your results carefully to make sure you are getting what you want to get.

Let's illustrate the difference between an INNER JOIN and an Outer Join using example one. The first SQL statement below uses a LEFT JOIN to get all the artists and their titles, if any. Notice that for the artists without titles, the title is listed as Null. The second SQL statement below changes the LEFT JOIN to an INNER JOIN. Now all the artists without titles just drop out of the results.

```
Select Artistname, Title
From Artists A Left Join Titles T
ON A.ArtistID=T.ArtistID
```

```
Artistname                        Title
--------------------------------  --------------
The Neurotics                     Meet the Neurotics
The Neurotics                     Neurotic Sequel
Louis Holiday                     Louis at the Keys
Word                              NULL
Sonata                            Sonatas
The Bullets                       Time Flies
Jose MacArthur                    NULL
Confused                          Smell the Glove
The Kicks                         NULL
Today                             NULL
21 West Elm                       NULL
Highlander                        NULL


Select Artistname, Title
From Artists A Inner Join Titles T
ON A.ArtistID=T.ArtistID

Artistname                        Title
--------------------------------  --------------
The Neurotics                     Meet the Neurotics
Confused                          Smell the Glove
The Bullets                       Time Flies
The Neurotics                     Neurotic Sequel
Sonata                            Sonatas
Louis Holiday                     Louis at the Keys
```

Note

When you use Outer Joins on more than two tables or mix Outer and Inner Joins, things can get tricky. Since Inner Joins eliminate non-matching rows and Outer Joins maintain matching rows from one table only, the order in which you join them can make a big difference. You can force the order of joins by placing them in parentheses. The innermost parentheses will be handled first. The only rule of thumb here is to think through what your joins are doing. A good technique is to build the query one join at a time and check results against what you would expect at each step.

Using an Outer Join to Duplicate NOT IN Functionality

We saw earlier in the chapter that an Inner Join could do the same thing as using IN with a subquery. An Outer Join with just a bit more work can do the same thing as using NOT IN with a subquery.

In Chapter 3 we looked at the following example, which reports artists who do not have titles:

```
Select Artistname
From Artists
Where ArtistID NOT IN(Select ArtistID
                      From Titles)
```

Let's do an Outer Join on Artists and Titles and examine the data.

```
Select A.ArtistID, Artistname, T.ArtistID
From Artists A Left Join Titles T
On A.ArtistID = T.ArtistID
```

```
ArtistID    Artistname                  ArtistID
----------- --------------------------- ------------
1           The Neurotics               1
1           The Neurotics               1
2           Louis Holiday               2
3           Word                        NULL
5           Sonata                      5
10          The Bullets                 10
14          Jose MacArthur              NULL
15          Confused                    15
17          The Kicks                   NULL
16          Today                       NULL
18          21 West Elm                 NULL
11          Highlander                  NULL
```

We're doing this just for illustration. Both the first and the third column report ArtistID. From the SQL code you can tell that the first column comes from the Artists table while the third column comes from the Titles table. The artists without matching records in the Titles table have Null for the third column. We can use that Null to find the artists without titles. In the SQL code below, we test for the matching ArtistID in the Titles table being Null.

This displays a list that is identical to the results obtained with NOT IN and a subquery. But there is a difference. If you had thousands of rows of data, the Outer Join would often, but not always, be noticeably faster depending on many factors including the number of rows in the subquery, the number of rows in the outer query, and the idiosyncrasies of each database engine. Before implementing any complex SQL statement into a production situation, it is a good idea to test it. The more often this SQL statement will be run, the more you should test.

```
Select Artistname
From Artists A Left Join Titles T
On A.ArtistID=T.ArtistID
Where T.ArtistID Is Null

Artistname
-------------------
Word
Jose MacArthur
The Kicks
Today
21 West Elm
Highlander
```

Joining Tables You Don't Select From

Suppose we want to report the names of all artists and the studios where they have recorded. The artist names are in the Artists table, and the studio names are in the Studios table. These two tables are not related to each other. Do you write the query with just these two tables and leave them unrelated? Absolutely not. To leave the tables unrelated would create a Cartesian product, which is almost never what you want. How do you write the query? You must include in the query any other tables you need to make those tables related. Referring to the relationship diagram in Appendix A, we see that in this particular case the Titles table relates to both artists and studios. By adding Titles we bring the other tables into relationship. We won't be selecting anything from the Titles table. It's only purpose is to create a relationship chain to the other tables. So we can write the query as:

```
Select Artistname, Studioname
From Artists Inner Join Titles ON Artists.ArtistID=Titles.ArtistID
Inner Join Studios On Studios.StudioID=Titles.StudioID

Artistname                    Studioname
--------------------------    ---------------------
The Neurotics                 MakeTrax
Confused                      Lone Star Recording
The Bullets                   Pacific Rim
The Neurotics                 MakeTrax
Sonata                        Lone Star Recording
Louis Holiday                 Pacific Rim
```

Outer Joins and Mixed Joins with More Than Two Tables

Earlier we saw some examples of doing Inner Joins with more than two tables. With each table joined in an INNER JOIN, you limit the resulting recordset to those records that have matching records in the other table or tables. Joining more than two tables is a little more complicated with Outer Joins or with mixed Inner and Outer Joins. Because you are including unmatched records, it makes a difference which table you join first.

Consider the following three tables:

Zip1
zip
46011
46012
46013
46015
46017
46018
46019

Zip2
zip
46011
46012
46013
46014

Zip3
zip
46013
46016

Let's write a couple of different Outer Join queries using these tables and see what we get.

```
Select zip1.zip
From zip1 Left Join zip2 On zip1.zip = zip2.zip
Left Join zip3 On zip1.zip = zip3.zip

Zip
------
46012
46011
46013
46015
46017
46018
46019
```

Since we are left joining zip1 to each of the other tables, what we end up with is zip1. But let's mix the LEFT JOIN with a RIGHT JOIN and see what happens.

```
Select zip1.zip
From zip1 Left Join zip2 On zip1.zip = zip2.zip
Right Join zip3 On zip1.zip = zip3.zip

Zip
-------
46013
Null
```

What produced this result? First the query did the LEFT JOIN, taking all the records from zip1 and matching records from zip2. This preliminary result is essentially the same a zip1. But then this result is RIGHT JOINed to zip3, taking all the records of zip3 and any matching records of zip1. The zip 46013 is in both tables. The Null represents the 46016 zip that is in zip3 and has no match in zip1.

The situation is more complicated with mixed INNER and OUTER JOINs. Let's see what the following query gives us with these same three tables:

```
Select zip1.zip
From (zip1 Inner Join zip2 On zip1.zip = zip2.zip)
Left Join zip3 On zip1.zip = zip3.zip

zip
--------
46012
46011
46013
```

You'll notice that parentheses were added to the query. This isn't required, except in Access. However, the parentheses make the query more understandable. The INNER JOIN is done first, yielding a preliminary result of just those rows common to zip1 and zip2. This would be 46011, 46012, and 46013. This is then Left Joined to zip3, resulting in all the rows from the preliminary result and any matching records from zip3.

What have we learned from these examples? The most important lesson is to be careful with using multiple OUTER JOINs or mixing INNER and OUTER JOINs. Use parentheses to make sure the joins are handled in the proper order. Also, do some reality checks on the resulting data to make sure you are getting what you want.

Joining on More Than One Column

Depending on your table structure, you may need to do a Join on more than one column. It is pretty easy. You just include an AND in your ON clause (if you use an Inner or Outer Join) or WHERE clause (if you use an Equi Join).

For example, suppose you decided to have the Lyric Music database support WAV, AIFF, and other audio file formats beside mp3 and Real Audio. That might call for splitting the mp3 and RealAud fields out of the Tracks table and putting them in a new AudioFiles table structured like this:

TitleID	TrackNum	AudioFormat
4	1	MP3
4	1	Real
4	1	WAV
4	2	AIFF
4	2	MP3
4	3	MP3
5	1	AIFF
5	2	Real

As with the Tracks table, it takes both TitleID and TrackNum to identify a particular track (since TrackNum repeats for each title). So if we were going to join these two tables we would need to join on both identifying columns.

```
Select TrackTitle From
Tracks T Inner Join AudioFiles A
On T.TitleID = A.TitleID And T.Tracknum = A.Tracknum
Where AudioFormat = 'MP3'

TrackTitle
-------------------------
Bob's Dream
Third's Folly
My Wizard
Leather
Hot Cars Cool Nights
Music in You
Don't Care About Time
Kiss
Pizza Box
Goodbye
```

```
You could write the same query with Equi Join syntax.

Select TrackTitle From
Tracks T, AudioFiles A
Where T.TitleID = A.TitleID And T.Tracknum = A.Tracknum
And AudioFormat = 'MP3'
```

Self Join

A ***Self Join*** is a table that is joined to itself. The Self Join can be either an INNER or OUTER JOIN. Self Joins can also be confusing. They are not used often, but when they are needed they are very useful.

SalesID	FirstName	LastName	Initials	Base	Supervisor
1	Bob	Bentley	bbb	$100.00	4
2	Lisa	Williams	lmw	$300.00	4
3	Clint	Sanchez	cls	$100.00	1
4	Scott	Bull	sjb		

The typical example for a Self Join is an employee table, similar to the Salespeople table in Lyric, as shown above. The Supervisor field for each row refers to the employee who is the supervisor for the employee in that row. In other words, the supervisor for Bob Bentley is SalesID 4, who is Scott Bull. The supervisor for Clint Sanchez is SalesID 1, who is Bob Bentley.

A Self Join always uses two fields in a table. One field is the foreign key to the table's primary key. Once we have that concept straight, writing the Self Join is fairly straightforward. You join the foreign key and primary key as you would with any other Inner or Outer Join. The only thing special you must do is use table aliases with the tables and with all columns. That is because once you join the table to itself, you essentially have two instances of the table, and SQL needs to know which one you are referring to with each table and column reference.

```
Select Sales.Firstname As EmpFirst, Sales.Lastname As EmpLast,
Sup.Firstname As SupFirst, Sup.Lastname As SupLast
From Salespeople Sales Inner Join Salespeople Sup On
Sales.Supervisor = Sup.SalesID
```

```
EmpFirst          EmpLast          SupFirst         SupLast
--------------    -------------    -----------      ---------
Bob               Bentley          Scott            Bull
Lisa              Williams         Scott            Bull
Clint             Sanchez          Bob              Bentley
```

Think through the example SQL above. The tricky part often is identifying the ON clause. Should it be Sales.Supervisor=Sup.SalesID or Sup.Supervisor = Sales.SalesID? You could easily think it should be the second because it associates the table alias Sup with the Supervisor ID. But that is precisely why that is the wrong answer. You want to associate the Supervisor field of the Sales version of the table with the SalesID field of the Sup version of the table, as visualized below.

Sales version

SalesID	FirstName	LastName	Initials	Base	Supervisor
1	Bob	Bentley	bbb	$100.00	4
2	Lisa	Williams	lmw	$300.00	4
3	Clint	Sanchez	cls	$100.00	1
4	Scott	Bull	sjb		

Sup version

Notice that in the above results, the sales record for Scott Bull dropped out. That is because we did an Inner Join and Scott has no supervisor. We could include him by changing the Inner Join to an Outer Join. In fact, we could list any salespeople without a supervisor with the following SQL:

```
Select Sales.Firstname As EmpFirst, Sales.Lastname As EmpLast
From Salespeople Sales Left Join Salespeople Sup On
Sales.Supervisor=Sup.SalesID Where Sales.Supervisor Is Null
```

```
EmpFirst              EmpLast
------------------    -------------
Scott                 Bull
```

<table>
<tr><th colspan="2">Self Join</th></tr>
<tr><th colspan="2">Access, SQL Server, Oracle, MySQL</th></tr>
<tr><td>Syntax</td><td><pre>SELECT Table1.Field, Table2.Field, Table1.Field
FROM Table1 Inner | Left | Right Join Table2
On Table1.Field = Table2.Field

SELECT Table1.Field, Table2.Field, Table1.Field
FROM Table1, Table2 Where Table1.Field =
Table2.Field</pre></td></tr>
<tr><td>Oracle 9i, SQL Server, MySQL, Access</td><td>1a. List the names of all salespeople who have supervisors along with the names of their supervisors.<pre>Select Sales.Firstname As EmpFirst, Sales.Lastname
As EmpLast, Sup.Firstname as SupFirst, Sup.Lastname
As SupLast
From Salespeople Sales Inner Join Salespeople Sup
On Sales.Supervisor = Sup.SalesID</pre></td></tr>
<tr><td>Oracle (all versions), SQL Server, MySQL, Access</td><td>1b. List the names of all salespeople who have supervisors along with the names of their supervisors.<pre>Select Sales.Firstname As EmpFirst, Sales.Lastname
As EmpLast, Sup.Firstname As SupFirst, Sup.Lastname
As SupLast
From Salespeople Sales, Salespeople Sup
Where Sales.Supervisor = Sup.SalesID</pre></td></tr>
</table>

Joining Two Subqueries

Suppose we wanted to produce a list of all the artists with members in Georgia. To do this we need to join the Members and Artists table. They don't join directly because there is a many-to-many relationship between these two tables. In other words, an artist can have several members, and a member can be part of more than one artist (or group). The XrefArtistsMembers table (part of which is shown below) handles this joining between these two tables as well as adding a field that indicates the responsible party.

MemberID	ArtistID	RespParty
20	2	-1
31	14	-1
3	1	-1
10	3	-1
13	3	0

So we could write SQL to list the artists with members in Georgia as shown below. We have used parentheses in the joins so it will work in Access.

```
Select Distinct Artistname
From (Artists A Inner Join XRefArtistsMembers X
On A.ArtistID = X.ArtistID)
Inner Join Members M
On M.MemberID = X.MemberID
Where M.Region='GA'

Artistname
------------
Confused
```

There are other ways to write this using a subquery. Below we have created a subquery that selects just the Georgia MemberIDs from Members. That subquery is then joined to the other two tables.

```
Select distinct Artistname
From Artists A inner join XRefArtistsMembers X
On A.ArtistID=X.ArtistID
Inner Join (Select MemberID from Members where Region='GA') M
On M.MemberID=X.MemberID

Artistname
--------------
Confused
```

This selects the same data. Why would you want to do it with a subquery? Though it won't be noticeable with this small amount of data, the subquery would be faster. Remember the Cartesian product that is built of a JOIN? In our first SQL statement with 23 members, 11 artists, and 23 records in XRefArtistsMembers, that would yield a Cartesian product of 23 x 11 x

23 = 5,819 rows! The second SQL uses the WHERE clause to reduce the number of members to just 3 rows before the Cartesian product is built. That yields a Cartesian product of 3 x 11 x 23 = 759 rows. That makes the join easier to do and, hence, faster.

Note

When using a subquery in the FROM clause, you must select every column you will need outside the subquery in the outer query's SELECT or WHERE clause. Also, the subquery must be given an alias so it can be joined to the other tables in the query.

Here is another way to do this same query:

```
Select Distinct Artistname
From Artists A Inner Join (
Select ArtistID From Members M Inner Join XRefArtistsMembers X
On M.MemberID = X.MemberID Where M.Region='GA') SC
On A.ArtistID = SC.ArtistID

Artistname
-----------
Confused
```

This may take a little analysis. The parentheses denote the subquery. This time a subquery joins two of three tables and makes the Georgia selection. The subquery has to select both ArtistIDs so that the subquery can be joined to Artists. This probably would not be faster because it is forcing a large join before applying a WHERE condition. But it is another way of doing the same thing, and with some queries, this would be faster.

These will work great in SQL Server and Oracle. Of course, no subqueries work in MySQL. In Access 97 and earlier you cannot use subqueries in the FROM clause, though you can accomplish the same thing by saving the subquery as a separate Access query and then joining to that. But since Access 2000, subqueries in the FROM clause are supported.

<table>
<tr><th colspan="2">Subqueries in FROM Clause</th></tr>
<tr><th colspan="2">SQL Server, Oracle, MySQL, Access 2000+</th></tr>
<tr><td>Syntax</td><td><pre>SELECT Field | Field, Field, Field | *
FROM Table1 Inner | Left | Right Join
(SELECT Field, Field FROM Table Where condition) Alias
On Table1.Field = Alias.Field

SELECT Field | Field, Field, Field | * FROM Table1 ,
(SELECT Field, Field FROM Table
Where condition) AliasWhere Table1.Field = Alias.Field</pre></td></tr>
<tr><td rowspan="2">SQL Server, Oracle 9i, Access 2000+</td><td>1a. List all artists with members in Georgia.<pre>Select Distinct Artistname
From Artists A Inner Join XRefArtistsMembers X
On A.ArtistID = X.ArtistID
Inner Join (Select MemberID From Members M
Where M.Region='GA') M
On M.MemberID = X.MemberID]</pre></td></tr>
<tr><td>1b. List all artists with members in Georgia.<pre>Select Distinct Artistname
From Artists A Inner Join
(Select ArtistID From Members M
Inner Join XRefArtistsMembers X
On M.MemberID = X.MemberID Where M.Region='GA') SC
On A.ArtistID = SC.ArtistID</pre></td></tr>
<tr><td rowspan="2">SQL Server, Oracle 8i and earlier</td><td>1c. List all artists with members in Georgia.<pre>Select Distinct Artistname
From Artists A, XRefArtistsMembers X,
(Select MemberID From Members M Where M.Region='GA') M
Where A.ArtistID = X.ArtistID And M.MemberID = X.MemberID</pre></td></tr>
<tr><td>1d. List all artists with members in Georgia.<pre>Select Distinct Artistname
From Artists A,
Select ArtistID From Members M, XRefArtistsMembers X
Where M.MemberID = X.MemberID And M.Region='GA') SC
Where A.ArtistID = SC.ArtistID</pre></td></tr>
</table>

Full Join

We have seen that an Outer Join can report all the records in one table plus matching records in a second table. What if you want to see all the records in both tables whether they match or not? This is what a *FULL JOIN* does. It essentially does a LEFT JOIN and a RIGHT JOIN at the same time.

Full Join	
SQL Server, Oracle	

Syntax	`SELECT Field | Field, Field, Field | *`
	`FROM Table1 FULL JOIN Table 2`
	`On Table1.Field = Table2.Field`

SQL Server, Oracle	1. List all phone numbers from either of two tables.
	`Select phone1.phone As firstphone, phone2.phone`
	`As secondphone`
	`From Phone1 Full Join Phone2`
	`On Phone1.phone=phone2.phone`

There are not many situations in which you need to do a FULL JOIN. But here is one example. Suppose a telemarketing company has two tables of phone numbers purchased from independent sources and they want to combine the lists, taking the unique phone numbers from each list. We have displayed two very small sample tables like that below.

Phone 1
Phone
1112223333
2223334444
3334445555
4445556666
5556667777
6667778888
7778889999

Phone 2
Phone
5556667777
6667778888
7778889999
8889990000
9990001111
0001112222

We can do a Full Join on these tables with the following SQL statement. The Null values in one column or the other indicate which values are missing from each table.

```
Select phone1.phone As firstphone, phone2.phone As secondphone
From Phone1 Full Join Phone2
On Phone1.phone = phone2.phone

firstphone secondphone
---------- ------------
1112223333 NULL
2223334444 NULL
```

```
3334445555 NULL
4445556666 NULL
5556667777 5556667777
6667778888 6667778888
7778889999 7778889999
NULL       0001112222
NULL       9990001111
NULL       8889990000
```

Now if we combine the Full Join with a CASE statement we can get a list of all the unique phone numbers from either table.

```
Select Case
  When phone1.phone is null Then phone2.phone
  Else phone1.phone
End As phone
From Phone1 Full Join Phone2
On Phone1.phone=phone2.phone

phone
-----------
1112223333
2223334444
3334445555
4445556666
5556667777
6667778888
7778889999
0001112222
9990001111
8889990000
```

Pretty cool, huh? Though you will rarely ever use a Full Join, it's nice to know it's there in your toolbox, at least in Oracle and SQL Server. Access and MySQL do not support Full Join.

Cross Join

A Full Join has few real world applications; a *CROSS JOIN* has fewer. A Cross Join essentially builds a Cartesian product of the rows from two tables. Because of this, it uses no ON keyword. When would you want such a thing? One example would be when you were filling a database with sample data for performance testing. If you created a table with 50 common first names and another table with 50 common last names, you could then generate a combination of 50 x 50 = 2500 records of first and last names. Of course, the Cross Join itself does not create a table, but it can be combined with the data definition and data manipulation commands we will see in later chapters. Cross Join is supported by SQL Server, Oracle, and MySQL.

Cross Join	
SQL Server, Oracle, MySQL	
Syntax	`SELECT Field | Field, Field, Field | *` `FROM Table1 CROSS JOIN Table 2`

SQL Server, Oracle, MySQL	1. List all possible combinations of salespeople and genres.
	`Select firstname, lastname, genre`
	`From salespeople cross join genre`

Chapter Summary

SQL has tremendous power to select information from multiple tables. The Equi Join and Inner Join are two different ways to report all the rows of two different tables that match on a shared field. When you do that, you can then report any column from either of the tables. An Outer Join allows you to report all the rows of one table plus the matching rows from another table. When doing an Outer Join you have to specify which table to pull all the rows from. The keywords LEFT JOIN and RIGHT JOIN accomplish this by pointing to the table from which you want to pull all the rows. A Full Join reports all the rows from both tables. A Cross Join builds a Cartesian product of all rows from two tables.

You can join any number of tables with multiple joins. You can even join tables to subqueries in Oracle and SQL Server. If doing multiple Outer Joins or mixing Inner and Outer Joins, you need to carefully watch the order in which you join the tables. You can specify the order by placing joins in parentheses.

Key Terms

Cartesian product
Cross Join
Equi Join
Full Join
Inner Join
Join
Left Join
Outer Join
Right Join
Self Join
table alias

Review Questions

1. What is a Cartesian product? How is it used in the SQL Join process?
2. What do you get if you do an Equi Join and leave out the WHERE clause that specifies the table relationship?
3. When combining Outer Joins and Inner Joins, what can you do to specify the joining order?
4. Which syntax form do you prefer: Equi Join or Inner Join? Why?
5. Why are table aliases helpful in doing Joins?
6. What is the difference between a Left Join and a Right Join?
7. Why does order of joining tables matter with Outer Joins and not Inner Joins?
8. Which of our target database systems supports joining to a subquery?
9. What is a Full Join?
10. Why must table and column aliases always be used in Self Joins?

Exercises

Using any SQL tool, write SQL commands to do the following:

1. List each title from the Title table along with the name of the studio where it was recorded.
2. List each title from the Title table along with the name of the studio where it was recorded, the name of the artist, and the number of tracks on the title.
3. List each genre from the genre table and the total length in minutes of all tracks recorded for that genre if any.
4. List the names of responsible parties along with the artist name of the artist they are responsible for.
5. Report the names of all artists that came from e-mail that have not recorded a title. Use NOT IN to create this query.
6. Report the names of all artists that came from e-mail that have not recorded a title. Use a Join to create this query.
7. Report the name of the title and number of tracks for any title with fewer than nine tracks.
8. List each artist name and a count of the number of members assigned to that artist.
9. List any salesperson whose supervisor is supervised by no one.
10. Each member is given his or her salesperson as a primary contact name and also the name of that salesperson's supervisor as a secondary contact name. Produce a list of member names and the primary and secondary contacts for each.

Additional References

HelpFixMyPC.Com – Joins Tutorial	**http://www.helpfixmypc.com/sql/join.htm**
A Gentle Introduction to SQL	**http://sqlzoo.net/**
Interactive SQL Tutorial - Performing a join	**http://www.xlinesoft.com /interactive_sql_tutorial /Performing_a_join.htm**

5 Database-Specific Statements and Functions

Chapter Overview

Each database vendor has tweaked and added to SQL for its particular system. Sometimes this has been to add much-needed functionality. Sometimes this has been to make its implementation of SQL more consistent with other products offered by the vendor or simply to differentiate the database system from competitors. Wise SQL programmers know when they are using ANSI-SQL and when they are using database-specific SQL. It makes a difference should you ever have to move your back-end data to a different system. This chapter will discuss how each of our four target database systems handles concatenation and other kinds of text manipulation, date manipulation, null manipulation, and datatype conversion. The chapter will also discuss features specific to only one database system, such as Access IIF and Oracle Decode.

Chapter Objectives

In this chapter, we will:

- Concatenate text fields
- Perform different kinds of text manipulation
- Perform date manipulation
- Study how to test for and manipulate null values
- Convert data from one datatype to another
- Write SQL with Access using IIF and Choose functions
- Write Oracle SQL with Decode

Microsoft Access Statements and Functions

Microsoft has tweaked SQL for Access to make it more like Visual Basic. If you are familiar with Visual Basic, Visual Basic for Applications, or VBScript, you should feel right at home with the functions described below.

Concatenation

Concatenation is the combination of two or more text values into one text value. The Access concatenation operator is the ampersand (&). You can concatenate multiple fields or fields with constant text. A common task is to concatenate a space between two other fields. You can make a space by placing a space between two quotes (' ').

Concatenation	
	Access
Syntax	Field & Field | 'Text' & Field

Examples	1. List the full name of each member.
	`Select Firstname & ' ' & Lastname As Fullname`
	`From Members`

	2. Report the City, State, and Zip of each member, formatted as City, State Zip.
	`Select City & ', ' & Region & ' ' & Postalcode As MailAddr`
	`From Members`

	3. Report each lead source preceded by the text, 'source: ' along with a count of the number of artists leads from that source.
	`Select 'source: ' & Leadsource As Source, Count(*) As NumLead`
	`From Artists`
	`Group By 'source: ' & Leadsource`

Text and Data Formatting Functions

Access has several functions for manipulating text fields and for formatting fields of other datatypes. The table below shows the major ones.

<table>
<tr><th colspan="2">Text Functions</th></tr>
<tr><th colspan="2">Access</th></tr>
<tr><td>Len(expression)
Left(expression, length)</td><td>Returns the length in characters of the text
Returns text containing the specified number of characters from the left side of a text value. If Length is greater than the length of the text value, the entire text value is returned.</td></tr>
<tr><td>Right(expression, length)</td><td>Returns text containing the specified number of characters from the right side of a text value. If Length is greater than the length of the text value, the entire text value is returned.</td></tr>
<tr><td>Mid(expression, start, length)</td><td>Returns any specified portion of a text value. Start specifies the first character position to include. Length specifies the number of characters to include.</td></tr>
<tr><td>InStr(start,Text1, Text2, compare)</td><td>Returns the starting position of the first occurrence of one text value within another. Start is optional and specifies the position within Text1 to start the search, starting from 1. If not specified, the search will begin at the first character. Text1 is the text being searched. Text2 is the text being searched for. Compare is used to specify the kind of comparison to make:
<table>
<tr><th>Constant</th><th>Value</th><th>Description</th></tr>
<tr><td>vbBinaryCompare</td><td>0</td><td>Perform a binary comparison.</td></tr>
<tr><td>vbTextCompare</td><td>1</td><td>Perform a textual comparison.</td></tr>
<tr><td>VbDatabaseCompare</td><td>2</td><td>Perform a comparison based on information in database.</td></tr>
</table>
If either string is null, this function will return a null. If Text1 is zero-length or if the search string is not found, it will return a 0. If Text2 is zero-length, the function will return the Start position. If Text2 is found in Text1 from the Start position on, the position of the match will be returned.</td></tr>
</table>

Text Functions (continued)	
Access	
Trim(expression), LTrim(expression), RTrim(expression)	Returns a copy of a text value without leading spaces (LTrim), trailing spaces (RTrim), or both leading and trailing spaces (Trim).
Ucase(expression), Lcase(expression)	Returns a copy of a text value converted to uppercase (Ucase) or lowercase (Lcase).
Format(expression, format)	The Format function is a powerful Access function that allows you to display data formatted in practically any way. Expression is the value or expression you want to format. Format is either an Access-named or user-defined format. Format can also have optional arguments for date formatting that specify the first day of the week and the first day of a fiscal year, but they will not be documented here. Here is a list of the common named formats: General Number, Currency, Fixed, Standard, Percent, Scientific, Yes/No, True/False, On/Off, General Date, Long Date, Medium Date, Short Date, Long Time, Medium Time, Short Time. User-defined formats can be a combination of set characters ($, %, -, etc) and symbols. The following are the most common symbols:

Symbol	**Meaning**
0	Display a numeric digit or a zero.
#	Display a numeric digit or nothing.
@	Display a text character or a space.
&	Display a text character or nothing.
<	Display as lowercase.
>	Display as uppercase.
ddddd	Display a date/time value formatted as mm/dd/yy according to the computer's short date format setting.
d, dd, ddd, dddd	Display the day of a date/time value as a number without a leading zero (d), a number with a leading zero (dd), a text abbreviation (ddd), or the full text day name (dddd)
M, mm, mmm, mmmm	Display the month of a date/time value as a number without a leading zero (m), a number with a leading zero (mm), a text abbreviation (mm), or the full text month name (mmmm)
yy, yyyy	Display the year of a date/time value in either two-digit or four-digit format
ttttt	Display the time of a date/time value formatted as hh:mm:ss according to the computer's time format setting

Let's put some of these functions to work. We'll start by listing all of the first letters of members' last names and a count of the number of members for each.

```
Select Left(lastname,1) As Initial, Count(*) As NumMembers
From Members
Group By Left(lastname,1)
```

```
Initial     NumMembers
-----       -----
A           1
B           1
C           3
F           3
G           2
H           2
I           1
K           1
L           1
M           2
P           1
R           1
S           1
T           1
W           2
```

Let's find out which track has the longest track name. Notice that you can use a function as an expression for an aggregate function.

```
Select Tracktitle
From Tracks
Where len(Tracktitle) = (Select max(len(Tracktitle))
                         From Tracks)
```

```
Tracktitle
---------------
Violin Sonata No. 1 in D Major
Violin Sonata No. 2 in A Major
Violin Sonata No. 4 in E Minor
```

For any artist whose name begins with "The," list the name formatted as: Rolling Stones, The. Notice in this example that the ***Len*** function is used to calculate the length setting for the

Right function. Also notice the concatenation.

```
Select Right(Artistname,Len(artistname)-4) & ', The' As NewName
From Artists
Where Left(Artistname,4) = 'The '

NewName
———————
Neurotics, The
Bullets, The
Kicks, The
```

Report a list of all of the domains that are used by members for e-mail. The domain is the part of the e-mail address after the @. Eliminate duplicates from the list.

```
Select Distinct Right(Email, Len(Email)-Instr(0,'@',Email,2))
From Members
Where Email Is Not Null

Expr1000
————————
bitspeed.com
cookery.com
corkscrew.com
daviscorp.com
dowop.com
irvingnet.com
ispl.com
mightyhost1.com
signon.com
tamilla.org
uptime.net
wmorrow.com
```

Date Manipulation

Being able to subtract dates, determine the current date, and calculate the number of days between two dates are all crucial database functions. All date manipulation stems from how Access stores dates internally. Access stores dates as a numeric value, such as 37544.6431481481. The whole number to the left of the decimal place is the number of days since Dec 31, 1899. The portion of the number to the right of the decimal place indicates the time as a percentage of one day (noon=.5, 6 P.M.=.75, etc.).

<table>
<tr><th colspan="2">Date Manipulation</th></tr>
<tr><th colspan="2">Access</th></tr>
<tr><td>Now(),
Date()</td><td>Now() returns the current date and time. Date() returns the current date. No arguments are placed between the parentheses.</td></tr>
<tr><td>IsDate(expression)</td><td>Returns True if the expression is a valid date and False if it is not.</td></tr>
<tr><td>Day(expression),
Month(expression),
Year(expression)</td><td>Day returns the day of the month of a specified date. Monthreturns a number between 1 and 12, representing the month of a specified date. Year returns the year of a specified date.</td></tr>
<tr><td>DateAdd(interval, num, date)</td><td>Adds or subtracts a specified time interval to a date or time. Interval is the date/time interval you want to add (see table below). Num is the number of those intervals you want to add; use negative number to subtract. Date is the date to which the interval is to be added.

<table>
<tr><th>Interval</th><th>Meaning</th></tr>
<tr><td>"yyyy"</td><td>Year</td></tr>
<tr><td>"q"</td><td>Quarter</td></tr>
<tr><td>"m"</td><td>Month</td></tr>
<tr><td>"y"</td><td>Day of year</td></tr>
<tr><td>"d"</td><td>Day</td></tr>
<tr><td>"w"</td><td>Weekday</td></tr>
<tr><td>"ww"</td><td>Week of year</td></tr>
<tr><td>"h"</td><td>Hour</td></tr>
<tr><td>"n"</td><td>Minute</td></tr>
<tr><td>"s"</td><td>Second</td></tr>
</table></td></tr>
</table>

Date Manipulation (continued)	
Access	
DateDiff(interval, date1, date2, firstdayofweek)	Returns the number of intervals between two dates. Interval is the date/time interval used to calculate the differences between the two days (see table under DateAdd). Firstdayofweek is optional and is assumed to be Sunday if not otherwise set. It is set with a number between 1 and 7 where 1 indicates Sunday and 7 indicates Saturday.
DateSerial(year, month, day) DateValue(date expression)	Both of these functions return a date value that can be inserted into a date field. The difference is the arguments passed. DateSerial takes three numeric arguments that indicate the year, month, and day. DateValue takes a single text argument that is in any format that Access can recognize, including 'Oct 15, 2002'; 'October 15, 02'; and '10/15/02'. The DateValue expression must be enclosed in quotes.

List the names and birthdays of all members with June birthdays

```
Select lastname, firstname, birthday
From Members
Where Month(birthday)=6

Lastname      firstname    birthday
------------  -----------  ----------
MacArthur     Jose         6/24/1978
Irving        Terry        6/22/1959
Sanders       Bryce        6/11/1966
Crum          Bobby        6/10/1965
```

List each artist name and that artist's one-year anniversary date.

```
Select artistname, DateAdd('yyyy', 1, entrydate) As Anniv
From Artists

artistname        Anniv
---------------   ----------
The Neurotics     5/14/2004
Louis Holiday     6/3/2004
Word              6/8/2004
Sonata            6/8/2004
The Bullets       8/10/2004
Jose MacArthur    8/17/2004
Confused          9/14/2004
The Kicks         12/3/2004
Today             10/7/2004
21 West Elm       2/5/2004
Highlander        8/10/2003
```

Datatype Conversions

In order to do certain kinds of data manipulation you may need to convert data from one datatype to another. Actually, Access can do most of these kinds of ***datatype conversions*** without being asked, so you may never need these functions. But here they are in case you ever do.

Datatype Conversions	
Access	
Cbool(expression)	Converts expression to Boolean datatype.
CByte(expression)	Converts expression to Byte datatype.
CCur(expression)	Converts expression to Currency datatype.
CDate(expression)	Converts expression to Date datatype.
CDbl(expression)	Converts expression to Double-precision datatype.
CInt(expression)	Converts expression to Integer datatype.
CLng(expression)	Converts expression to Long Integer datatype.
CSng(expression)	Converts expression to Single-precision datatype.
CStr(expression)	Converts expression to String (text) datatype.
Int(expression)	Returns the integer value of a numeric expression.

This example shows how the CInt function will round to the nearest whole number:

```
Select Tracktitle, LengthSeconds/60 As Sec_Div_By_60,
CInt(LengthSeconds/60) As Whole_Min
From Tracks Where TitleID=4

Tracktitle               Sec_Div_By_60     Whole_Min
-----------------------  ----------------- -----------
Bob's Dream              3.08333333333333  3
Third's Folly            5.86666666666667  6
My Wizard                3.88333333333333  4
Leather                  3.08333333333333  3
Hot Cars Cool Nights     3.2               3
Music in You             3.4               3
Don't Care About Time    3.68333333333333  4
Kiss                     3.63333333333333  4
Pizza Box                3.05              3
Goodbye                  4                 4
```

Note

If you want to round to a certain number of decimal places, a Round function is available in Access 2000 and later versions. Its syntax is: Round(expression, num_places).

Handling Nulls

Every database needs some way to determine if a value is null. Access provides two such functions: ***IsNull*** and ***Nz***. IsNull returns True if the expression is null and False if it is not. If displayed, this will show -1 for True and 0 for False. Note that this is different from the SQL Server

IsNull function. The Nz function operates like the SQL Server IsNull function. It takes as an argument a value to use as a replacement if the expression is null.

Handling Nulls	
Access	
Syntax	IsNull(expression) Nz(expression, replacement_value_if_null)
Examples	1. List the web address of each artist and whether or not the web address is null. `Select IsNull(WebAddress) As Is_It_Null From Artists`
	2. List the web address of each artist. If the web address is null, list "no website." `Select Nz(WebAddress,'No website') From Artists`

If Logic

If logic allows you to evaluate an expression and display one thing or another based on the value of that expression. In Chapter 2 we saw how this was accomplished by the simple CASE and searched CASE SQL keywords, which Access does not support. Here are some functions that Access does support:

If Logic	
Access	
IIF(expression,display_if_true, display_if_false)	IIF provides a True and False choice. It takes three arguments. The first argument is a logical test. The second argument shows what to display or use if the test evaluates as True. The third argument shows what to display or use if the test evaluates as False.
Choose(expression,display_if_1, display_if_2, display_if_3,...)	Choose can have any number of arguments. The first argument is a numeric field value. The second argument shows what to display or use if the field value is 1. The third argument shows what to display or use if the field value is 2. This continues until all possible values are accounted for.

The first example uses the IsNull(WebAddress) we looked at earlier and places it as the logical test for the ***IIF*** function. If the WebAddress is in fact Null, the IIF function will report "No Website." Otherwise, it will report the value of the WebAddress field. This is another way of doing the Nz function.

```
Select IIF(IsNull(WebAddress),'No Website',WebAddress) As Web
From Artists

Web
------------------------
www.theneurotics.com
No Website
No Website
www.classical.com/sonata
No Website
www.josemacarthur.com
No Website
www.today.com
www.21westelm.com
No Website
```

The second example using the ***Choose*** function has to do several gyrations to work. First the Access Abs function takes the absolute value of the ReadAud and mp3 fields. This is because in Access a True value is stored as -1. Choose needs positive numbers, so Abs makes the value positive. Also, 1 is added to the value of RealAud+mp3 because Choose evaluates numbers starting with 1 and RealAud+mp3 by itself could equal 0 if both were False. The WHERE clause serves just to limit the number of rows being returned.

```
Select RealAud, MP3,
Choose(Abs(RealAud+MP3)+1,'Neither','Real or MP3','Both') As Status
From Tracks
Where TitleID = 3 or TitleID = 7

RealAud     MP3   Status
----------- ----- --------
-1          -1    Both
-1          -1    Both
-1          -1    Both
-1          -1    Both
-1          -1    Both
-1          -1    Both
```

```
0          -1    Real or MP3
0          -1    Real or MP3
0          -1    Real or MP3
0          -1    Real or MP3
0          -1    Real or MP3
-1         -1    Both
-1         -1    Both
-1         -1    Both
0          0     Neither
0          0     Neither
0          0     Neither
0          0     Neither
```

Microsoft SQL Server Statements and Functions

The SQL Server extensions to SQL are called Transact-SQL (or T-SQL).

Concatenation

Concatenation is the combination of two or more text values into one text value. The SQL Server concatenation operator is the plus sign (+). You can concatenate multiple fields or fields with constant text. A common task is to concatenate a space between two other fields. You can make a space by placing a space between two quotes (' ').

Concatenation	
	SQL Server
Syntax	Field + Field | 'Text' + Field
Examples	1. List the full name of each member. `Select Firstname + ' ' + Lastname As Fullname From Members`
	2. Report the City, State, and Zip of each member, formatted as City, State, Zip. `Select City + ', ' + Region + ' ' + Postalcode As MailAddr From Members`
	3. Report each lead source preceded by the text 'source: ' along with a count of the number of artist leads from that source. `Select 'source: ' + Leadsource As Source, Count(*) As NumLead From Artists Group by 'source: ' + Leadsource`

Text Functions

SQL Server has several functions for manipulating text fields. The "Text Functions" table shows the major ones.

Text Functions	
SQL Server	
Len(expression) Left(expression, length)	Returns the length in characters of the text Returns text containing the specified number of characters from the left side of a text value. If Length is greater than the length of the text value, the entire text value is returned.
Right(expression, length)	Returns text containing the specified number of characters from the right side of a text value. If Length is greater than the length of the text value, the entire text value is returned.
Substring (expression, start, length)	Returns any specified portion of a text value. Start specifies the first character position to include. Length specifies the number of characters to include.
CharIndex (expression, text, start)	Returns the starting position of the first occurrence of one text expression within another. Expression is the text being searched for. Text is the text being searched. Start is optional and specifies the position within Text to start the search, starting from 1. If not specified, the search will begin at the first character. If Text is null the function will return null. If Expression is not found within Text, the function will return 0.
LTrim(expression), RTrim(expression)	Returns a copy of a text value without leading spaces (LTrim), or trailing spaces (RTrim).
Upper(expression), Lower(expression)	Returns a copy of a text value converted to uppercase (Upper) or lowercase (Lower).
Replicate (expression,num_times)	Returns the expression the given number of times.

Let's put some of these functions to work. We'll start by listing all of the first letters of members' last names and a count of the number of members for each.

```
Select Left(lastname,1) As Initial, Count(*) As NumMembers
From Members
Group By Left(lastname,1)

Initial      NumMembers
------  ------
A            1
B            1
C            3
F            3
G            2
H            2
I            1
K            1
L            1
M            2
P            1
R            1
S            1
T            1
W            2
```

Let's find out which track has the longest track name. Notice that you can use a function as an expression for an aggregate function.

```
Select Tracktitle
From Tracks
Where len(Tracktitle) = (Select max(len(Tracktitle))
                         From Tracks)

Tracktitle
---------------
Violin Sonata No. 1 in D Major
Violin Sonata No. 2 in A Major
Violin Sonata No. 4 in E Minor
```

For any artist whose name begins with "The" list the name formatted as: Rolling Stones, The. Notice in this example that the Len function is used to calculate the length setting for the Right function. Also notice the concatenation:

```
Select Right(Artistname,Len(artistname)-4) + ', The' As NewName
From Artists
Where Left(Artistname,4) = 'The '

NewName
---------------
Neurotics, The
Bullets, The
Kicks, The
```

Report a list of all of the domains that are used by members for e-mail. The domain is the part of the e-mail address after the @. Eliminate duplicates from the list.

```
Select Distinct Right(Email, Len(Email)-Charindex('@',Email))
From Members
Where Email Is Not Null

-------------------
bitspeed.com
cookery.com
corkscrew.com
daviscorp.com
dowop.com
irvingnet.com
ispl.com
mightyhostl.com
signon.con
tamilla.org
uptime.net
wmorrow.com
```

Date Manipulation

Being able to subtract dates, determine the current date, and calculate the number of days between two dates are all crucial database functions. All date manipulation stems from how SQL Server stores dates internally. SQL Server stores dates as a numeric value, such as 37544.6431481481. The whole number to the left of the decimal place is the number of days since Jan 1, 1900. The portion of the number to the right of the decimal place indicates the time as a percentage of one day (noon=.5, 6 P.M.=.75, etc.).

Date Manipulation	
SQL Server	
GetDate()	GetDate () returns the current date and time. No arguments are placed between the parentheses, but they are required.
IsDate(expression)	Returns True if the expression is a valid date and False if it is not.
Day(expression), Month(expression), Year(expression)	Day returns the day of the month of a specified date. Month returns a number between 1 and 12, representing the month of a specified date. Year returns the year of a specified date.
DateAdd(interval, num, date)	Adds or subtracts a specified time interval to a date or time. Interval is the date/time interval you want to add (see table below). Num is the number of those intervals you want to add; use negative number to subtract. Date is the date to which the interval is to be added. Unlike Access, the Interval is not placed within quotation marks.
DateDiff(interval, date1, date2, firstdayofweek)	Returns the number of intervals between two dates. Interval is the date/time interval used to calculate the differences between the two days (see table under DateAdd).

Interval	Meaning
yyyy	Year
q	Quarter
m	Month
y	Day of year
d	Day
dw	Weekday
ww	Week of year
hh	Hour
n	Minute
s	Second

List the names and birthdays of all members with June birthdays.

```
Select lastname, firstname, birthday
From Members
Where Month(birthday)=6

Lastname        firstname      birthday
------------    -----------    ----------
MacArthur       Jose           6/24/1978
Irving          Terry          6/22/1959
Sanders         Bryce          6/11/1966
Crum            Bobby          6/10/1965
```

List each artist name and that artist's one-year anniversary date.

```
Select artistname, DateAdd(yyyy, 1, entrydate) As Anniv
From Artists

artistname          Anniv
---------------     -------------
The Neurotics       5/14/2004
Louis Holiday       6/3/2004
Word                6/8/2004
Sonata              6/8/2004
The Bullets         8/10/2004
Jose MacArthur      8/17/2004
Confused            9/14/2004
The Kicks           12/3/2004
Today               10/7/2004
21 West Elm         2/5/2004
Highlander          8/10/2003
```

Datatype Conversions and Data Formatting

In SQL Server you often need to explicitly convert the values of a field to another datatype. For instance, an integer divided by something will report only integer (whole number) values unless you explicitly convert it to a decimal datatype. SQL Server offers two datatype conversion functions: Convert and Cast. Both do essentially the same thing, although Convert also does some date formatting conversions that Cast does not. However, Cast is ANSI SQL99 syntax and Convert is ODBC syntax. So Cast is more likely to port to other database systems. ***Floor*** simply reports the integer value of a numeric expression.

In SQL Server, formatting data often involves casting or converting it. As shown below, Convert has several style options for formatting dates. Formatting numbers often involves casting or converting the number to a character value so that leading zeros, commas, dollar signs and other formatting options can be added.

Datatype Conversions	
	SQL Server
Syntax	Floor(expression) Cast(expression as datatype) Convert(datatype, expression, style*)

*Selected Styles (optional)

Convert datetime or smalldatetime to character data

2-digit year	4-digit year	Style
1	101	mm/dd/yy
2	102	yy.mm.dd
3	103	dd/mm/yy
6	106	dd mon yy
7	107	mon dd, yy
8	108	hh:mm:ss
10	110	mm-dd-yy
12	112	yymmdd

Convert float or real to character data

0	6 digits maximum; use in scientific notation, if appropriate.
1	8 digits; must be used in scientific notation.
2	16 digits; must be used in scientific notation.

Convert money or smallmoney to character data

0	2 digits to the right of the decimal point and no commas.
1	2 digits to the right of the decimal point and commas to the left of the decimal point every 3 digits.
2	4 digits to the right of the decimal point and no commas to the left of the decimal point.

Datatype Conversions (continued)	
SQL Server	
Examples	1. For each track from Title 4 report the track title and the length in minutes without rounding or truncating to whole minutes. `Select Tracktitle, Cast(LengthSeconds As Decimal)/60 As LengthMin From Tracks Where TitleID=4`
	2. For each track from Title 4 report all in one column the track title followed by a colon (:) and the length in seconds. `Select Tracktitle + ':' + Convert(Char, LengthSeconds) From Tracks Where TitleID=4`
	3. Report the name and yearly base of each salesperson formatted with commas and two decimal places. `Select firstname + ' ' + lastname, Convert(char,base*52,1) From salespeople`
	4. Report the name and birthday of each member in mm/dd/yyyy format. `Select firstname + ' ' + lastname, Convert(char,birthday,101) From members`

Let's look at the results from Example 1. Without doing the Cast (or a Convert), the calculation of LengthSeconds divided by 60 would stay a small integer and thus would report only whole numbers.

```
Select Tracktitle, Cast(LengthSeconds As Decimal)/60 As LengthMin
From Tracks
Where TitleID = 4

Tracktitle                                          LengthMin
--------------------------------------------------  ------------
Bob's Dream                                         3.083333
My Wizard                                           3.883333
Third's Folly                                       5.866666
Leather                                             3.083333
Hot Cars Cool Nights                                3.200000
Music in You                                        3.400000
Don't Care About Time                               3.683333
```

```
Kiss                                                  3.633333
Pizza Box                                             3.050000
Goodbye                                               4.000000
```

In Example 2 we couldn't concatenate a small integer to a text value. But if we Convert (or Cast) the small integer into a character datatype, then we can concatenate them.

```
Select Tracktitle + ':' + Convert(Char, LengthSeconds)
From Tracks
Where TitleID = 4

_______________

Bob's Dream:185
My Wizard:233
Third's Folly:352
Leather:185
Hot Cars Cool Nights:192
Music in You:204
Don't Care About Time:221
Kiss:218
Pizza Box:183
Goodbye:240
```

The following demonstrates using the optional style argument with Convert. It is the best way to display just the date portion or just the time portion of a datetime or smalldatetime value.

```
Select getdate(), Convert(char, getdate(),101)

--------------------------    ----------------
2002-10-16 21:43:32.293       10/16/2002
```

Handling Nulls

Every database needs some way to determine if a value is null. SQL Server provides an IsNull function. Note that this is different from the Access IsNull function. The SQL Server IsNull function takes as an argument a value to use as a replacement if the expression is null.

Handling Nulls	
SQL Server	
Syntax	IsNull(expression, replacement_value_if_null)
Examples	1. List the web address of each artist. If the web address is null, list 'no website.' `Select IsNull(WebAddress,'No website') From Artists`

```
Select IsNull(WebAddress,'No website')
From Artists

-----------------------------------------
www.theneurotics.com
No website
No website
www.classical.com/sonata
No website
www.josemacarthur.com
No website
www.today.com
www.21westelm.com
No website
```

MySQL Statements and Functions

MySQL is in some ways similar to and in other ways different from Oracle, SQL Server, and Access. It lacks a few features in some places, but adds some features not found in the others.

Concatenation

Concatenation is the combination of two or more text values into one text value. MySQL provides two functions for concatenation. Concat will concatenate a series of text values separated by commas. Concat_WS (meaning with separator) takes as an argument a separator that is then placed between each of the text values. These two functions also differ in how they handle nulls. If any of the arguments for Concat is null, then the function will return a null. Concat_WS will ignore nulls unless the separator is a null, in which case it returns a null.

Concatenation	
MySQL	
Syntax	Concat(expression1, expression2, expression3) Concat_WS(separator, expression1, expression2, expression3)
Examples	1. List the full name of each member. `Select Concat_WS(' ',Firstname, LastName) As Fullname From Members`
	2. Report the City, State, and Zip of each member, formatted as City, State, Zip. `Select Concat(City,', ',Region ,' ',Postalcode) As MailAddr From Members`
	3. Report each lead source preceded by the text 'source: ' along with a count of the number of artist leads from that source. `Select Concat('source: ',Leadsource) As Source, Count(*) As NumLead From Artists Group by Source`

Text Functions

MySQL has several functions for manipulating text fields. The table below shows the major ones.

Text Functions	
MySQL	
Length(expression)	Returns the length in characters of the text.
Left(expression, length)	Returns text containing the specified number of characters from the left side of a text value. If Length is greater than the length of the text value, the entire text value is returned.
Right(expression, length)	Returns text containing the specified number of characters from the right side of a text value. If Length is greater than the length of the text value, the entire text value is returned.
Substring (expression, start, length)	Returns any specified portion of a text value. Start specifies the first character position to include. Length specifies the number of characters to include.
Locate(expression,text,start)	Returns the starting position of the first occurrence of one text expression within another. Expression is the text being searched for. Text is the text being searched. Start is optional and specifies the position within Text to start the search, starting from 1. If expression is not found, the function will return a 0.
Trim(expression), LTrim(expression), RTrim(expression)	Returns a copy of a text value without leading spaces (LTrim), trailing spaces (RTrim), or both leading and trailing spaces (Trim).
Upper(expression), Lower(expression)	Returns a copy of a text value converted to uppercase (Upper) or lowercase (Lower).
LPad(string, num_char,pad_chars), RPad(string,num_char, pad_chars)	Makes a string a certain length (num_char) by adding a certain set of pad characters (pad_chars) to the left (LPad) or right (RPad).

Let's put some of these functions to work. We'll start by listing all of the first letters of members' last names and a count of the number of members for each.

```
Select Left(lastname,1) As Initial, Count(*) As NumMembers
From Members
Group By Left(lastname,1)
```

```
Initial     NumMembers
----------- ------------
A           1
B           1
C           3
F           3
G           2
H           2
I           1
K           1
L           1
M           2
P           1
R           1
S           1
T           1
W           2
```

For any artist whose name begins with "The," list the name formatted as: Rolling Stones, The. Notice in this example that the Len function is used to calculate the length setting for the Right function. Also notice the concatenation.

```
Select Concat(Right(Artistname,Length(artistname)-4),', The') As
NewName
From Artists
Where Left(Artistname,4) = 'The '

NewName
-------
Neurotics, The
Bullets, The
Kicks, The
```

Report a list of all of the domains that are used by members for e-mail. The domain is the part of the e-mail address after the @. Eliminate duplicates from the list.

```
Select Distinct Right(Email, Length(Email)-Locate('@',Email,1))
From Members
Where Email Is Not Null

----------------
bitspeed.com
```

```
cookery.com
corkscrew.com
daviscorp.com
dowop.com
irvingnet.com
ispl.com
mightyhostl.com
signon.con
tamilla.org
uptime.net
wmorrow.com
```

Report in a single column a list of studio names and the cities. Pad the studio name so that the city names line up.

```
Select RPad(StudioName, 40, ' ') || City As StudioNamesAndCities
From Studios;

STUDIONAMESANDCITIES
-------------------------------------    --------------
MakeTrax                                 Anderson
Lone Star Recording                      Davis
Pacific Rim                              Santa Theresa
```

Date Manipulation

MySQL has all the functionality of other database systems to subtract dates, determine the current date, and calculate the number of days between two dates. MySQL stores dates in ISO 8601 format (YYYY-MM-DD).

<table>
<tr><th colspan="2">Date Manipulation</th></tr>
<tr><th colspan="2">MySQL</th></tr>
<tr><td>Now(),CurDate(), CurTime()</td><td>Now() returns the current date and time. CurDate() returns the current date. CurTime() returns the current time. No arguments are placed between the parentheses, but they are required.</td></tr>
<tr><td>DayOfMonth (expression), Month(expression), Year(expression)</td><td>DayofMonth returns the day of the month of a specified date. Month returns a number between 1 and 12, representing the month of a specified date. Year returns the year of a specified date.</td></tr>
<tr><td>AddDate(date, Interval expression type),SubDate(date, Interval expression type)</td><td>Adds or subtracts a specified time interval to a date or time. Interval is the literal word Interval. Expression is the number of those date intervals you want to add or subtract. Type indicates the interval size. The available types include: Second, Minute, Hour, Day, Month, Year, Minute_Second, Hour_Minute, Day_Hour, Year_Month, Hour_Second, Day_Minute, and Day_Second</td></tr>
<tr><td>To_Days(date)</td><td>Given a date, returns a daynumber. To subtract two dates use To_Days on each and subtract the daynumbers.</td></tr>
<tr><td>Date_Format (date,format)</td><td>Displays a date formatted to the format specifications. Use one or more of the format codes shown below (partial list). You may also include literals. Enclose the entire format string in quotes.</td></tr>
<tr><td>Date_Format (date,format) (continued)</td><td>
<table>
<tr><th>Format</th><th>Meaning</th></tr>
<tr><td>%M</td><td>Month name (January..December)</td></tr>
<tr><td>%W</td><td>Weekday name (Sunday..Saturday)</td></tr>
<tr><td>%Y</td><td>Year, numeric, 4 digits. Use %y for 2 digits</td></tr>
<tr><td>%a</td><td>Abbreviated weekday name (Sun..Sat)</td></tr>
<tr><td>%d</td><td>Day of the month (00..31) Use %e to drop leading 0s</td></tr>
<tr><td>%m</td><td>Month, numeric (00..12) Use %c to drop leading 0s</td></tr>
<tr><td>%b</td><td>Abbreviated month name (Jan..Dec)</td></tr>
<tr><td>%H</td><td>Hour (00..23) Use %k to drop leading 0s</td></tr>
<tr><td>%h</td><td>Hour (01..12) Use %l to drop leading 0s</td></tr>
<tr><td>%i</td><td>Minutes, numeric (00..59)</td></tr>
<tr><td>%r</td><td>Time, 12-hour (hh:mm:ss [AP]M)</td></tr>
<tr><td>%T</td><td>Time, 24-hour (hh:mm:ss)</td></tr>
<tr><td>%s</td><td>Seconds (00..59)</td></tr>
<tr><td>%p</td><td>AM or PM</td></tr>
</table>
</td></tr>
<tr><td>Last_Day(date)</td><td>Returns the last day of the month for the given date.</td></tr>
</table>

List the names and birthdays of all members with June birthdays.

```
Select lastname, firstname, birthday
From Members
Where Month(birthday)=6

Lastname       firstname     birthday
-------------  ------------  ----------
MacArthur      Jose          6/24/1978
Irving         Terry         6/22/1959
Sanders        Bryce         6/11/1966
Crum           Bobby         6/10/1965
```

List each artist name and that artist's one-year anniversary date.

```
select artistname, AddDate(entrydate, Interval 1 Year) From artists

artistname         Anniv
----------------   ----------
The Neurotics      5/14/2004
Louis Holiday      6/3/2004
Word               6/8/2004
Sonata             6/8/2004
The Bullets        8/10/2004
Jose MacArthur     8/17/2004
Confused           9/14/2004
The Kicks          12/3/2004
Today              10/7/2004
21 West Elm        2/5/2004
Highlander         8/10/2003
```

Let's use the To_Days function to report the age in days of members from Georgia. Your results will vary depending on which day you run this.

```
Select lastname, firstname, birthday, To_Days(Current_TimeStamp)-
To_Days(birthday) as AgeInDays
From Members
Where Region='GA'

Lastname     firstname   birthday                AgeInDays
-----------  ----------  ----------------------  -----------
Finney       Doug         1963-08-04 00:00:00    14318
```

```
Irving        Terry        1959-06-22 00:00:00    15822
Henderson     Michelle     1964-03-15 00:00:00    14094
```

Finally, lets use the Date_Format function to report the artistname and entry date of each artist in mm-dd-yyyy format.

```
Select Artistname, Date_Format(entrydate,'%m-%d-%Y') as Entered
From Artists

Artistname                Entered
----------------------    -----------
The Neurotics             05-14-2003
Louis Holiday             06-03-2003
Word                      06-08-2003
Sonata                    06-08-2003
The Bullets               08-10-2003
Jose MacArthur            08-17-2003
Confused                  09-14-2003
The Kicks                 12-03-2003
Today                     10-07-2003
21 West Elm               02-05-2003
Highlander                08-10-2002
```

Datatype Conversions

MySQL automatically handles many kinds of datatype conversions without the use of special functions. For an example consider the following SQL statement. LengthSeconds has a small integer datatype. Yet the result of the division is reported rounded to two decimal places. To do that in SQL Server you would need to use a Cast or Convert function.

```
Select Tracktitle, LengthSeconds/60 As LengthMin
From Tracks
Where TitleID = 4

Tracktitle                LengthMin
----------------------    -----------
Bob's Dream               3.08
My Wizard                 3.88
Third's Folly             5.87
Leather                   3.08
Hot Cars Cool Nights      3.2
Music in You              3.4
```

```
Don't Care About Time    3.68
Kiss                     3.63
Pizza Box                3.05
Goodbye                  4
```

Similarly, the following SQL illustrates that you can concatenate a text field, constant text, and a small integer together without any special data conversion functions:

```
Select  Concat(Tracktitle,':',LengthSeconds)
From Tracks
Where TitleID = 4

------------------------------
Bob's Dream:185
My Wizard:233
Third's Folly:352
Leather:185
Hot Cars Cool Nights:192
Music in You:204
Don't Care About Time:221
Kiss:218
Pizza Box:183
Goodbye:240
```

MySQL also offers the same datatype conversion functions as SQL Server: Convert and Cast. However, Cast and Convert are implemented differently in MySQL than they are in SQL Server, with fewer (and different) datatypes and without the style option on Convert. Plus Cast and Convert are not available prior to MySQL 4.0.2. Cast () is ANSI SQL99 syntax and Convert() is ODBC syntax. So Cast is more likely to port to other database systems. ***Truncate*** reports the value of a numeric expression truncated (not rounded) to the specified number of decimal places.

Datatype Conversions	
MySQL	
Syntax	Cast(expression as datatype) Convert(datatype, expression) Truncate(number, num_decimal_places) Datatype must be one of the following: Binary, Date, Datetime, Signed {Integer}, Time, Unsigned {Integer}

```
Select truncate(3.1415926,3)

-----
3.141
```

Handling Nulls

Every database needs some way to determine if a value is null. MySQL provides two functions. The IsNull function works similarly to the Access IsNull function. IsNull returns True if the expression is null and False if it is not. If displayed, this will show 1 for True and 0 for False.

The *IfNull* function works similar to the SQL Server IsNull function. It takes as an argument a value to use as a replacement if the expression is null.

Handling Nulls	
MySQL	
Syntax	IsNull(expression) IfNull(expression,display_if_expression_is_null)
Examples	1. List the web address of each artist and whether or not the web address is null. `Select WebAddress, IsNull(WebAddress) As Is_It_Null From Artists`
	2. List the web address of each artist. If the web address is null, list 'no website.' `Select IfNull(WebAddress,'No website') From Artists`

Miscellaneous Functions

Here are some functions that MySQL offers that sometimes come in handy. Greatest and Least take any number of arguments, all of which are numeric values to be compared. The greatest or least of them will be reported. These functions are useful when a table has multiple numeric columns that need to be compared. Example 1 below simply demonstrates how the functions work. Example 2 uses the Least function to detect tracks missing either an mp3 or Real Audio recording. If either is missing, the Least value will be 0.

Format displays a numeric value rounded to the number of decimal places indicated and with commas every three digits on the left of the decimal point.

Misc Functions	
MySQL	
Syntax	Greatest(number1, number2, number3) Least(number1, number2, number3) Format(number, num_decimal_places
Examples	1. List the largest of the following numbers: 3, 5, 7, and 9. `Select Greatest(3,5,7,9)`

	2. List any tracks that lack either an mp3 or Real Audio recording.
	`Select TrackTitle From Tracks`
	`Where Least(mp3,RealAud)=0`

	3. Report the name and yearly base of each salesperson formatted with commas and two decimal places.
	`Select Concat(firstname, lastname), Format(base*52,2)`
	`From salespeople`

Oracle Statements and Functions

If you have read the previous sections on Access, SQL Server, and MySQL, you will find that Oracle does all the same things. As with the other database systems, the Oracle syntax is often slightly different.

Concatenation

Concatenation is the combination of two or more text values into one text value. Oracle's concatenation operator is two vertical bars (||). Oracle also offers a Concat function that will concatenate two values separated by commas. Unlike Concat in MySQL, Oracle's Concat function can handle only two arguments, so the vertical bars operator is a much more flexible tool. A common task is to concatenate a space between two other fields. You can make a space by placing a space between two quotes (' ').

Text Functions

The "Text Functions" table shows the major functions available in Oracle for manipulating text.

Concatenation	
Oracle	
Syntax	Field_or_Text || Field_or_Text || Field_or_Text Concat(Field_or_Text, Field_or_Text)

Examples	1. List the full name of each member.
	`Select Firstname || ' ' || Lastname As Fullname`
	`From Members`

	2. Report the City, State, and Zip of each member, formatted as City, State, Zip.
	`Select City || ', ' || Region || ' ' || Postalcode`
	`As MailAddr From Members`

	3. Report each lead source preceded by the text, 'source: ' along with a count of the number of artists leads from that source.
	`Select Concat('source: ', Leadsource) As Source, Count(*)`
	`As NumLead From Artists Group by Concat('source: ', Leadsource)`

Text Functions	
Oracle	
Length(expression)	Returns the length in characters of the text.
Substr (expression, start, length)	Returns any specified portion of a text value. Start specifies the first character position to include. Length specifies the number of characters to include. Unlike our other target databases, Oracle has no Left or Right functions. Left(expression,1) is equivalent to Substr(expression, 1,1). Right(expression,1) is equivalent to Substr(expression, Length(expression),1).
InStr(text, expression)	Returns the starting position of the first occurrence of one text expression within another. Expression is the text being searched for. Text is the text being searched. If Expression is not found within Text, the function will return 0.
LTrim(expression), RTrim(expression), Trim(expression)	Returns a copy of a text value without leading spaces (LTrim), without trailing spaces (RTrim), or without both leading and trailing spaces (Trim).
Upper(expression), Lower(expression), Initcap(expression)	Returns a copy of a text value converted to uppercase (Upper), to lowercase (Lower), or with a capitalized first letter (Initcap).
LPad(string, num_char,pad_chars), LPad(string, num_char,pad_chars)	Makes a string a certain length (num_char) by adding a certain set of pad characters (pad_chars) to the left (LPad) or right (RPad).

Let's put some of these functions to work. We'll start by listing all of the first letters of members' last names and a count of the number of members for each.

```
Select Substr(lastname,1,1) As LastInit, Count(*) As NumMembers
From Members
Group By Substr(lastname,1,1)

Initial      NumMembers
----------   -------------
A            1
B            1
C            3
F            3
G            2
H            2
I            1
K            1
L            1
M            2
P            1
R            1
S            1
T            1
W            2
```

Let's find out which track has the longest track name. Notice that you can use a function as an expression for an aggregate function.

```
Select Tracktitle
From Tracks
Where length(Tracktitle) = (Select max(length(Tracktitle))
                            From Tracks)

Tracktitle
_______________
Violin Sonata No. 1 in D Major
Violin Sonata No. 2 in A Major
Violin Sonata No. 4 in E Minor
```

For any artist whose name begins with "The," list the name formatted as: Rolling Stones, The. Notice in this example that the Length function is used to calculate how much text remains after the "The." Also notice the concatenation.

```
Select Substr(Artistname,5,Length(Artistname)-4) || ', The' As
NewName From Artists
Where Substr(Artistname,1,4) = 'The '

NewName
---------------
Neurotics, The
Bullets, The
Kicks, The
```

Report a list of all of the domains that are used by members for e-mail. The domain is the part of the e-mail address after the @. Eliminate duplicates from the list. This is harder than the last example because we don't know where the @ is in the text. The ***Instr*** function finds it, and the ***Substr*** function reports everything beyond it (using the Instr once more in that calculation).

```
Select Distinct Substr(Email, Instr(Email,'@')+1, Length(Email)-
Instr(Email,'@'))
From Members
Where Email is Not Null

-----------------
bitspeed.com
cookery.com
corkscrew.com
daviscorp.com
dowop.com
irvingnet.com
ispl.com
mightyhostl.com
signon.con
tamilla.org
uptime.net
wmorrow.com
```

Report in a single column a list studio names and the cities. Pad the studio name so that the city names line up.

```
Select RPad(StudioName, 40, ' ') || City As StudioNamesAndCities From
Studios;

STUDIONAMESANDCITIES
-------------------------------------------------------
MakeTrax                                Anderson
Lone Star Recording                     Davis
Pacific Rim                             Santa Theresa
```

Date Manipulation

Being able to subtract dates, determine the current date, and calculate the number of days between two dates are all crucial database functions. All date manipulation stems from how Oracle stores dates internally. Oracle stores dates as a numeric value, such as 37544.6431481481. The whole number to the left of the decimal place is the number of days since Jan 1, 1900. The portion of the number to the right of the decimal place indicates the time as a percentage of one day (noon=.5, 6 P.M.=.75, etc.).

List the names and birthdays of all members with June birthdays:

```
Select lastname, firstname, birthday
From Members
Where to_char(birthday,'mm')= 6

Lastname      firstname    birthday
------------- ------------ ----------
MacArthur     Jose         6/24/1978
Irving        Terry        6/22/1959
Sanders       Bryce        6/11/1966
Crum          Bobby        6/10/1965
```

List each artist name and that artist's one-year anniversary date:

```
Select artistname, Add_months(To_date(entrydate),12) As Anniv
From Artists

artistname         Anniv
------------------ ----------
The Neurotics      5/14/2004
Louis Holiday      6/3/2004
Word               6/8/2004
Sonata             6/8/2004
The Bullets        8/10/2004
```

Date Manipulation	
Oracle	
Sysdate	Sysdate returns the current date. This contains the current time, but does not show it unless you specifically format it. For instance, to format sysdate to show date and time, you could use: Select To_char(sysdate,'YYYYMMDD HH24:MI:SS') from dual;To format sysdate to show just the time, you could use:Select To_char(sysdate,'fmHH24:MM:SS') from dual;The to_char function is discussed below under Datatype Conversions. Dual is a special Oracle table that has only one row and one column. It exists so you can select from it when you don't have a regular table to select from.
To_char(expression,'dd'), To_char(expression,'mm'), To_char(expression,'yyyy')	These will respectively return the day, month, and year of a date expression.
To_date(expression)+num	Adds or subtracts a given number of days to a date. Expression is the base date. Num is the number of days you want to add (using +) or subtract (using -).
Add_months (To_date(expression),num)	Adds or subtracts a given number of months to a date. Expression is the base date. Num is the number of months you want to add (using +) or subtract (using -).
To_date(date1) - To_date(date2)	Returns the number of days between two dates.
Last_Day(date)	Returns the last day of the month for the given date.
Next_Day(date,DayOfWeek)	Returns the date of the next named day of the week after the given date. Valid values for DayOfWeek are 'SUNDAY', 'MONDAY', etc.

```
Jose MacArthur     8/17/2004
Confused           9/14/2004
The Kicks          12/3/2004
Today              10/7/2004
21 West Elm        2/5/2004
Highlander         8/10/2003
```

Welcome cards are sent out on the Monday following an artist's EntryDate. List the artist name and the Monday following each EntryDate in August 2003.

```
Select ArtistName, Next_Day(EntryDate,'MONDAY') As CardDay
 From Artists
 Where EntryDate Between '01-Aug-2003' And '31-Aug-2003';

ARTISTNAME                                                 CARDDAY
---------------------------------------------------------- ------------
The Bullets                                                11-AUG-03
Jose MacArthur                                             11-AUG-03
```

Datatype Conversions

Oracle automatically handles many kinds of datatype conversions without using special functions. For example, consider the following SQL statement. LengthSeconds has a small integer datatype. Yet the result of the division is reported rounded to two decimal places. To do that in SQL Server you would need to use a Cast or Convert function.

```
Select Tracktitle, LengthSeconds/60 As LengthMin
From Tracks
Where TitleID = 4

Tracktitle               LengthMin
__________    _____-
Bob's Dream              3.08
My Wizard                3.88
Third's Folly            5.87
Leather                  3.08
Hot Cars Cool Nights     3.2
Music in You             3.4
Don't Care About Time    3.68
Kiss                     3.63
Pizza Box                3.05
Goodbye                  4
```

Similarly, the following SQL illustrates that you can concatenate a text field, constant text, and a small integer together without any special data conversion functions.

```
Select Tracktitle || ':' ||LengthSeconds
From Tracks
Where TitleID = 4

-----------------------------
Bob's Dream:185
My Wizard:233
```

```
Third's Folly:352
Leather:185
Hot Cars Cool Nights:192
Music in You:204
Don't Care About Time:221
Kiss:218
Pizza Box:183
Goodbye:240
```

However, there are still times that you need to tell Oracle to explicitly convert the datatype of a value. The To_Date function used in the Date Manipulation section is an example of this. Oracle offers three such functions: ***To_Char***, ***To_Date***, and ***To_Number***.

<table>
<tr><th colspan="2">Datatype Conversions</th></tr>
<tr><th colspan="2">Oracle</th></tr>
<tr><td>To_Char(value)
Or
To_Char(value,format)</td><td>Converts a number or date to a text value. It is also used to control the display formatting of dates and numbers. To_Char can be used with just the numeric or date argument to be converted to text. Optionally you can add a second argument that specifies how to format the number or date. Use one or more of the format codes shown below (partial list). You may also include literals. Enclose the entire format string in quotes. The entire format argument should be enclosed in quotes.

<table>
<tr><th>Format</th><th>Meaning</th></tr>
<tr><td>MM</td><td>Month number</td></tr>
<tr><td>MON</td><td>Three-letter month abbreviation</td></tr>
<tr><td>MONTH</td><td>Month fully spelled out</td></tr>
<tr><td>DD</td><td>Day of month</td></tr>
<tr><td>DY</td><td>Three-letter day of week abbreviation</td></tr>
<tr><td>YYYY</td><td>Four-digit year</td></tr>
<tr><td>YY</td><td>Two-digit year</td></tr>
<tr><td>YEAR</td><td>Year spelled out</td></tr>
<tr><td>Q</td><td>Number of quarter</td></tr>
<tr><td>HH</td><td>Hour of day (12-hour)</td></tr>
<tr><td>HH24</td><td>Hour of day (24-hour)</td></tr>
<tr><td>MI</td><td>Minutes of hour</td></tr>
<tr><td>SS</td><td>Seconds of minute</td></tr>
<tr><td>A.M.</td><td>AM or PM</td></tr>
<tr><td>9</td><td>Number or blank</td></tr>
<tr><td>0</td><td>Number or zero</td></tr>
</table>
</td></tr>
</table>

Datatype Conversions (continued)	
Oracle	
To_Date(value) Or To_Date(value,format)	Converts a number or text value to a date. This can be used for converting text-equivalent dates to a date datatype for inserting into a table. To_Date can be used with just the numeric or text argument to be converted to a date. Optionally you can add a second argument that specifies how to format the date. The format argument can include literals. The entire format argument should be enclosed in quotes. See the format options under To_Char
To_Number()	Converts a text value to a number.
Floor(expression) Trunc(number, num_dec_places)	Floor reports the integer value of a numeric expression.Trunc truncates a number to a number of decimal places.

The SQL below will report the name of each salesperson and his or her yearly base formatted with two digits to the right of the decimal point and commas every third digit on the left of the decimal point.

```
Select firstname || ' ' || lastname As Salesperson,
To_Char(base*52,'999,999.00') As YearlyBase
From salespeople;

SALESPERSON                               YEARLYBASE
----------------------------------------  -------------
Bob Bentley                                   5,200.00
Lisa Williams                                15,600.00
Clint Sanchez                                 5,200.00
```

List the names and birthdays of all members with June birthdays with the birthday formatted as Jan 01, 2004.

```
Select lastname, firstname, to_char(birthday,'MON DD, YYYY')
From Members
Where to_char(birthday,'mm')= 6

LASTNAME                  FIRSTNAME                  TO_CHAR(BIRT
------------------------- -------------------------- --------------
MacArthur                 Jose                       JUN 24, 1978
```

```
Irving                      Terry                       JUN 22, 1959
Sanders                     Bryce                       JUN 11, 1966
Crum                        Bobby                       JUN 10, 1965
```

The SQL below will truncate pi to three decimal places.

```
Select trunc(3.1415926,3)
From dual;

-------------------------
3.141
```

Handling Nulls

Every database needs some way to determine if a value is null. Oracle provides an ***Nvl*** function. Nvl takes as an argument a value to use as a replacement if the expression is null.

Handling Nulls	
	Oracle
Syntax	Nvl(expression, replacement_value_if_null)
Examples	1. List the web address of each artist. If the web address is null, list 'no website.' `Select Nvl(WebAddress,'No website') From Artists`

```
Select Nvl(WebAddress,'No website')
From Artists

------------------------------------
www.theneurotics.com
No website
No website
www.classical.com/sonata
No website
www.josemacarthur.com
No website
www.today.com
www.21westelm.com
No website
```

Miscellaneous Functions

Here are some functions that Oracle offers that sometimes come in handy. Greatest and Least take any number of arguments, all of which are numeric values to be compared. The greatest or least of them will be reported. These functions are useful when a table has multiple numeric columns that need to be compared. Floor returns the integer value of a number. Example 1 below simply demonstrates how the functions work. Example 2 uses the Least function to detect tracks missing either an mp3 or Real Audio recording. If either is missing, the least value will be 0.

Misc Functions	
	Oracle
Syntax	Greatest(number1, number2, number3) Least(number1, number2, number3)
Examples	1. List the largest of the following numbers: 3, 5, 7, and 9. `Select Greatest(3,5,7,9) from dual`

	2. List any tracks that lack either an mp3 or Real Audio recording.
	`Select TrackTitle From Tracks`
	`Where Least(mp3,RealAud)=0`

Decode

Decode operates similar to the Simple CASE statement discussed in Chapter 2. It allows you to evaluate a value, and based on it return one of several other values. If the expression is equal to the first value supplied, the function will return result1. If the expression is equal to the second value supplied, then the function will return result2. This can continue through any number of values. If the expression is not equal to any of the values, the function will return the final default result.

<table>
<tr><th colspan="2">Decode</th></tr>
<tr><th colspan="2">Oracle</th></tr>
<tr><td>Syntax</td><td>SELECT Decode(Field | Expression, value1, result1, value2, result2, ... default_result) FROM Table</td></tr>
<tr><td>Examples</td><td>1. List the first names of every member and a column that identifies sex as either man or woman.
<code>Select Firstname,
Decode(Gender,'F','woman','M','man')As Sex
From Members</code></td></tr>
<tr><td></td><td>2. List the name, region, and an area identifier for each artist.
<code>Select Artistname,
Region,Decode(Region,
'NC','South',
'VA','South',
'IL','Midwest',
'VT','New England',
'Somewhere Else') As Area
From Artists</code></td></tr>
</table>

Chapter Summary

Every database vendor has extended the power of SQL with special functions and commands. Some are the same across different database systems, but many are unique. Some duplicate the power of ANSI-SQL statements. This chapter has not discussed all such commands and functions, but it has discussed many of the major ones.

Every database system provides a method of concatenating or combining text values. Access does this with the ampersand (&) operator. SQL Server does it with the plus sign (+) operator. Oracle uses two vertical bars (||). MySQL uses the Concat and Concat_WS functions.

The database systems also provide ways to manipulate text, using functions such as Length (or Len), Left, and Right. The syntax of these text functions varies among the various database systems, but the conceptual use of them is always the same. Another common SQL extension is date manipulation. Each database system offers varying ways to generate the current system date, to add and subtract dates, and to report a formatted portion of a date.

Users of some database systems often need to explicitly convert a field value from one datatype to another. This is especially true of SQL Server. Other database systems handle most datatype conversions implicitly. But every database system provides ways to do these conversions when necessary. Finally, every database system provides one or more functions to handle nulls, logic processing functionality, and miscellaneous functions.

It is important to know the differences between these database systems. It is not uncommon for a database to be moved from one database engine to another. By sticking as closely as possible to ANSI-SQL, you can avoid some reprogramming later. In addition, knowledge of these differences can guide any reprogramming you do have to do.

Key Terms

Choose
concatenation
datatype conversion
DateAdd, AddDate
DateDiff
Decode
Floor, Int
IIF
Instr, CharIndex, Locate
IsNull, Nz, Nvl, IfNull
Left
Len, Length
Mid, Substring, Substr
Right
To_Char
To_Date
To_Number
Trim
Trunc, Truncate

Review Questions

1. Why do database vendors make their versions of SQL different from other versions of SQL?
2. How do you concatenate text values in each of our four target database systems?
3. What are the closest Access, Oracle, and MySQL equivalents to the SQL Server IsNull function?
4. What ANSI-SQL statement is Oracle's Decode function most like?
5. How does each of our four target database systems store dates?
6. Why do you need to explicitly convert datatypes?
7. How could you duplicate the InitCap function of Oracle using SQL Server's text functions?
8. If you were migrating an Oracle Decode function to Access, what would you use? What would be the limitations of it?
9. What is the difference between MySQL's Concat and Concat_WS functions?
10. What is the Oracle equivalent of MySQL's CurTime() function?

Exercises

Using any SQL tool, write SQL commands to do the following:

1. Report the artist name and member name for each member who is the responsible party for each artist. Concatenate the first and last name of each member with a space between.
2. Modify the SQL for Exercise #1 to also report the home phone number, formatted as (xxx) xxx-xxxx.

3. Report the studio name and the first name of each studio contact. *Hint:* the first name is the part before the space.
4. Report the studio name and the last name of each studio contact. *Hint:* the last name is the part that follows the space.
5. Report the longest track title.
6. Report the artist name and the age in years of the responsible member for each artist at the time of that artist's entry date.
7. List every genre from the Genre table and the names of any titles in that genre if any. For any genres without titles, display 'No Titles' in the Title column.
8. List each artist name and a lead source designation. If the lead source is 'Ad', then report 'Ad' for the lead source designation. If the lead source is anything else, then report 'Not Ad' for the lead source designation. If doing this with Oracle, use Decode to accomplish this.
9. Report all the genres from the Genre table, capitalizing the first letter of each.
10. Report the track title and time of each track in 'Time Flies,' formatting the time as min:seconds. *Hint:* Use Modulo (see Chapter 2) to obtain seconds. Use formatting or string manipulation to keep leading zeros from dropping.

Additional References

MySQL Date and Time Functions	**http://www.mysql.com/documentation/mysql/bychapter/manual_Reference.html#Date_and_time_functions**
MySQL String Functions	**http://www.mysql.com/documentation/mysql/bychapter/manual_Reference.html#String_functions**
Oracle Migration Workbench for MS Access Reference Guide	**http://download-east.oracle.com/docs/pdf/Z26073_02.pdf**
SQL Server Built-In Functions	**http://www.cs.sfu.ca/CourseCentral/Software/Sybase/TRANSACT-SQL/node11.html**
Oracle 8i Tutorials – Character Functions	**http://www.llcsystems.com/FAQ/oracle_SQL/oracle_SQL_11.htm**

6 Advanced Queries

Chapter Overview

This chapter discusses both advanced SQL syntax and advanced ways to use SQL. Many of these techniques are things you will seldom or rarely do, but it seems that a need is always popping up for one or another of these techniques, so this is good knowledge to have. Specifically, the chapter will focus on the UNION keyword, the INTERSECT and MINUS capabilities of Oracle, and advanced uses of subqueries.

Chapter Objectives

In this chapter, we will:

- Study how to create queries with UNION and UNION ALL
- Study how to create INTERSECT and MINUS queries
- Use subqueries in the SELECT clause
- Create correlated subqueries
- Use Exists with subqueries
- Write nested subqueries

Union Queries

Union queries are not all that complex, but you can do some advanced things with them, as we will see. A *UNION* is similar to a Join in that both involve connecting two tables. But a Union combines the data from two tables in a way that is totally unlike a Join. As we have seen, when you join two tables you then can select columns from either of the tables. It is as if the two tables have been joined up side-by-side to give you more columns to choose from.

In contrast, a UNION joins two tables top to bottom, combining the rows of each. We'll look at an example to help you visualize it. Suppose Lyric Music wants to send out Christmas cards to all members and all studios. Wouldn't it be nice to combine the data from both tables into a master Christmas card list? That's what a Union query does. You simply write one query, add the keyword UNION to the bottom of it, and then write the second query.

```
Select Firstname, LastName, Address, City, Region, PostalCode
From Members
Union
Select Studioname, ' ', Address, City, Region, PostalCode
From Studios
```

```
Firstname            LastName   Address             City            Region  PostalCode
-------------------- ---------- ------------------- --------------- ------- ----------
Lone Star Recording             PO Box 221          Davis           TX      76382
MakeTrax                        3000 S St Rd 9      Anderson        IN      46012
Pacific Rim                     681 PCH             Santa Theresa   CA      99320
Bryce                Sanders    PO Box 1292         Peterson        NC      27104
Warren               Boyer      167 Alamo Dr        Alverez         TX      75601
Kerry                Fernandez  15 Midway           Lynchberg       VA      21223
Doug                 Finney     2020 Dubois         Savannah        GA      30003
Bonnie               Taft       RR4                 Alamaba         VT      05303
Michelle             Henderson  201 Bonaventure     Savannah        GA      30005
Brian                Ranier     23 Gregory Lane     London          ONT     M6Y 2Y7
Louis                Holliday   15 Davis Ct         Clinton         IL      63882
Tony                 Wong       115 Maple St        McKensie        ONT     M8H 3T1
Terry                Irving     18a 7th St          Tybee Island    GA      30004
Frank                Payne      5412 Clinton        New Rochelle    NY      10014
Roberto              Goe        14 Gray Rd          Columbus        OH      48110
Jose                 MacArthur  51444 Vine          Santa Rosa      CA      99999
Aiden                Franks     167 East 38th       Alverez         TX      75601
Davis                Goodman    2020 Country Rd     Columbus        OH      48318
Caroline             Kale       1515 Stone Church Rd Allen          VA      20321
Bobby                Crum       RR2                 Pine            VT      05412
Marcellin            Lambert    142 Sample Rd       Alexandria      VA      20102
Vic                  Cleaver    100 Maple           Reston          VT      05544
Carol                Wanner     787 Airport Rd      Alverez         TX      75601
Roberto              Alvarez    Rt 1                Anderson        IN      46019
William              Morrow     PO Box 1882         New Rochelle    NY      10014
Mary                 Chrisman   1772 East 117th     Fishers         IN      46123
```

This simple example illustrates several things about Union queries. First, you have to select the same number of fields from each table. Since we selected six fields from Members, we had to select six fields from Studios. We had only five fields with relevant data in Studios (since it has only a Studio name instead of a first name and a last name), so we had to compensate by selecting ' ' as a dummy field.

Second, this example illustrates that the fields do not have to be named the same. We used Studioname from one table and Lastname from the other table both in column one. When the corresponding fields do not have the same name, the column name from the first table is used as the heading in the results.

Third, although the corresponding fields do not have to have the same name, they must have the same datatype. You could not, for example, do a union of address and lengthseconds. In other words, to be "union compatible" two recordsets must have the same number of fields and have corresponding fields with the same datatype.

The independent queries of the union can have their own joins, WHERE conditions, and anything else you can do in a query. Suppose we only wanted to send Christmas cards to studios and to members who were the responsible party for each artist.

```
Select Firstname, LastName, Address, City, Region, PostalCode
From Members M Inner Join XRefArtistsMembers X On M.MemberID = X.MemberID
Where RespParty = 1
Union
Select Studioname, ' ', Address, City, Region, PostalCode
From Studios
```

```
Firstname            LastName   Address          City           Region  PostalCode
-------------------- ---------- ---------------- -------------- ------- ----------
Lone Star Recording             PO Box 221       Davis          TX      76382
MakeTrax                        3000 S St Rd 9   Anderson       IN      46012
Pacific Rim                     681 PCH          Santa Theresa  CA      99320
William              Morrow     PO Box 1882      New Rochelle   NY      10014
Brian                Ranier     23 Gregory Lane  London         ONT     M6Y 2Y7
Warren               Boyer      167 Alamo Dr     Alverez        TX      75601
Roberto              Goe        14 Gray Rd       Columbus       OH      48110
Jose                 MacArthur  51444 Vine       Santa Rosa     CA      99999
Roberto              Alvarez    Rt 1             Anderson       IN      46019
Bonnie               Taft       RR4              Alamaba        VT      05303
Marcellin            Lambert    142 Sample Rd    Alexandria     VA      20102
Louis                Holliday   15 Davis Ct      Clinton        IL      63882
Terry                Irving     18a 7th St       Tybee Island   GA      30004
Bryce                Sanders    PO Box 1292      Peterson       NC      27104
```

Let's add one more thing to the example. Let's add an S or M to each row to identify where it is a studio or member. This is just a calculated column, and a pretty simple one at that.

```
Select 'M' As Src, Firstname, LastName, Address, City, Region, PostalCode From Members
M Inner Join XRefArtistsMembers X On M.MemberID = X.MemberID
Where RespParty = 1
Union
Select 'S', Studioname, ' ', Address, City, Region, PostalCode
From Studios
```

```
Src Firstname            LastName  Address         City          Region PostalCode
--- -------------------- --------- --------------- ------------- ------ ----------
S   Lone Star Recording            PO Box 221      Davis         TX     76382
S   MakeTrax                       3000 S St Rd 9  Anderson      IN     46012
S   Pacific Rim                    681 PCH         Santa Theresa CA     99320
M   Roberto              Alvarez   Rt 1            Anderson      IN     46019
M   Jose                 MacArthur 51444 Vine      Santa Rosa    CA     99999
M   Warren               Boyer     167 Alamo Dr    Alverez       TX     75601
M   Bonnie               Taft      RR4             Alamaba       VT     05303
M   William              Morrow    PO Box 1882     New Rochelle  NY     10014
M   Bryce                Sanders   PO Box 1292     Peterson      NC     27104
M   Roberto              Goe       14 Gray Rd      Columbus      OH     48110
M   Marcellin            Lambert   142 Sample Rd   Alexandria    VA     20102
M   Brian                Ranier    23 Gregory Lane London        ONT    M6Y 2Y7
M   Terry                Irving    18a 7th St      Tybee Island  GA     30004
M   Louis                Holliday  15 Davis Ct     Clinton       IL     63882
```

Let's do a more simple union to illustrate an important point. We have mentioned before that the Lyric Music data has 11 artists and 23 members. However, the following Union query of the city and region from each has only 18 rows. If you examine the table data in Appendix A, you will find three members in Alverez, TX, and two in Columbus, OH, as well as other duplicates. Union queries eliminate duplicates.

```
Select city, region
From artists
Union
Select city, region
From members
```

```
city                      region
------------------------- ---------------------
Allen                     VA
Fishers                   IN
Lynchberg                 VA
McKensie                  ONT
Pine                      VT
Reston                    VT
Savannah                  GA
Alexandria                VA
Anderson                  IN
Alabama                   VT
London                    ONT
New Rochelle              NY
Peterson                  NC
Alverez                   TX
Tybee Island              GA
Columbus                  OH
Clinton                   IL
Santa Rosa                CA
```

Union All

If you don't want the duplicates eliminated, use ***Union All*** instead of Union. Let's look at the above SQL with the addition of the word ALL.

```
Select city, region
From artists
Union All
Select city, region
From members
```

```
city                      region
------------------------  --------------
Peterson                  NC
Clinton                   IL
Anderson                  IN
Alexandria                VA
Alverez                   TX
Santa Rosa                CA
Tybee Island              GA
New Rochelle              NY
London                    ONT
```

```
Alamaba             VT
Columbus            OH
Anderson            IN
Santa Rosa          CA
Fishers             IN
Alverez             TX
Savannah            GA
Tybee Island        GA
Savannah            GA
New Rochelle        NY
New Rochelle        NY
Alverez             TX
Peterson            NC
Alverez             TX
London              ONT
Alexandria          VA
Allen               VA
Lynchberg           VA
McKensie            ONT
Alamaba             VT
Clinton             IL
Pine                VT
Reston              VT
Columbus            OH
Columbus            OH
```

Order By Clause in a UNION

These results have not been sorted in any particular order. There are a couple of special rules for ORDER BY in a Union. First, a Union can have only one ORDER BY clause. Second, it must be placed at the end of the statement, controlling the sorting of everything in the Union. Third, the ORDER BY must refer to column names or aliases used in the first SELECT clause. Let's apply an ORDER BY to our first Union example.

```
Select city, region
From artists
Union
Select city, region
From members
Order by region, city
```

```
city                      region
------------------------- ------------------
Santa Rosa                CA
Savannah                  GA
Tybee Island              GA
Clinton                   IL
Anderson                  IN
Fishers                   IN
Peterson                  NC
New Rochelle              NY
Columbus                  OH
London                    ONT
McKensie                  ONT
Alverez                   TX
Alexandria                VA
Allen                     VA
Lynchberg                 VA
Alamaba                   VT
Pine                      VT
Reston                    VT
```

You can do a Union of more than two tables or queries. Just keep adding UNION followed by another query. Union is supported by Access, SQL Server, Oracle, and MySQL version 4 and higher.

Union	
Access, SQL Server, Oracle, MySQL 4	

Syntax	`SELECT Field | Field, Field, Field | *`
	`FROM Table1`
	`UNION | Union All`
	`SELECT Field | Field, Field, Field | *`
	`FROM Table2`
	`Order By Field, Field`

Access, SQL Server, Oracle, MySQL 4	1. List all studios and members who are the responsible party for an artist, identifying the source as S or M.
	`Select 'M' As Src, Firstname, LastName, Address, City, Region, PostalCode`
	`From Members M Inner Join XRefArtistsMembers X`
	`On M.MemberID = X.MemberID`
	`Where RespParty=1`
	`Union`
	`Select 'S', Studioname, ' ', Address, City, Region, PostalCode`
	`From Studios`

Using Union to Report Both Detail and Total

A Union query can do more than report data from two tables. It can also report the data from a single table massaged in different ways. For instance, you can use Union to join the detail from a table with the aggregate from a table to report both detail and totals together. For an example, let's report each track of TitleID 4 plus the total time of all those tracks.

```
Select TrackNum, TrackTitle, LengthSeconds
From Tracks
Where TitleID = 4
Union
Select 99, 'Total', Sum(LengthSeconds)
From Tracks
Where TitleID = 4
Order by TrackNum
```

```
TrackNum    TrackTitle                       LengthSeconds
----------- -------------------------------- -------------
1           Bob's Dream                      185
2           My Wizard                        233
3           Third's Folly                    352
4           Leather                          185
5           Hot Cars Cool Nights             192
6           Music in You                     204
7           Don't Care About Time            221
8           Kiss                             218
9           Pizza Box                        183
10          Goodbye                          240
99          Total                            2213
```

The trick is to get the total to show up on the bottom. In this case we did it by assigning a TrackNum of 99 to the total. If you didn't want to display the TrackNum, you could sort by TrackTitle and assign a TrackTitle of 'xxTotal' or something similar to the total.

Using Union to Report Multiple Summary Statistics

You can also use Union to make multiple independent aggregates of some data and report all the results together. Suppose we wanted to see a count of tracks that were less than two minutes, between two and three minutes, and more than three minutes. We could write that with a Union.

```
Select 1, '< 2 minutes' As Length, Count(*) As NumTracks
```

```
From Tracks
Where LengthSeconds < 240
Union
Select 2, '2-3 minutes', Count(*)
From Tracks
Where LengthSeconds Between 240 and 360
Union
Select 3, '>3 minutes', Count(*)
From Tracks
Where LengthSeconds > 360

            Length        NumTracks
----------- ------------- ----------
1           < 2 minutes   21
2           2-3 minutes   22
3           >3 minutes    7
```

Again, the first column serves only to report the results in the order we want them. It should be noted that this could also be written with a CASE statement. Not only would it be easier to write, it would also run faster. But if you are working in Access, which does not support CASE, this may be your only option.

Using Union to Treat Multiple Columns As One Column

A final handy use of Union is to realign multiple columns into one virtual column to which you can then apply a WHERE or ORDER BY clause. If you have a poor data design, you may have to do this often. But even with well-designed data you may sometimes want to treat multiple columns as one. The SQL below uses a Union as a subquery to report all the MP3 files and all the Real Audio files in a single column. Then it counts the column and reports the total. The Union All is needed to retain duplicates; the way the Union is written, it is nothing but duplicates.

```
Select Count(SoundFile) As Num_Electronic_Files From
(Select MP3 As SoundFile From Tracks Where MP3=1
Union All
Select RealAud From Tracks Where RealAud=1) UnionQuery

Num_Electronic_Files
----------------------
80
```

Note

The Union Query alias is needed because whenever a subquery is used in the FROM clause, it must be given an alias.

Note

The above SQL will not run in Access 97 (or earlier versions) because (as noted in Chapter 4) those versions of Access do not support subqueries in the FROM clause. However, you can save the Union as a separate Access query and use that in the FROM clause.

As you can see, Union is a very useful tool. But you shouldn't use it often. For one thing—as pointed out above—Union is one way to overcome a poor data design, so if you are using too many Unions, it may be a bad sign. Secondly, Union queries often run much more slowly than Joins. For Joins the database can generally take advantage of indexes on primary and foreign keys to speed up the Join. But a Union (especially if run without the All option) has to compare all the columns from every SELECT statement in the UNION. This can take some time. So use Unions sparingly, only when you truly need them.

Intersect and Minus

The INTERSECT keyword is used to determine which rows exist in both of two recordsets. This is an ANSI-standard SQL command, though of our four target databases, INTERSECT is supported only in Oracle. It is written similar to a UNION.

The INTERSECT keyword can be illustrated with our two phone lists used earlier. The SQL statement below will report the three phone numbers that are both in phone1 and in phone2:

```
Select phone
From phone1
Intersect
Select phone
From phone2

PHONE
------------
5556667777
6667778888
7778889999
```

Intersect	
Oracle	

Syntax	`SELECT Field | Field, Field, Field | *`
	`FROM Table1`
	`Intersect`
	`SELECT Field | Field, Field, Field | *`
	`FROM Table2`

Oracle	1. List all cities and regions that have both members and artists.
	`Select city, region`
	`From members`
	`Intersect`
	`Select city, region`
	`From artists`

The MINUS keyword eliminates rows from the first recordset that match the second recordset. So this could give us another way to find unmatched rows. Let's use this to find the genres that do not have recorded titles. In the first recordset we will list all the genres, then we'll use MINUS to take away all the genres with recorded titles.

```
Select genre
From Genre
Minus
Select genre
From Titles

GENRE
-----------
R&B
pop
rap
```

Minus	
Oracle	

Syntax	`SELECT Field | Field, Field, Field | *`
	`FROM Table1`
	`Minus`
	`SELECT Field | Field, Field, Field | *`
	`FROM Table2`

Oracle	1. List all genres that do not have recorded titles.
	`Select genre`
	`From Genre`
	`Minus`
	`Select genre`
	`From Titles`

Of our four target databases, the MINUS keyword is implemented only in Oracle. It is equivalent to the ANSI-standard EXCEPT keyword, which is not implemented in any of our four databases.

Simple SubQueries in the Select Clause

We have already seen the use of subqueries in the WHERE clause (which Access, SQL Server, and Oracle can do) and in the FROM clause (which SQL Server, Oracle, and Access 2000 or higher do). Using subqueries in the SELECT clause gets more complicated. But we will begin with the easiest possible way of doing it.

<table>
<tr><th colspan="2">Subqueries in SELECT Clause</th></tr>
<tr><th colspan="2">Access 2000+, SQL Server, Oracle</th></tr>
<tr><td>Syntax</td><td><pre>SELECT Field, Field, (Select Field From Table2)
FROM Table1</pre></td></tr>
<tr><td>Examples</td><td>1. List track title, length in seconds, and the total seconds for the entire CD for all tracks in TitleID 4.<pre>Select TrackTitle, LengthSeconds,
  (Select Sum(lengthseconds)
  From tracks
  Where titleid = 4) As TotSec
From Tracks
Where titleid = 4</pre></td></tr>
<tr><td></td><td>2. List track title, length in seconds, and the length as a percentage of the total time for the CD for all tracks in TitleID 4.<pre>Select TrackTitle, LengthSeconds,
Cast(Cast(LengthSeconds as Decimal(5,2))/(Select
Sum(lengthseconds)
From Tracks
Where titleid=4)*100 As Decimal(5,2)) As PctTime
From Tracks
Where titleid=4</pre></td></tr>
</table>

Let's analyze this using the second example. If you run the subquery by itself, it returns the total seconds for the entire CD.

```
Select Sum(lengthseconds)
From Tracks
Where titleid = 4

-----------
2213
```

We can use the subquery to place this number in the SELECT clause and use it in a calculation with the length of each track. One interesting thing about this query is the use of Cast within Cast. The inner Cast on LengthSeconds is only to keep the division from ending up with a whole number (which since this is percentage calculation would always be zero). The outer Cast controls the formatting to two decimal places.

So the total query runs like this:

```
Select TrackTitle, LengthSeconds,
Cast(Cast(LengthSeconds as Decimal(5,2))/(Select Sum(lengthseconds)
From Tracks where titleid=4)*100 As Decimal(5,2)) As PctTime
From Tracks Where titleid=4

TrackTitle                    LengthSeconds PctTime
----------------------------  ------------  ----------
Bob's Dream                    185            8.36
My Wizard                      233            10.53
Third's Folly                  352            15.91
Leather                        185            8.36
Hot Cars Cool Nights           192            8.68
Music in You                   204            9.22
Don't Care About Time          221            9.99
Kiss                           218            9.85
Pizza Box                      183            8.27
Goodbye                        240            10.85
```

One key thing to note about this is that in these examples the subquery returns only one row and one column. If any more than that is returned, you would have to use one of the more complicated queries discussed below. But for these examples it just so happens that we want that one column and one row in every row of our outer query.

Since simple SELECT clause subqueries are limited to queries with one row and one column, they are primarily used for cases just like the one above when query information is used in conjunction with a single aggregate from the same or another table.

Correlated Subqueries

A *correlated subquery* returns multiple rows and uses as WHERE clause in the subquery to join each row of the subquery to the appropriate row of the outer query. Suppose we wanted to extend the above query to report multiple titles. We would need to have the subquery return multiple rows, one for each title as shown below:

```
Select TitleID, Sum(lengthseconds)
From Tracks
Group by TitleID

TitleID
---------    -----
1            2237
3            2129
4            2213
5            2087
6            2662
7            2476
```

To link this with the outer query we would write it as follows. To keep the results short we will report only the first track of each title, but that part has nothing to do with making the subquery correlated:

```
Select TrackTitle, LengthSeconds,
  (Select Sum(lengthseconds)
   From Tracks SC
   Where SC.TitleID=T.TitleID) As TotSec
From Tracks T
Where TrackNum = 1

TrackTitle                          LengthSeconds TotSec
----------------------------------  ------------- -------
Bob's Dream                         185           2213
Fat Cheeks                          352           2129
Hottie                              233           2237
Violin Sonata No. 1 in D Major      511           2662
Song 1                              285           2087
I Don't Know                        201           2476
```

At first glance this query seems to violate some of the laws of SQL. The subquery returns multiple rows without a GROUP BY clause and a non-aggregate in SELECT. But it has to be that way simply because a correlated subquery can return only one column—the column that is displayed or used in a calculation. It also seems strange to refer to the T table alias in the subquery when that alias exists only in the outer query. But, again, that is how a correlated subquery is written.

Because of this unique syntax and unlike other subqueries, the subquery portion of a correlated subquery cannot be used as an independent query. This makes correlated subqueries more difficult to debug. But that's why this is in the chapter on advanced queries.

Note

Table aliases are not always required in correlated subqueries. They are required in the above example because the same table is used in both the subquery and the outer query.

<table>
<tr><th colspan="2">Correlated Subqueries</th></tr>
<tr><th colspan="2">SQL Server, Oracle, MySQL 4</th></tr>
<tr><td>Syntax</td><td><pre>SELECT Field, Field,
 (Select Field
  From Table2
  Where Table2.Field = Table1.Field)
FROM Table1</pre></td></tr>
<tr><td>Examples</td><td>1. For the first track on each title, list the track title, length in seconds, total total length for that title, and the length as a percentage of the total time for that title.
<pre>Select TrackTitle, LengthSeconds,
 (Select Sum(lengthseconds)
  From Tracks SC
  Where SC.TitleID = T.TitleID) As TotSec,
  Cast(Cast(LengthSeconds as Decimal(5,2))/
 (Select Sum(lengthseconds)
  From Tracks SC
  Where SC.TitleID = T.TitleID)*100 As Decimal(5,2))
    as PctTime
From Tracks T
Where TrackNum = 1</pre></td></tr>
</table>

The above example builds on what we first did with correlated subqueries. This correlates two subqueries. The first yields the TotSec column. The second yields the PctTime column. We cannot just use TotSec in place of the second subquery, as SQL does not remember what this column alias stands for. Both subqueries can use the SC table alias, since in both cases it exists entirely inside the subquery.

```
Select TrackTitle, LengthSeconds,
  (Select Sum(lengthseconds)
   From Tracks SC
   Where SC.TitleID=T.TitleID) As TotSec,
   Cast(Cast(LengthSeconds as Decimal(5,2))/
  (Select Sum(lengthseconds)
   From Tracks SC
   Where SC.TitleID=T.TitleID)*100 As Decimal(5,2)) as PctTime
From Tracks T
Where TrackNum = 1

TrackTitle                          LengthSeconds TotSec      PctTime
----------------------------------- ------------- -------
Bob's Dream                         185           2213        8.36
Fat Cheeks                          352           2129        16.53
Hottie                              233           2237        10.42
Violin Sonata No. 1 in D Major      511           2662        19.20
Song 1                              285           2087        13.66
I Don't Know                        201           2476        8.12
```

By the way, in this example the PctTime values will not add up to 100. They are the time for each Track 1 as a percentage of the total time for that title. In other words, they are not percentages of the same total.

Correlated subqueries are useful in the right situation. But often the same thing can be accomplished with a FROM clause subquery. Plus using a FROM clause subquery allows you to use any subquery column aliases in the outer query. So for most SQL programmers the following SQL is more understandable than the above correlated subquery and does the same thing.

```
Select TrackTitle, LengthSeconds, TotSec,
Cast(Cast(LengthSeconds as Decimal(5,2))/TotSec*100 as Decimal(5,2))
As PctTime
From Tracks T Inner Join (Select TitleID, Sum(lengthseconds) As
TotSec From Tracks Group by TitleID) SC
On SC.TitleID = T.TitleID
Where TrackNum = 1

TrackTitle                          LengthSeconds TotSec      PctTime
----------------------------------- ------------- ----------- -------
Bob's Dream                         185           2213        8.36
Fat Cheeks                          352           2129        16.53
Hottie                              233           2237        10.42
Violin Sonata No. 1 in D Major      511           2662        19.20
```

```
Song 1                                     285          2087        13.66
I Don't Know                               201          2476        8.12
```

Using EXISTS with Subqueries

EXISTS is a special keyword operator that, like IN, can be used with a subquery and return a True or False value. However, while IN looks for matches between an expression and the values from the subquery, EXISTS just looks at whether or not any rows are returned in the subquery. In other words, EXISTS checks for the existence of data in the subquery. Data is either there (True) or it isn't (False). EXISTS doesn't care what the data looks like as long as some data of some kind exists.

In most cases, EXISTS is used as a WHERE clause subquery but with correlated subquery syntax. For example, suppose we wanted to return a list of all artists with more than one member. Let's start with the inner subquery:

```
Select ArtistID, Count(MemberID)
From XRefArtistsMembers
Group By ArtistID
Having Count(MemberID)> 1

ArtistID
----------- -----
3           2
5           3
10          3
11          2
15          3
16          2
17          2
18          3
```

So far, so good. Now let's make that a subquery in a query with the Artists table. We'll use EXISTS, correlating the ArtistID of the subquery with the ArtistID from the Artists table.

```
Select Artistname
From Artists A
Where Exists (Select ArtistID, Count(MemberID)
              From XRefArtistsMembers X
              Where X.ArtistID= A.ArtistID
              Group By ArtistID
```

```
              Having Count(MemberID)>1)

Artistname
------------
Word
Sonata
The Bullets
Confused
The Kicks
Today
21 West Elm
Highlander
```

Let's examine this code. All we do is add the correlated subquery WHERE clause syntax to the subquery. What SQL does is this: for each row in the Artists table, it runs the subquery for just that ArtistID. That will return either one row for that artist or zero rows if that artist has fewer than two members. If it has zero rows, the subquery data does not "exist," and the outer query will not report that row.

I know what you're thinking. Why not just join the subquery to the Artists table? It is easier to write and easier to think through. For instance, here is SQL using join to accomplish the same thing:

```
Select Artistname From Artists A
Inner Join
 (Select ArtistID, Count(MemberID) as NumMem From XRefArtistsMembers
Group By ArtistID Having Count(MemberID)>1) SQ
On A.ArtistID = SQ.ArtistID

Artistname
-------------
Word
Sonata
The Bullets
Confused
The Kicks
Today
21 West Elm
Highlander
```

So why give yourself a headache by thinking through an EXISTS subquery when a Join will do? Because the EXISTS subquery will be faster. With an EXISTS subquery, SQL does not have to perform a full row-by-row join, building the Cartesian product and then tossing out the unmatched rows. It simply runs the subquery for each row of the outer query. In fact, in some cases it doesn't even have to run the entire subquery, since as soon as it finds one good record it knows that at least some data exists.

That would not be the case in the above example that returns at most one record for each artist. But suppose we wanted a list of artists who had produced one or more titles. We could write it this way:

```
Select Artistname
From Artists A
Where Exists
  (Select ArtistID
   From Titles T
   Where T.ArtistID = A.ArtistID)

Artistname
---------------
The Neurotics
Louis Holiday
Sonata
The Bullets
Confused
```

Some artists have zero titles, some have one, and some have two or more. As soon as the subquery finds the first match for a given artist, SQL can go ahead and include the artist name. So while EXIST subqueries can be a little confusing, they are definitely powerful.

A rule of thumb in the real world is to balance speed of execution with maintainability. If a query will be run every day and the database is large, it is worthwhile to write the query for the best possible performance, such as using correlated subqueries. But if you will run the query just once or rarely, performance is not as big a factor as is understanding what you are doing and being able to maintain the code later. In that case, trade off some performance and use a Join.

Nested Subqueries

SQL allows you to nest subqueries within subqueries. SQL Server, for example, allows subqueries to be nested 32 levels deep. However the number of levels of nesting allowed is not that important because you will get confused well before SQL ever does. The issue of performance versus maintainability really becomes important with ***nested subqueries***.

Let's just extend the above example and list the names of all the artists who have recorded a title with ten or more tracks.

<table>
<tr><th colspan="2">Using EXISTS With Subqueries</th></tr>
<tr><th colspan="2">SQL Server, Oracle, MySQL 4</th></tr>
<tr><td>Syntax</td><td><pre>SELECT Field, Field,
From Table
FROM Table1
Where Exists (Select Field, Field from Table2
Where Table1.Field=Table2.Field)</pre></td></tr>
<tr><td>Examples</td><td>1. List the names of all artists who have recorded a title.<pre>Select Artistname
From Artists A
Where Exists
  (Select ArtistID
   From Titles T
   Where T.ArtistID = A.ArtistID)</pre></td></tr>
</table>

```
Select Artistname
From Artists A
Where Exists
  (Select ArtistID
   From Titles T
   Where T.ArtistID = A.ArtistID
   And Exists
     (Select TitleID, Count(TrackNum)
      From Tracks TR
      Where TR.TitleID = T.TitleID
      Group by TitleID
      Having Count(Tracknum)>= 10))

Artistname
------------------------
The Bullets
Confused
```

What is this doing? The first subquery now has an AND added to its WHERE clause. This second test uses EXISTS with a nested subquery that reports all titles with 10 or more tracks. Let's do a simpler join to verify our results:

```
Select Artistname, Title, Count(Tracknum) As NumTracks
From Artists A Inner Join Titles T  On T.ArtistID= A.ArtistID
Inner Join Tracks TR On TR.TitleID = T.TitleID
Group by Artistname, Title

Artistname                 Title                          NumTracks
-------------------------  ------------------------------ ----------
Louis Holiday              Louis at the Keys              8
The Neurotics              Meet the Neurotics             8
The Neurotics              Neurotic Sequel                9
Confused                   Smell the Glove                10
Sonata                     Sonatas                        5
The Bullets                Time Flies                     10
```

In the real world you won't find many situations where writing SQL with nested subqueries is the most advisable approach. But those situations do exist (no pun intended), and it is nice to have this tool available for them.

Chapter Summary

While Joins connect tables side by side, UNION, INTERSECT, and MINUS are ways of connecting tables top to bottom. UNION reports all rows from multiple queries, eliminating duplicates. UNION ALL reports all rows from multiple queries, without eliminating duplicates. INTERSECT is an Oracle-only feature that reports all the rows that are only in both of two tables or queries. MINUS is an Oracle-only feature that eliminates rows from the first recordset that matches the second recordset.

This chapter also discussed advanced uses of subqueries, including using subqueries in the SELECT clause, correlated subqueries, and using subqueries with EXISTS. In simple SELECT clause subqueries, the subquery can have only one column and one row, and so they are primarily used to include a single aggregated value in the SELECT list. Correlated subqueries can have multiple columns and rows and use WHERE syntax to link the rows of the subquery with the rows of the outer query. EXISTS can also be used with correlated subqueries. EXISTS simply looks at whether or not any matching rows are returned in the subquery. If some rows exist, then EXISTS reports True. Otherwise it reports False.

Key Terms

correlated subqueries
EXISTS
Intersect
Minus
nested subqueries
Union
Union All

Review Questions

1. What makes two recordsets "union compatible?"
2. What is the difference between Union and Union All?
3. What is the difference between IN and EXISTS before a subquery?
4. Why is EXISTS with a subquery faster than a Join?
5. What does INTERSECT do?
6. What does MINUS do?
7. What does EXISTS with a subquery return to the outer query?
8. What is the difference between how two tables are combined with a Union compared to a Join?
9. If you want the results of a Union query sorted, where do you place the ORDER BY clause(s)?
10. A definition for the word correlated is, "to put into a complementary or reciprocal relationship." What does that definition have to do with what goes on in a correlated subquery?

Exercises

Using any SQL tool, write SQL commands to do the following:

1. Using EXISTS, list the names of all artists who have not recorded a title (Can be done only with SQL Server or Oracle).
2. Produce a single list of studio names with their web addresses and artist names with their web addresses. Eliminate from the list any studios or artists without a web address.
3. The following SQL statement uses an Intersect to list all cities and regions that have both members and artists: Select city, region from members Intersect Select city, region from artists. Unfortunately, you cannot use Intersect in any of our databases except Oracle. Write a query that would run in the other databases, using a Join to accomplish the same thing.

4. Report the title name, number of tracks, and total time in minutes for each title (Can be done only with SQL Server, Oracle, or Access 2000+).
5. Produce a list of all of the area codes used in both member's home phones and studio's phones along with a count of the phone numbers for each area code.
6. For each artist, list the artist name and the first and last name (together in one column) of every member associated with that artist. On the next line, follow that information with a count of the number of members associated with that artist. Include all artists whether they have members or not. *Hints:* Depending on which database you use, you may have to cast or convert the count into a text value. To get the sorting to work, the use of a dummy file will likely be required.
7. Use a correlated subquery to list all genres that do not have recorded titles (Can be done only with SQL Server or Oracle).

Additional References

HotOracle.com – The Union Clause
http://www.hot-oracle.com/articles.html?articleId=25&page=1

HotOracle.com – The Intersect Clause
http://www.hot-oracle.com/articles.html?articleId=25&page=2

HotOracle.com – The Minus Clause
http://www.hot-oracle.com/articles.html?articleId=25&page=3

SmartSoft Computing LTD – Advanced SQL Tutorial
http://www.smart-soft.co.uk/Oracle/advanced-sql-tutorial.htm

DevGuru – Beyond the Basics with SQL
http://www.devguru.com/features/tutorials/AdvancedSQL/advancedSQL.html

7

Data Manipulation

Chapter Overview

SQL is not just for reading information from a database. SQL can also add, edit, and delete records. In this chapter we will learn the powerful INSERT, DELETE, and UPDATE commands. These can operate with specified values or with data read from other tables. The chapter will also discuss the concept of transactions, which let you group individual commands and require they be completed or not completed as a group. The chapter will demonstrate the use of Commit and Rollback for controlling transactions and provide a brief look at procedural programming to SQL Server and Oracle to issue Commits and Rollbacks based on errors. Finally, this chapter will discuss the issues of concurrency, data locking, and the problem of deadlock.

Chapter Objectives

In this chapter, we will:

- Study the concepts of front-end and back-end as they relate to database applications
- Add rows to a table using INSERT
- Delete rows from a table using DELETE
- Edit data in existing rows using UPDATE
- Study the concept of transactions and using Commits and Rollbacks
- Learn how SQL Server and Oracle can rollback transactions on errors
- Understand the concepts of concurrency, locking, and deadlock

DML and Front-End Programming

In this chapter we will do more than just view data from a database. The SQL commands discussed here will add new records, edit existing records, and delete records.

This is a good time to bring up the concept of ***back-end*** vs. ***front-end*** as it relates to database applications. The term back-end refers to the data in your database, as well as the database engine that controls it. The term front-end refers to the user interface. In the exercises in this book, our back-end has been the Lyric Music database and SQL Server, Oracle, Access, or MySQL. The front-end we have used has been SQL Server's Query Analyzer, Oracle's SQL Plus, MySQL Manager, Access's query interface, or the SQL Test web page.

However, in a real-world database application the front-end would be much more complex and user-friendly. The front-end might be a web application written in ASP, PHP, JSP or other technologies. It might be a Visual Basic program connected to a remote database. It might even be a program on a hand-held computer with wireless connectivity to the back-end database. Whatever it is, the front-end program might use SQL SELECT statements to allow the user to browse records from the database and display an entire record on the screen. It might use SQL SELECT statements to fill in drop-down choices on a form. It could also use the commands we will learn in this chapter to edit, delete, and add new records to the tables. Many of the concepts we will discuss in this chapter, including transactions and locking, impact front-end programming greatly.

There is even a class of back-end programming that can do a lot of the functions required by a front-end, but do them in the more safe and controlled environment of the back-end database. These are stored procedures. This chapter will not cover stored procedure programming, as that is beyond the scope of this book. However, we will look briefly at Oracle's PL/SQL and SQL Server's script processing, which is the first step into that world of database programming.

Note

SQL data manipulation commands will not work on the SQL Test web page on the textbook web site. If you have set up your own web server with the SQL Test web page or you are running SQL directly against a database, these commands should work fine.

Insert

You can use SQL to add new records to a table. There are two general forms of the syntax. One is for inserting a single new record using specific values. The other is for inserting one or more records using the results of a query. In both cases the ***INSERT*** statement has two parts. The first part lists the table and the fields that will receive the data. The second part specifies the values to be inserted into the table.

Insert (using specific values)	
Access, SQL Server, Oracle, MySQL	
Syntax	`INSERT INTO Table (Field, Field, Field)` `  Values (value, value, value)`

Examples	1. Add 'Hip-Hop' as a new genre in the Genre table.
	
	`Insert into Genre(Genre)`
	`  Values('hip-hop')`

	2. Add new title as TitleID 8, which has been recorded by Word (ArtistID 3) called 'Word Live,' recorded in StudioID 2 in the genre 'pop.'
	
	`Insert into Titles(TitleID,ArtistID,Title,`
	`StudioID,Genre)`
	`  Values(8,3,'Word Live',3,'pop')`

	3. Add a new salesperson as SalesID 5 named Bryce Sanders with initials of bgs, a base salary of 200, and supervised by SalesID 1.
	
	`Insert into Salespeople`
	`  Values(5,'Bryce','Sanders','bgs',200,1)`

Example 1 is about as simple as you can get. We are inserting a record into a table with only one field. So the field list has only one entry, and the values list has only one entry. Notice that quotes are placed around the text value in the values list. The value you place into a column must always be of the correct datatype and, if needed, have the proper characters enclosing it.

Example 2 is more interesting. Now we are inserting five fields for a single record. Commas separate each of the fields in the field list. Commas also separate each of the values in the values list. The numeric values do not need to have quotes around them. If you check Appendix A you will see that Titles also has a UPC field, which we are not providing a value for. It is possible to leave a field blank if the table is set up to allow null values in that field or if the table is set up to provide a default value for that field. We will see how to do those things in Chapter 8.

Note

When inserting records to a table, you must supply values to all fields except those that autogenerate, those with default values, and those that can have null values. This means that you must understand the back-end database you are working with if you want to successfully use SQL manipulation commands. If you want to explicitly insert a null value you should use the value Null without quotes. SQL will not allow you to use two commas together with nothing between them. Foreign Key constraints, discussed in Chapter 8, may further limit the kinds of values you can insert into tables.

Example 3 lacks a field list. If you are inserting values for every field in a record, you can dispense with the field list and just list each value in proper field order. Though this is handy, it isn't recommended for most applications. For one thing, this code does a pretty poor job of documenting itself. More importantly, if for whatever reason the fields were created in a different order than you thought they were, the insert would probably fail. Worse, it might not fail but put the values into the wrong fields.

If you run any of these commands you will notice that INSERT returns no records. If you want to see the inserted record, you can then do a SELECT.

Insert (using a query)	
Access, SQL Server, Oracle, MySQL	

Syntax	`INSERT INTO Table1 (Field, Field, Field)`
	`SELECT Field, Field, Field`
	`FROM Table2`

Access, SQL Server, Oracle, MySQL	1. Populate the AudioFile table with all the mp3s from the Tracks table.
	
	`Insert into Audiofiles(TitleID, Tracknum, AudioFormat)`
	`Select TitleID, Tracknum, 'mp3'`
	`From Tracks Where MP3 = 1`

Access, SQL Server, Oracle	2. Add a new salesperson as SalesID 6, named Courtney Mulligan with initials of cgm, a base salary of 200, and supervised by Bob Bentley. Assign her the next available SalesID.
	
	`Insert into Salespeople (SalesID, Firstname, Lastname, Initials, Base, Supervisor)`
	`Select 6, 'Courtney','Mulligan','cgm',200, SalesID`
	`From Salespeople`
	`Where Firstname = 'Bob' And Lastname='Bentley'`

When inserting records with a query you simply follow the field list with a SELECT statement. The SELECT statement can be any valid SQL SELECT and can include the use of Joins, subqueries, and anything else supported by the database system. However, an ORDER BY clause will be ignored. The SELECT statement must produce the same number of columns, in the same order, and with the same datatype as either the field list or, if the field list is omitted, the fields of the table. Since a SELECT statement might return multiple records, this version of INSERT can insert many records with one statement.

That is what is shown with Example 1. This Audiofiles table does not actually exist in the Lyric Music database. But if it did, this statement could populate the table with all the MP3 audio files. Notice that the SELECT statement includes a text value "mp3" to be used in every record.

Example 2 uses a mix of specific values and looked-up table values. The SalesID of the supervisor, Bob Bentley, is looked up from the table. This example will not run in MySQL. MySQL will not accept an INSERT statement using a SELECT statement that pulls from the same table you are inserting into. According to MySQL documentation, this is because SELECT could find records inserted earlier during the same INSERT and lead to unpredictable results. Despite that good reason, this example will run in our other target databases.

Delete

Of the three commands we will look at in this chapter, DELETE is the simplest. It will delete one or more rows from a table. The syntax is simply DELETE FROM followed by a table name and a WHERE condition that specifies which row or rows to delete.

Delete	
Access, SQL Server, Oracle, MySQL	

Syntax	`DELETE`
	`FROM Table`
	`WHERE Condition`

Access, SQL Server, Oracle, MySQL	1. Delete the salesperson with SalesID 6.
	
	`Delete`
	`From Salespeople`
	`Where SalesID = 6`

	2. Delete the salesperson named Courtney Mulligan.
	
	`Delete`
	`From Salespeople`
	`Where Firstname = 'Courtney'`
	`And Lastname = 'Mulligan'`

Access, SQL Server, Oracle	3. Delete all records in the Audiofiles table related to the CD, Time Flies.
	
	`Delete`
	`From Audiofiles`
	`Where TitleID =(Select TitleID`
	`From Titles`
	`Where Title = 'Time Flies')`

Example 1 shows a simple DELETE using the primary key field to identify the row to be deleted. If you want to delete a single row, identify that row with the primary key, since it is always unique. Example 2 deletes the same record but using two non-primary key fields to identify the record. While this works, there is always a chance of having more records with these first and last names. Therefore, it is always much safer to delete using the primary key.

Example 3 shows how to delete multiple rows in one table with a WHERE clause that refers to a second table. SQL does not support using a Join in a DELETE statement. So if you need to refer to a second table, it has to be with a subquery. Of course, MySQL does not support subqueries, so it is limited to deleting rows based only on the fields of the same table. Most of the time, that is not a severe limitation, as you will normally delete rows based on that table's primary key.

Note

As with INSERT commands, Foreign Key constraints, discussed in Chapter 8, may further limit the kinds of values you can delete into tables.

Update

The *UPDATE* command will modify existing data in a table. The syntax in its simplest form is to specify the table to be updated followed by SET and field=value. If you are setting multiple values, use SET only once and separate each field=value pair with a comma. The value that you set the field(s) to can be a specific values, the old value plus new information, the result of a mathematical calculation, or a value from another field. Use a WHERE clause to specify which records to change.

Single Table Update Statements

The most straightforward UPDATE statements are those that use a single table. The examples below illustrate setting a field to a value (Example 1), setting a field to its previous value plus new information (Example 2), setting a field to the value of another field (Example 3), updating multiple fields (Example 4), and updating a single field based on multiple criteria (Example 5).

Update (single table)	
	Access, SQL Server, Oracle, MySQL

Syntax	`UPDATE Table`
	`SET Field = Value, Field = Value`
	`WHERE Condition`

Examples	1. Change the Base for SalesID 3 to $200.
	`Update Salespeople`
	`Set Base = 200`
	`Where SalesID = 3`
	2. Give salesperson Bob Bentley a $50 raise in Base.
	`Update Salespeople`
	`Set Base = Base+50`
	`Where Firstname = 'Bob'`
	`And Lastname = 'Bentley'`

	3. Member Frank Payne works from his home. Set his Workphone number to the value of his Homephone number.
	`Update Members`
	`Set Workphone = Homephone`
	`Where Firstname = 'Frank' And Lastname = 'Payne'`

	4. Change the record for the title Time Flies to set the UPC to 1828344222 and the Genre to 'pop'.
	`Update Titles`
	`Set UPC = '1828344222', Genre = 'pop'`
	`Where Title = 'Time Flies'`

	5. All members who live in Virginia and who have previously been handled by the salesperson with SalesID 3 will now be handled by the salesperson with SalesID 4.
	`Update Members`
	`Set SalesID = 4`
	`Where Region = 'VA' And SalesID = 3`

Multi-Table Update Statements

Sometimes either the values to be used for updating or the criteria to be used for selecting records to update come from a different table than the one being updated. The syntax and the capabilities for doing this vary among the databases.

SQL Server

<table>
<tr><th colspan="2">Update (multi-table)</th></tr>
<tr><th colspan="2">SQL Server</th></tr>
<tr><td>Syntax</td><td><pre>UPDATE Table1
SET Field = Value, Field = Value|Subquery
FROM Table1 INNER|LEFT|RIGHT JOIN Table2
ON Table1.Field = Table2.Field
WHERE Condition</pre></td></tr>
<tr><td rowspan="2">Examples</td><td>1. All the members of the group Confused now have e-mail addresses that are the member's firstname followed by @confused.com. Update the member records appropriately.<pre>Update Members
Set Email = firstname+'@confused.com'
From Members M
Inner Join Xrefartistsmembers X
On M.MemberID = X.MemberID
Inner Join Artists A
On A.ArtistID = X.ArtistID
Where Artistname = 'Confused'</pre></td></tr>
<tr><td>2. All members who live in Virginia and who have previously been handled by salesperson Scott Bull will now be handled by salesperson Clint Sanchez.<pre>Update Members
Set SalesID=(Select SalesID From Salespeople
Where Firstname='Clint' And Lastname='Sanchez')
From Members Inner Join Salespeople
On Members.SalesID=Salespeople.SalesID
Where Region='VA' And Salespeople.Firstname='Scott'
And Salespeople.Lastname='Bull'</pre></td></tr>
</table>

In SQL Server, a multi-table UPDATE requires a small change in the syntax from the single-table UPDATE. Between the SET and WHERE clauses, you can add a FROM clause where you can join multiple tables and an ON clause to specify the join relationships. You can also use Equi

Join syntax by just listing the tables separated by commas and specifying the join relationships in the WHERE clause.

Example 1 joins three tables to identify the appropriate records by the name "Confused." Example 2 uses a two-table Join so that it can identify members handled by Scott Bull. However, that Join does not give the query access to the SalesID for Clint Sanchez. That is brought in with a subquery in the SET statement.

Oracle

<table>
<tr><th colspan="2">UPDATE (multi-table)</th></tr>
<tr><th colspan="2">Oracle</th></tr>
<tr><td>Syntax</td><td><pre>UPDATE Table|Subquery
SET Field = Value, Field = Value|subquery
WHERE Condition</pre></td></tr>
<tr><td rowspan="2">Examples</td><td>1. All the members of the group Confused now have e-mail addresses that are the member's firstname followed by an @confused.com. Update the member records appropriately.<pre>Update Members
Set Email = firstname||'@confused.com'
Where MemberID IN
(Select M.MemberID From Members M
Inner Join Xrefartistsmembers X
On M.MemberID = X.MemberID
Inner Join Artists A
On A.ArtistID = X.ArtistID
Where Artistname = 'Confused')</pre></td></tr>
<tr><td>2. All members who live in Virginia and who have previously been handled by salesperson Scott Bull will now be handled by salesperson Clint Sanchez.<pre>Update (Select Members.SalesID
From Members Inner Join Salespeople
On Members.SalesID=Salespeople.SalesID
Where Region='VA' And Salespeople.Firstname='Scott'
And Salespeople.Lastname='Bull')
Set SalesID=(Select SalesID From Salespeople
Where Firstname='Clint' And Lastname='Sanchez')</pre></td></tr>
</table>

The above examples show two ways of doing multi-table updates in Oracle. Example 1 uses the table name in the UPDATE statement and a subquery in the WHERE clause to limit the rows in the table being updated. Example 2 uses a subquery in the UPDATE statement. For this to work the table being updated must be "key preserved" within the subquery or you will get an error. Basically that means you need to have primary keys properly defined, but sometimes it gets more complicated than that. Example 1's use of IN would not have the performance of a subquery, but it would get the job done.

MySQL

<table>
<tr><th colspan="2">UPDATE (multi-table)</th></tr>
<tr><th colspan="2">MySQL 4.0+</th></tr>
<tr><td>Syntax</td><td><pre>UPDATE Table1, Table2
SET Field = Value, Field = Value
WHERE Table1.Field=Table2.Field
AND Condition</pre></td></tr>
<tr><td>Examples</td><td>1. All the members of the group Confused now have e-mail addresses that are the member's firstname followed by an @confused.com. Update the member records appropriately.<pre>Update Members M, Xrefartistsmembers X, Artists A
Set Email = Concat(firstname,'@confused.com')
Where M.MemberID = X.MemberID
And A.ArtistID = X.ArtistID
And Artistname = 'Confused'</pre></td></tr>
<tr><td></td><td>2. All members who live in Virginia and who have previously been handled by salesperson Scott Bull will now be handled by salesperson Clint Sanchez.<pre>Update Members,Salespeople
Set SalesID=3
Where Members.SalesID=Salespeople.SalesID
And Region='VA'
And Salespeople.Firstname='Scott'
And Salespeople.Lastname='Bull'</pre></td></tr>
</table>

The MySQL syntax (which works only in version 4.04 and higher) uses what is essentially an Equi-Join to do the multi-table update. Notice, however, that in Example 2 MySQL cannot use a subquery in the SET clause. The only solution is to first look up Clint Sanchez's SalesID (3) and then use that value in the SET clause.

Access

UPDATE (multi-table)	
Access	

Syntax	`UPDATE Table`
	`SET Field = Value, Field = Value|subquery`
	`WHERE Condition`

Examples	1. All the members of the group Confused now have e-mail addresses that are the member's firstname followed by an @confused.com. Update the member records appropriately.
	`Update Members`
	`Set Email = firstname&'@confused.com'`
	`Where MemberID IN(Select M.MemberID`
	`From (Members M Inner Join Xrefartistsmembers X`
	`On M.MemberID = X.MemberID) Inner Join Artists A`
	`On A.ArtistID = X.ArtistID`
	`Where Artistname = 'Confused')`

	2. All members who live in Virginia and who have previously been handled by salesperson Scott Bull will now be handled by salesperson Clint Sanchez, who is SalesID 3.
	`Update MembersSet SalesID=3`
	`Where MemberID IN(Select Members.MemberID`
	`From Members Inner Join Salespeople`
	`On Members.SalesID=Salespeople.SalesID`
	`Where Region='VA' And Salespeople.Firstname='Scott'`
	`And Salespeople.Lastname='Bull')`

Access is more limited. Example 1 works with the same syntax as for Oracle, except that parentheses are needed to group the Joins. However, Example 2 demonstrates that Access cannot use a subquery in the SET clause. If you try, you will get an error saying you must use an updateable query. The only solution is to first look up Clint Sanchez's SalesID (3) and then use that value in the SET clause.

Transactions

Suppose you wanted to add a new CD title and all its tracks. Adding the title is one INSERT. Adding the tracks is one or more separate INSERT(s). Suppose something happens at some point in this process. It could be anything. Perhaps the database server goes down. Perhaps another user is trying to add a different title but with the same TitleID, and so there is a conflict. If, for whatever reason, only some of these new records are added, we have a problem. That problem is inconsistent data. By looking at the Titles table you would think the title was added just fine, but it isn't.

It is for these kinds of situations that ***transactions*** exist. Transactions let you group individual commands and require that they be completed or not completed as a group. A transaction is a logical unit of work made up of a series of statements (SELECTs, INSERTs, UPDATEs, or DELETEs). If no errors are encountered during the transaction, then all of the modifications in the transaction become a permanent part of the database. If errors are encountered, then none of the modifications are made to the database.

There are four major properties of transactions that make up the acronym ACID:

- ***Atomicity***—A transaction is a logical unit of work that should be completely done or else not done at all.
- ***Consistency***—When completed, data is consistent with itself. There will be no orphan records. There will be no discrepancy between detail and totals.
- ***Isolation***—No other users see any parts of transaction until it is completed.
- ***Durability***—When finished, all parts of the transaction persist.

Basic Transaction Syntax

With some variation among our target databases, we have three tools for making transactions work: BEGIN, ***ROLLBACK***, and ***COMMIT***. BEGIN marks the start of the transaction. If at any point the transaction is cancelled, it undoes everything back to BEGIN. ROLLBACK cancels the transaction. COMMIT writes all data to the permanent tables and ends the transaction. Let's take as an example deleting a title and all its tracks.

SQL Server

```
Begin Tran
Delete From Tracks Where TitleID=44
Delete From Titles Where TitleID=44
Commit Tran
```

MySQL

```
Begin;
Delete From Tracks Where TitleID=44;
Delete From Titles Where TitleID=44;
Commit;
```

Oracle

```
Commit;
```

```
Delete From Tracks Where TitleID=44;
Delete From Titles Where TitleID=44;
Commit;
```

As you can see, there is little difference in the syntax. SQL Server uses BEGIN TRANS (or BEGIN TRANSACTION) and COMMIT TRANS (or COMMIT TRANSACTION). In MySQL, the transaction commands are simply BEGIN, ROLLBACK, and COMMIT. However, when using transactions each of these commands as well as each SQL statement must end with a semi-colon (;). Oracle does not have BEGIN TRANSACTION command. A transaction is defined as the statements that fall between two COMMIT commands. As with MySQL, each transaction command and each SQL statement must end with a semi-colon (;). Microsoft Access does not support transactions in SQL. Access SQL can process only one statement at a time, so transactions are impossibile. You can, however, use transactions in Access Visual Basic for Applications (VBA).

Note

MySQL has various kinds of table types. Unless specified when the table is created, the table type will default to MyISAM, which is not capable of processing transactions. Only InnoDB and or BDB table types support transactions. See Chapter 8 to see how to create a table with a particular table type.

In the examples above, BEGIN TRAN (or Begin or the first Commit) marks the beginning of the transaction. Although the first DELETE is processed, the changes are not permanently written to the database until COMMIT TRAN (or Commit) is encountered. Between those two points, all the statements in the transaction can be rolled back as if they never happened.

Note

In the above example we deleted the related records from the child table, Tracks, before deleting the parent record in Titles. If you have set up a foreign key constraint to enforce the integrity of your data, as discussed in Chapter 8, you must delete child records before deleting parent records.

If instead of committing the transaction, you wanted to roll back the transaction you could use:

SQL Server

```
Begin Tran
Delete From Tracks Where TitleID=44
```

```
Delete From Titles Where TitleID=44
Rollback Tran
```

MySQL

```
Begin;
Delete From Tracks Where TitleID=44;
Delete From Titles Where TitleID=44;
Rollback;
```

Oracle

```
Commit;
Delete From Tracks Where TitleID=44;
Delete From Titles Where TitleID=44;
Rollback;
```

You could put anything between BEGIN TRAN and ROLLBACK TRAN, even a command to drop the entire database, and it would not be permanently done.

Rolling Back on Errors

Suppose we have two genres to add to the Genre table. For whatever reason we want both to be added or neither to be added. We write the following transaction (SQL Server syntax):

```
Begin Tran
Insert into Genre(genre) Values('classical')
Insert into Genre(genre) Values('ska')
Commit Tran
```

If we have a primary key set up on the genre field, the first INSERT will fail because we already have a classical genre, and primary keys must have unique values. However, if you run this transaction you will find that the second INSERT will still be committed into the database. In other words, an error does not by itself stop a transaction. To make these statements commit together or not at all, we need to add some code to test for whether an error has happened and then issue either a Rollback or a Commit, depending on whether or not there was an error. That concept is straightforward, but to implement it in SQL is not. In addition, each database system takes a different approach.

Below we will discuss how to rollback on errors using SQL Server scripts and Oracle PL/SQL. MySQL provides no native If logic processing that will allow us to trap, test, and respond to errors. That doesn't mean that you cannot handle errors in transactions with MySQL. It simply means that, as with Microsoft Access, if you use MySQL you need to handle transaction errors through your front-end programming.

Rollback on Error in SQL Server

In SQL Server you test for an error condition using the @@Error global variable. SQL Server maintains a powerful set of ***global variables*** always available in any SQL statement. These variables give you access to the last error that occurred (@@Error), the last identity value generated (@@Identity), the number of tows affected by the last statement (@@Rowcount), the server name (@@Servername), and many other things.

The use of @@Error has to be paired with some form of IF logic. The syntax for IF logic in SQL Server is:

```
If condtion action_to_take
Else alternative_action_to_take
```

The ELSE is optional. You can even have multiple lines of actions and alternative actions as long as you begin each list with the word BEGIN (not to be confused with BEGIN TRANS) and end with the word END.

So you might think we could write our code like this:

```
Begin Tran
Insert into Genre(genre) Values('classical')
Insert into Genre(genre) Values('ska')
If @@Error <>0 Rollback Tran
Else Commit Tran
```

You might think that, but you would be wrong. The reason is that @@Error is reset with every SQL command. The above code tests for problems with the last INSERT only. We need to introduce one more concept: local variables. Local variables are variables you define yourself. They begin with one @ sign followed by a name you make up. You have to ***declare*** each variable with a datatype. So here would be one way to write a rollback on error that would work:

```
Begin Tran
Declare @ErrCheck int
Insert into Genre(genre) Values('classical')
Set @ErrCheck = @@Error
Insert into Genre(genre) Values('ska')
Set @ErrCheck = @ErrCheck + @@Error
If @ErrCheck <>0 Rollback Tran
Else Commit Tran
```

What does this code do? After beginning the transaction, the DECLARE creates our local variable @ErrCheck as an integer. Then we do the first INSERT and capture into @ErrCheck whatever is in @@Error—it will be either 0 for no error or some other number. Next we do the second INSERT and add any error code from that to what is already in @ErrCheck. At this point @ErrCheck is the sum of the errors (if any) from the two INSERT commands. We check if it is equal to zero (meaning no errors) and either Rollback or Commit. This procedure does nothing to keep track of different kinds of errors and handle them appropriately. It just fails or succeeds. But for us it succeeds in demonstrating how to rollback errors.

Rollback on Error in Oracle

To rollback transaction errors in Oracle, we have to move from regular SQL to PL/SQL. ***PL/SQL*** is a procedural programming language that can be used in SQL *Plus. PL/SQL not only uses all the regular SQL commands that you have seen up to this point, it also implements IF logic structures, looping, and more. All we can do in this section is give you the briefest introduction to PL/SQL to demonstrate how you might handle transaction errors.

PL/SQL programs are structured in the following blocks. All lines except DECLARE, BEGIN, and EXCEPTION must end with a semi-colon (;). The slash (/) character actually executes the PL/SQL script.

```
DECLARE
  Local variable declarations
BEGIN
  Body of PL/SQL code
EXCEPTION
  Error handling code
END;
/
```

In Oracle errors are called exceptions. There are a few predefined exceptions, including TOO_MANY_ROWS and NO_DATA_FOUND. Other kinds of errors are called undefined exceptions. To handle an undefined exception, you must explicitly declare the exception and associate it with a specific Oracle error code. You can find an Oracle error code by deliberately issuing an SQL statement that causes an error. For example, here is how we can learn that violating a unique constraint is error code 00001:

```
SQL> Insert into Genre Values('classical');
Insert into Genre Values('classical')
*
ERROR at line 1:
ORA-00001: unique constraint (TEST.PK_GENRE) violated
```

Below is PL/SQL code that will rollback when an error occurs while inserting either of our two records:

```
DECLARE
  e_PK EXCEPTION;
  PRAGMA EXCEPTION_INIT(e_PK, -00001);
BEGIN
  Commit;
  Insert into Genre(genre) Values('classical');
  Insert into Genre(genre) Values('ska');
  Commit;
EXCEPTION
  When e_PK Then
  Rollback;
END;
/
```

Let's analyze this code line by line. In the DECLARE block, we declare (or create) one local variable (e_PK) as an exception. The PRAGMA EXCEPTION_INIT command tells the PL/SQL compiler to associate the e_PK exception name with the specific Oracle error code. The BEGIN block simply begins our transaction with the first Commit, issues the two INSERT commands, and does a second Commit to end the transaction.

Here's the key to this code. If an error occurs while processing any of the commands in the BEGIN block, the program will immediately jump to the EXCEPTION block. So if an error occurs, the second Commit will never happen. Instead, the EXCEPTION block tests for the e_PK exception. If that happens, a Rollback is issued. Other errors are not explicitly handled in this code.

Concurrency

In the real world, multiple people use a database simultaneously. Some may be running reports. Some may be entering new records. Others may be updating or deleting existing records. All these database commands and transactions are running concurrently.

Sometimes that can cause a problem. Suppose User A enters a new CD title record and then enters all the tracks for that title. Meanwhile, User B runs some calculations on the average number of tracks per title. What if User B's calculations are processed between the time that User A enters the title and the time User A enters the tracks? The tracks per title calculation will be in error.

There are four different kinds of ***concurrency*** problems:

- ***Dirty reads*** occur when one user reads a record that is part of another user's incomplete transaction. That is what the above example illustrates. In a worst-case scenario, the first user reads a record that is eventually rolled back. You would have a report showing data that never really existed in the database. Dirty reads are also called Uncommitted Dependency.
- ***Unrepeatable reads*** occur when a record is read twice during a transaction, and the second read is affected by a separate transaction. For instance, a front-end program might compare the number of records before an insert to the number of records after an insert to make sure the data was added. But if another transaction has in the meantime also added a record, that procedure will not work. Unrepeatable reads are also called Inconsistent Analysis.
- ***Phantoms*** occur with concurrent data manipulation actions. One user may be updating all the records in a table at the same time another user is inserting a new record to the table. The result can be that the update does not apply to the new record when it should or that the update does apply to the new record when it should not. In either case, the situation leads to unexpected results. Suppose a decision was made to change the R&B genre to Blues. User A could issue the update at the same time User B was inserting a new record that used the old R&B genre. User A might then look at the results and be surprised that one record still said R&B. Worse, if a foreign key constraint (discussed in Chapter 8) was in effect, User B could get an error.
- ***Lost updates*** occur when two transactions try to update the same record. Suppose User A is updating the tracktitle of a track while User B is updating the lengthseconds of that same track. If they are both using update commands that specify just one field, there won't be a problem. But generally database updates are handled through a front-end program that reads all fields, places them in a form, and then updates all fields back to the record. In that case, one of the users will think his or her update went through, only to find later that it has disappeared.

Locks

Databases solve these concurrency problems through locking. Generally, databases provide some level of automatic locking. Some databases lock individual records while an edit is going on. Other databases can lock only at the table level. Microsoft Access does what it called page-locking, which ***locks*** 2 KB of a table at a time. That could be one record or several records depending on the number and datatypes of the fields.

These automatic locks can prevent some concurrency problems, but not all of them. For instance, lost updates need to be handled by the front-end programming. One way of doing that is with a timestamp field that automatically records when a record was last changed. The front-end program can check the value of the timestamp just before it updates to make sure no other user has changed the record in the meantime. Front-end access methods, such as ActiveX Data Objects (ADO) allow the programmer to set the lock options that are appropriate for each transaction.

Locks need to be handled carefully. Obviously, the safest way to prevent concurrency problems would be to lock the entire database with each transaction. But that would be unacceptable. Can you imagine a popular e-commerce website such as Amazon.com only allowing one customer at a time to enter an order? This just illustrates that the more you lock, the more you hinder performance. But, of course, the less you lock, the more you risk concurrency problems.

Transactions can eliminate concurrency problems by making sure that groups of SQL commands are processed together or not at all. If a transaction is long and involved, other transactions may have to wait for that transaction to finish before they can continue. But a pause is better than an error or an unexpected result.

Sometimes two or more transactions can end up with a situation called ***deadlock***. Deadlock occurs when transaction A cannot finish because it is waiting for transaction B to clear a lock, but transaction B cannot finish because it is waiting for transaction A to clear a lock. Some databases have built-in procedures for solving deadlocks. For instance, SQL Server will detect a deadlock and select one transaction to kill based on the "cost" of undoing that transaction. But killing a deadlock transaction is still a pain to the user, who gets an error and had to redo some work. It is much better to prevent deadlocks. There are some things front-end programmers and stored procedure programmers can do to prevent them, such as always updating tables in the same order, keeping transactions as short as possible, and not placing user interaction in the middle of a transaction.

Chapter Summary

The INSERT, DELETE, and UPDATE commands allow SQL to write as well as read data. INSERT will add to records to a database table given either specific values or multiple rows of data from an SQL SELECT statement. DELETE will remove records from a table. All our sample databases can delete based on the value of one or more fields. All but MySQL can delete records in one table based on the value of a subquery that reads from a related table. UPDATE modifies existing data in a table. All our target databases can update data in a table either based entirely on values in that table or based on values from other tables. However, the capabilities and approach varies considerably among the various databases.

Transactions let you group individual commands and require that they be completed or not completed as a group. Transactions have the four properties of atomicity, consistency, isolation, and durability. Oracle, SQL Server, and MySQL all allow for SQL to create, commit, and rollback transactions. In addition, Oracle and SQL Server provide procedural processing for trapping errors and conditionally issuing either a commit or a rollback. A discussion of transactions leads to a general consideration of concurrency, the issues that arise when multiple people use a database simultaneously. Concurrency problems include dirty reads, unrepeatable reads, phantoms, and lost updates. Deadlock is a situation that occurs when two transactions are each waiting for the other to complete. Transactions, locks, and good front-end programming can solve these issues.

Key Terms

atomicity
back-end
COMMIT
concurrency
consistency
deadlock
declare
DELETE
dirty reads
durability
front-end
global variables
INSERT
isolation
local variables
locks
lost updates
phantoms
PL/SQL
ROLLBACK
transaction
unrepeatable reads
UPDATE

Review Questions

1. What is the difference between the front-end and the back-end in a database application?
2. How is the INSERT syntax different from the UPDATE syntax?
3. What are transactions and why are they important?
4. How can transactions be done if you are using an Access database?
5. What does the term *isolation* mean with regard to transactions?
6. What is a phantom and what can cause it?
7. If concurrency is such a problem, why don't database applications allow only one user a time to make changes in the data?
8. What similarities do you see between the SQL Server and the Oracle code shown above to rollback a transaction based on an error?
9. How is locking handled by both back-ends and front-ends?
10. What are some ways to prevent deadlocks from occurring?

Exercises

Using any SQL tool, write SQL commands to do the following:

1. The area code for Columbus, Ohio has been changed from 277 to 899. Update the homephone and workphone numbers of all members accordingly.
2. Salesperson Bob Bentley has agreed to turn over all his female members to salesperson Lisa Williams. Update the Members table accordingly. Unless you are using MySQL, do not use SalesIDs in the SQL except when joining tables.
3. Add a new artist with the following information. Use a database-specific function to automatically get today's date.

ArtistID	ArtistName	City	Region	Country	WebAddress	EntryDate	LeadSource
12	November	New Orleans	LA	USA	www.november.com	(today)	Directmail

4. Members Doug Finney and Terry Irving are forming a new artist to be called "Doug and Terry." Add this record to the Artists table, using ArtistID 13, the address information of Doug Finney, no web address, today's entry date, and no lead source. Don't hand-code any data for insert that can be looked up from the Members table.
5. Add the appropriate new records to the XrefArtistsMembers table for the artist "Doug and Terry" (see #4). Doug is the responsible party. Don't hand-code any data for insert that can be looked up from the Members table.
6. Write SQL to delete ArtistIDs 12 and 13 with one SQL command and then rollback that delete (Can be done only with SQL Server, Oracle, or MySQL).
7. Write SQL to delete all records in the XrefArtistsMembers table for ArtistID 13 and then rollback that delete (Can be done only with SQL Server, Oracle, or MySQL).
8. Write an SQL transaction to delete all records in the XrefArtistsMembers table for ArtistID 13, delete the artist record for ArtistID 13, and then commit the transaction (Can be done only with SQL Server, Oracle, or MySQL).
9. Write SQL to (1) begin a transaction, (2) delete all the tracks for TitleID 4, (3) select the track records for TitleID 4 to prove that they are really gone, (4) rollback the transaction, and (5) select the track records for TitleID 4 to prove that now they are not gone (Can be done only with SQL Server, Oracle, or MySQL).
10. Lyric Music has decided to set up a web page for every artist who doesn't have a web site. The web address will be www.lyricmusic.com/ followed by the artistID. Fill this in for every artist record that doesn't already have a Web site.

Additional References

ExtremeTech – Front-End, Back-End, All Across the Net
http://www.extremetech.com/article2/0,3973,11781,00.asp

HotOracle.com
http://www.hot-oracle.com/

Database Journal – SQL Server Locking
http://databasejournal.com/features/mssql/article.php/1440371

MSDN – Concurrency
http://msdn.microsoft.com/library/default.asp?url=/library/en-us/acdata/ac_8_con_7a_3kqb.asp

8

Data Definition Language

Chapter Overview

In this chapter we will explore the Data Definition Language (DDL) commands of SQL. We will learn how to use SQL to create and alter tables. The chapter will also discuss the related concepts of constraints, indexes, and views. With these tools, the database developer can control the data entered to the database, increase performance, simplify things for the end user and front-end developer, and guard security. We will also introduce the concepts of stored procedures and triggers and discuss their use in a database system. Finally, we will discuss using scripts to assist the database developer to port SQL code from one database installation to another.

Chapter Objectives

In this chapter, we will:

- Study how databases are created in each of our target database systems
- Create and alter the field structure of tables
- Create and drop primary key constraints
- Create and drop unique constraints
- Create and drop default constraints
- Create and drop check constraints
- Create and drop foreign key constraints
- Create and drop indexes
- Create and drop views
- Learn about stored procedures and triggers
- Save and use DDL in scripts

Data Definition Language

Data Definition Language or *DDL* is a subset of SQL commands used to create and modify database objects, such as tables, constraints, indexes, and views. With these commands you can create an entire database using SQL rather than a graphical user interface. You might wonder why you wouldn't rather use a graphical user interface. The two main answers are control and portability. With DDL you gain more control over exactly what database objects are built and what they are named. Also, as we shall see, DDL saved into a script can be easily ported from one database installation to another.

Database Object-Naming Tips

As we work through this chapter, we will be creating and naming many things. If you don't want to live with regrets every time you work with your database, it is best to begin with a naming plan. Here are some tips for a naming plan:

- Figure out the names for all your tables and primary key fields before you begin. Then look over the list to make sure your names are consistent. Don't have, for instance, tables named Orders, Order_Details, and orderspymts. Instead, be obsessively consistent, naming them orders, orders_details, and orders_pymts or Orders, OrdersDetails, and OrdersPymts.
- Do not include spaces inside your table or fields. This is a requirement with MySQL. Our other databases allow you to create tables and fields with spaces in the names, but it is a bad idea. You will have to hassle with square brackets ([]) around any field or table names with embedded spaces. It also limits your portability to MySQL. Instead of spaces, just capitalize the first letter of each word in your table name. Some people like to use underscores (_) between words, but you may find it to also be a hassle since the underscore is hard to reach on most keyboards.
- Avoid the use of SQL reserved words and punctuation marks in table and field names. Order, Select, Case, and other reserved words can be used in some databases with square brackets around them. Think of other names instead.
- Keep names short, but long enough to be descriptive.
- Be consistent in your use of abbreviations. If you abbreviate number as Num in one name and No in another, you may confuse yourself later. Limit the abbreviations you use to those that would be instantly understandable by nearly anyone. For instance, in an insurance database you might think that Ins would be good abbreviation for insurance. But someone else could think it stood for Insert. Better to be clear than brief.

- Name primary key and foreign key fields consistently. If CustID is the primary key in the customer table, then don't use CustNum in another table as a foreign key that links to it. SQL won't get confused linking fields with different names, but you will.
- Avoid generic field names. Don't name a field ID or Date. You will later forget what date it is, and you will confuse that ID with another ID. Instead, use names like OrderID, and OrderDate.
- Some database administrators like to name all their tables beginning with tbl, all their indexes beginning with idx, all their primary keys beginning with pk, etc. The downside of this, especially with table names, is that it is more typing. The upside is that you always know what kind of object you are working with. We have not followed this convention with Lyric Music for the sole purpose of keeping the SQL as simple and readable as possible. But this is a good idea.
- Similarly, some database administrators like to name all their fields beginning with an abbreviation of the datatype. So you might have intEmpID, txtName, and dteHire. Again, we didn't do this in Lyric Music because it makes the SQL a little harder to type. But if you always know the datatype you are dealing with, it can save time and effort when you are writing your code.

Databases

All of the tables, indexes, views, and other objects you create reside within a database. The very term database has a slightly different implementation in each of our four target database systems.

In Access, a database is a .mdb file. Each Access database resides separately from all others on any computer. A database can be created in Access by launching the Access program and selecting Blank Access Database. An Access database can be accessed by other computers over a local area network. If the Access database is located on a web server, it can be accessed over the Internet. Technically, the access database file does not have to be physically located on the web server for Internet access, but for performance reasons it should be.

In SQL Server, a computer with SQL Server installed on it will function as a database server and can be accessed by other computers over a local area network or even across the Internet by a web server located anywhere in the world. Each installation of SQL Server is called an instance. Generally a given server computer will host just one instance, but it is possible for a given server to host multiple instances. Each instance can contain several databases. Each database exists essentially independent of all other databases on that SQL Server instance. However, each SQL Server instance also contains a centralized system catalog called the master database, which contains all database and table names, all SQL Server login accounts, all server configuration values, all system stored procedures, and more. Each database shares access to the master database.

A SQL Server database can be created on any SQL Server instance using the Create Database command. The command in its simplest form is just Create Database followed by the name to be used for the new database. However, it has many options for specifying the initial size, maximum size, and physical location of the database data file and log file. Specifying these locations allow a database administrator to balance the database load among various hard drives and even computers. These options are not germane to an SQL programming book. They are documented in the Transact-SQL Help component of Query Analyzer. You can switch between databases by typing Use followed by the database name.

The MySQL concept of database is very similar to that of SQL Server. An instance of MySQL running on a server computer can contain multiple databases. A new MySQL database can be created with Create Database followed by the name to be used for the new database. If there is a chance the database already exists and you want to prevent an error, you can type Create Database If Not Exists followed by the name of the database. There are no other options for the Create Database command. You can switch between databases by typing Use followed by the database name.

In Oracle, an instance is a set of server services required for Oracle to run, including background processes and memory buffers. Each Oracle instance runs just one database and is created when the Create Database command is executed So to create a new database in Oracle essentially means to create a separate instance of Oracle on the same server or a different server. To create and manage databases, Oracle provides create database scripts plus utilities that vary from version to version.When the Create Database command is executed the following operations are performed: creation of data files, creation of log files, creation of the SYSTEM tablespace, creation of the data dictionary, and mounting and opening the database for use.

Creating a Table

You may wonder why you would write SQL to create a table when most databases provide a nice graphical user interface for doing it. Actually, there are times when the graphical user interface is a lot faster and easier. But there are at least two reasons why you would want to create your tables in SQL. The first is control. With SQL you can specifically set every option and give each default, index, and other database object the exact name you want. The second reason is documentation. In an SQL script file, you have an exact record of how you created the database. Even better, you can apply that same script to another database server and have an exact copy of your database in seconds. This is actually very common in the real world, in which you do testing on a development server and then run all your development scripts against a production server.

The Create Table command has many options. You can create primary keys, defaults, and other constraints within the Create Table command. We will examine those options later. We will start with the most basic Create Table options. The words Create Table are followed by the name of the new table. Then you place your column list surrounded by parentheses. For each column, specify the column name followed by one or more spaces, the datatype followed by one or more spaces, and either Null or Not Null.

Null means that the field may contain null (empty) values. Not Null means that the field cannot contain null values. If a field is set as Not Null, either a default value must also be set up or else all Inserts must provide a value for that field. Similarly, Updates cannot set the value of a Not Null field to Null. So only use Not Null when a field must logically always have a value. Your primary key fields must be set to Not Null.

Create Table	
	SQL Server, Oracle, MySQL, Access

Syntax	`CREATE Table tablename (`
	`  Fieldname1 datatype NULL | NOT NULL,`
	`  Fieldname2 datatype NULL | NOT NULL`
	`)`

SQL Server	1a. Create a table called Contracts with the ArtistID from the Artists table and a ContractDate field.
	
	`Create Table tblContracts (`
	`  ArtistID Integer Not Null,`
	`  ContractDate SmallDateTime Not Null`
	`)`

Oracle	1b. Create a table called Contracts with the ArtistID from the Artists table and a ContractDate field.
	
	`Create Table tblContracts (`
	`  ArtistID Integer Not Null,`
	`  ContractDate Date Not Null`
	`)`

MySQL	1c. Create a table called Contracts with the ArtistID from the Artists table and a ContractDate field.
	
	`Create Table tblContracts (`
	`  ArtistID Int Not Null,`
	`  ContractDate Date Not Null`
	`)`

Access	1d. Create a table called Contracts with the ArtistID from the Artists table and a ContractDate field.
	
	`Create Table tblContracts (`
	`  ArtistID Long Not Null,`
	`  ContractDate DateTime Not Null`
	`)`

Note

A left parenthesis comes before the first column in the list. A comma follows each column entry in the list except the last one. The last column in the list is followed by a right parenthesis.

Note

In Oracle the final right parenthesis can be followed by the word *tablespace* and the name of a tablespace where this table will physically be stored.

You'll notice that the above examples are identical except for the names of the datatypes. Elsewhere in this chapter where this is the case, we will show the code for just one of the database systems. You can look up the equivalent datatypes in Appendix B or your database documentation to apply it to another database system.

Dropping a Table

Dropping a table deletes it from the database. You won't use this command very often in real life. But you will probably use it a lot while working with this chapter. You must drop tables before recreating them with revised code. The syntax for that is Drop Table tablename, and is the same in all our target databases.

Dropping a Table	
SQL Server, Oracle, MySQL, Access	
Syntax	`DROP Table tablename`
Examples	1. Remove the tblContracts table from the database. `Drop Table tblContracts`

Adding Columns to an Existing Table

It's never too late to add a column to a table. That is one of the many uses of the Alter Table command. Follow the words Alter Table with the table name and the word Add. Then define the column just as you would in the Create Table command.

Adding Columns to an Existing Table	
SQL Server, Oracle, MySQL, Access	
Syntax	`ALTER Table tablename ADD fieldname datatype NULL | NOT NULL`

MySQL, SQL Server (other databases vary only in datatypes)	1. Add a text field called ContractType with a length of 10 to the tblContracts table.
	`Alter Table tblContracts`
	`Add ContractType VarChar(10) Null`

Access users often dislike the fact that the SQL Alter Table command can add a column only to the end of the field list and not somewhere in the middle. It is true that in the Access graphical user interface you can move columns up and down the list and arrange them in an order that makes sense. You cannot do that with an SQL interface. But the order of the columns has nothing to do with performance and nothing to do with how you present them to users in a query.

Altering an Existing Column in an Existing Table

In most cases it is never too late to modify a column in a table. This is also done with the Alter Table command. In SQL Server and Access, follow the words Alter Table with the table name and the words Alter Column. Then redefine the column just as you would in the Create Table command. In Oracle and MySQL, follow the words Alter Table with the table name and the word Modify. Then redefine the column just as you would in the Create Table command. A further restriction in Oracle is that you will get an error and the command will not be processed if you set a column that is already null to Null or set a column that is already not null to Not Null. So don't include the entire column description, but just the part that needs to be changed.

Note

You need to know how a table is set up before you try to modify it. In Oracle and MySQL, use `Describe tablename` to see a list of the columns and datatypes for a table. In SQL Server's Query Analyzer use `Exec sp_help tablename`. In Access, use the graphical user interface to view the table design.

Altering Existing Columns	
Access 2000+, SQL Server, Oracle, MySQL	

Syntax	`ALTER Table tablename`
	`ALTER Column fieldname datatype NULL | NOT NULL`
	`ALTER Table tablename MODIFY fieldname datatype`

SQL Server, Access	1a. Change the length on the ContractType field to 15 in the tblContracts table. `Alter Table tblContracts Alter Column ContractType VarChar(15) Null`
Oracle, MySQL	1b. Change the length on the ContractType field to 15 in the tblContracts table. `Alter Table tblContracts Modify ContractType VarChar(15)`

This Alter Table command works great for changing the Null setting, lengthening or shortening the size of a text field, and even changing the datatype within reason. Most databases can convert one kind of numeric field to another or even convert numeric data to text. But there are limits to these implicit conversions. When in doubt, don't use this command but instead create a new column with the datatype you want, and then use and UPDATE statement to copy all the data from the old column to the new.

That same procedure (create a new column and then update it) is the only way within pure SQL to rename a column. However, individual databases or front-end programs may provide other ways to rename a column. For instance, SQL Server offers a built-in stored procedure called `Exec sp_rename` and Oracle has a `Rename` command.

Dropping Columns

Dropping a column is as easy as dropping a table. It also is done with the Alter Table command. This removes a column and all its data from the table.

Dropping a Column	
SQL Server, Oracle, MySQL, Access	
Syntax	`ALTER Table tablename DROP COLUMN columnname`
Examples	1. Remove the Contracttype column from the tblContracts table. `Alter Table tblContracts Drop Column ContractType`

Using Identity Columns and Sequences

Identity columns automatically generate a sequential number with each row that is inserted. Because the values in identity columns are always unique, they make excellent primary keys in cases where there is no naturally occurring primary key. If you define a column as an identity column, you will never have to insert a value to it, but it will always be unique within that table.

Access

In Access you create an identity column by just using the special Counter datatype. This is shown in the Create Table code below:

```
Create Table tblX (
  ID Counter Not Null,
  anotherfield int Null
  )
```

SQL Server

In SQL Server, Identity is a column modifier. It can only be used with an Integer (Int) datatype. When you define the identity, you can specify seed and increment values. Seed is the starting number for the identity. Increment is the number to increase the identity with each row. The syntax is Identity (seed, increment). If you use Identity without a seed and increment, they will each default to 1. This is shown in the Create Table code below:

```
Create Table tblX (
  ID int Identity(10000,1) Not Null,
  anotherfield int Null
  )
```

MySQL

In MySQL you create an identity column by using Auto_Increment as a column modifier after the datatype. The datatype can be any of the integer (whole number) datatypes. MySQL requires that the auto_increment field be set up as the primary key during the Create Table command. This is shown in the Create Table code below:

```
Create Table tblX (
  ID int auto_increment Not Null,
  anotherfield int Null,
  primary key(ID)
  )
```

Oracle

In Oracle you do not define an identity column but create a ***sequence*** to generate the incrementing values. A sequence is a database object that exists separately from the table. You can have as many sequences as you want, but each sequence should be used for just one field. The SQL code to create a sequence is shown below. It is simply Create Sequence followed by the name you want to use. A good practice is to name the sequence seq_ followed by the table name and field name it will be used for. Start is the starting number for the identity. Increment is the number to increase the identity with each row. The first line may or may not be needed, but is good practice. It will drop, or delete, the sequence if it already exists so that the create sequence will always run. If you tried to create a sequence that already existed, you would get an error and the sequence would be left unchanged.

```
Drop Sequence seq_tblX_ID;
Create Sequence seq_tblX_ID
  Start with 1
  Increment by 1;
```

Either before or after you create the sequence, you can create the table normally.

```
create table tblX (
  ID int Not Null,
  anotherfield int Null
  );
```

Whenever you insert records into the table, you can use the sequence to generate the next value. Notice the sequence syntax, which is the name of the sequence followed by .nextval to generate the next value. In our example below, 14 is merely the value to be placed into anotherfield and has nothing to do with the sequence:

```
Insert into tblX(ID,anotherfield) Values(seq_tblX_ID.nextval,14)
```

Note

Technically speaking, an identity column (or sequence) is unique within a given a table in a given database on a given server. In cases where a database is distributed to multiple locations, an identity column cannot be guaranteed to be unique across every instance of the table. This can cause problems if you use identity columns for primary keys in a distributed database. There are two solutions. One is to use the identity column in conjunction with a locationID as the primary key. The other is to use a ***Globally Unique Identifier (GUID)***, which is supported in some databases. A GUID is a 16-byte ID that is generated based on (among other things) the MAC address of the PC's network card. A GUID is guaranteed to be unique across every instance of a distributed database. The downside of GUIDs is that they are very cumbersome to work with. You might remember an identity of 1466332, but you would never remember a GUID of C1C5FCE2-879E-4A96-B845-9F3FC4A10EC8. Yes, that is really what they look like.

Constraints

A *constraint* is any kind of restriction placed on data inserted into a table. Constraints can take a number of forms. ***Primary key constraints*** enforce a unique value for each row. ***Foreign key constraints*** require that the data entered to a particular column in a child table must match existing data in a parent table. ***Default constraints*** ensure that data not specifically inserted will take an assumed default value. ***Check constraints*** require that data match certain patterns or have certain values. There are three main categories of constraints:

- ***Entity constraints*** ensure that the value in a column meets some criteria compared to other rows in the table. Examples of this are primary key constraints and unique constraints. They test the value of a column compared to the values for that column in all other rows to make sure that the value is unique.
- ***Domain constraints*** ensure that the value in a column meets some particular criteria without respect to any other row in the table. An example of this is a default constraint, which assures that a column will have some pre-specified value if the user fails to specify a value. Another example is a check constraint, which requires that the column value be less than or greater than some value, equal to one of a list of values, or practically anything else.
- ***Referential integrity constraints*** ensure that the value in a column matches a value in another column in a different table or (sometimes) the same table. Foreign key constraints are an example of this. For instance, in the Lyric Music database we could use a foreign key constraint to make sure that the genre entered for any title is one of the genres in the genre table.

Constraint Names

You sometimes have to refer to constraints by name, so it is good practice to name them consistently. One standard is to begin the constraints with two letters that indicate the type of constraint (pk for primary key, fk for foreign key, df for default, ck for check, and un for unique). Follow that with the table name. If it is a check, default, or unique constraint, follow the table name with the column being constrained. If it is a foreign key constraint, follow the table name with the name of the table it refers to. So, for instance, a primary key for Artists would be named pk_artists. A default for the SalesID field in the Artists table would be named df_artists_salesid. A foreign key constraint between Artists and Salespeople would be named fk_artists_salespeople. Oracle limits the length of constraint names, so you may have to abbreviate in some cases. In SQL Server and Oracle two constraints cannot have the same name, even if they are in different tables. You can develop your own naming scheme, but be consistent and you will thank yourself later.

Setting Primary Key Constraints

Primary keys are unique identifiers for each record in a database table. Suppose you are working at a job and your clocked hours are recorded in a database. Those hours will be recorded with some piece of information that identifies them as belonging to you. It might be your Employee ID number, a Social Security number, or something else. But that identifier needs to be there so that at the end of the week it can relate those hours to the record in the employee table that has your name and include them on your paycheck. Otherwise, someone else could get paid for your hours. See how important primary keys are? They provide the links for relating one table to another. They have to be unique so that there is no confusion about which record is which.

Adding a Primary Key Constraint with Alter Table

To add a primary key constraint on an existing table, you use Alter Table followed by the tablename, the words Add Constraint, the name you want to use for the constraint, the words Primary Key, and the field or fields that make up the primary key in parentheses. The syntax is identical in each of our target databases.

Adding a Primary Key Constraint with Alter Table	
SQL Server, Oracle, MySQL, Access	
Syntax	`ALTER Table tablename ADD CONSTRAINT constraintname PRIMARY KEY (fieldname1, fieldname2)`
Examples	1. Set the primary key of the tblContracts table to ArtistID and ContractDate. `Alter Table tblContracts Add Constraint pk_tblContracts Primary Key (ArtistID,ContractDate)`
	2. Set the primary key of tblX to the ID field. `Alter Table tblX Add Constraint pk_tblX Primary Key (ID)`

Adding a Primary Key Constraint with Create Table

You can create the primary key constraint right in your Create Table code. There are two forms of this syntax shown below. The first form simply adds the words Primary Key beside the primary key field in the field list. There are two limitations to this syntax. First, it cannot create only a multi-field primary key. Second, this first syntax form provides no way for you to name the primary key constraint. If you don't name it, the database system will name it, and it will not come up with as good a name as you would. If you ever have to drop or disable the constraint, you will want it to have a good name.

The second syntax form essentially adds regular Add Constraint syntax after the field list. Notice that in this case you add a comma after the last field and follow that with the constraint information prior to the final parenthesis. With this syntax you can name the constraint and use as many fields as you would like. Both forms of syntax work identically in all our target databases with variations only for datatypes.

<table>
<tr><th colspan="2">Adding a Primary Key Constraint with Create Table</th></tr>
<tr><th colspan="2">SQL Server, Oracle, MySQL, Access</th></tr>
<tr><td>Syntax</td><td>

```
Create Table tablename (
  fieldname1 datatype not null Primary Key,
  fieldname2 datatype null | not null
)

Create Table tablename (
  Fieldname1 datatype not null,
  Fieldname2 datatype null | not null,
  Constraint constraintname Primary Key (fieldname1,fieldname2)
)
```

</td></tr>
<tr><td rowspan="2">SQL Server (other databases vary only in datatypes)</td><td>1. Create a table called tblX with an integer ID field and integer anotherfield. Make ID the primary key.

```
Create Table tblX (
  ID int Not Null Primary Key,
  anotherfield int Null
  )
```

</td></tr>
<tr><td>2. Create a table called Contracts with the ArtistID from the Artists table and ContractDate field. Set the primary key to ArtistID and ContractDate.

```
Create Table tblContracts (
  ArtistID Integer Not Null,
  ContractDate SmallDateTime Not Null,
  Constraint pk_tblcontracts Primary Key
(ArtistID,ContractDate)
)
```

</td></tr>
</table>

Note

The first syntax above works with Access 2000 and XP. For Access 97, use the second syntax.

Setting Unique Constraints

If primary key values must be unique, then what is a ***unique constraint*** good for? Sometimes you want to make sure a non-primary key column has unique values. For instance, an employee table might use EmployeeID as a primary key but set a unique constraint on the Social Security Number column to help guard against typing errors or fraud. In database terms, these unique constraints are sometimes called *alternate keys* because they could be used as the primary key if you wished. As with primary key columns, those columns are set up to be used with unique constraints should be defined as Not Null.

A unique constraint can be composed of one or more columns. If multiple columns are used, then the unique constraint will require unique combinations of the column values. Once you create a unique constraint, you will receive an error if you try to enter a nonunique value.

Adding a Unique Constraint with Alter Table

Adding a Unique Constraint with Alter Table	
	SQL Server, Oracle, MySQL, Access
Syntax	`ALTER TABLE tablename ADD CONSTRAINT constraintname UNIQUE (fieldname1, fieldname2)`
Examples	1. Add a constraint to the Titles table so that UPC is unique. `Alter Table Titles Add Constraint un_titles_upc Unique (UPC)`
	2. Add a constraint to the Titles table so that the combination of ArtistID and Title is unique. `Alter Table Titles Add Constraint un_titles_artistid_title Unique (ArtistID, Title)`

Adding a Unique Constraint with Create Table

As with primary key constraints, you can create unique constraints with your Create Table code using either of two syntax forms. The second syntax form is preferred since it allows you to name the constraint and to create a multi-column constraint. Both forms of syntax work identically in all our target databases with variations only for datatypes.

<table>
<tr><th colspan="2">Adding a Unique Constraint with Create Table</th></tr>
<tr><th colspan="2">SQL Server, Oracle, MySQL, Access</th></tr>
<tr><td>Syntax</td><td><pre>CREATE TABLE tablename (
  Fieldname1 datatype NULL | NOT NULL PRIMARY KEY,
  Fieldname2 datatype NULL | NOT NULL UNIQUE
)

CREATE TABLE tablename (
  Fieldname1 datatype NULL | NOT NULL,
  Fieldname2 datatype NULL | NOT NULL,
  CONSTRAINT constraintname UNIQUE (fieldname1,
  fieldname2)
)</pre></td></tr>
<tr><td rowspan="2">SQL Server (other databases vary only in datatypes)</td><td>1. Create a table called tblX with an integer ID field an integer anotherfield. Make ID the primary key.<pre>Create Table tblX (
  ID int Not Null,
  anotherfield int Not Null Unique
)</pre></td></tr>
<tr><td>2. Create a table called Contracts with the ArtistID from the Artists table and a ContractDate field. Set the primary key to ArtistID and ContractDate.<pre>Create Table tblContracts (
  ArtistID Integer Not Null,
  ContractDate SmallDateTime Not Null,
  Constraint un_tblcontracts_artistid Unique
  (ArtistID)
)</pre></td></tr>
</table>

Setting Default Constraints

A default constraint automatically fills in a value if the user fails to supply a value. Three things to remember about default constraints are:

- They are only used with INSERTs. Once a row exists in a table, the default plays no part in setting the value.
- If the INSERT supplies a value for the column specified by a default, the INSERT's value is used instead of the default.
- If the INSERT does not supply a value, then the default value will be inserted.

Defaults are great for filling in the current date and/or time with each new record. They can also set initial values for things such as default credit terms, whether or not an item is taxable, whether or not an order is paid, or whether or not an order has been shipped. Defaults affect only one column. The default can specify some fixed value or use a system function; for instance, to get the current date.

Adding a Default Constraint with Alter Table

As shown below, SQL Server, Oracle, and MySQL have three slightly different syntax forms for setting default constraints. Microsoft Access does not support adding default constraints through the SQL query interface at all. However, you can set them up through the table design features of the graphical user interface or with VBA programming.

Adding a Default Constraint with Alter Table	
	SQL Server, Oracle, MySQL

Syntax	`(SQL Server) ALTER TABLE tablename ADD CONSTRAINT constraintname DEFAULT value FOR fieldname`
	
	`(Oracle) ALTER TABLE tablename MODIFY fieldname DEFAULT value`
	
	`(MySQL) ALTER TABLE tablename ALTER fieldname SET DEFAULT value`

SQL Server	1a. Make a default entry of 0 for the RespParty field of XRefArtistsMembers.
	
	`Alter Table XRefArtistsMembers`
	`Add Constraint df_xrefartistsmembers_respparty`
	`Default 0 for RespParty`

	2a. Set a default for the ContractDate of the tblContracts table to the current date and time.
	
	`Alter Table tblContracts`
	`Add Constraint df_tblcontracts_contractdate`
	`Default getdate() for ContractDate`

Oracle	1b. Make a default entry of 0 for the RespParty field of XRefArtistsMembers.
	
	`Alter Table XrefArtistsMembers Modify RespParty`
	`default 0`

	2b. Set a default for the ContractDate of the tblContracts table to the current date and time.
	
	`Alter Table tblContracts Modify ContractDate`
	`Default sysdate`

MySQL	1c. Make a default entry of 0 for the RespParty field of XRefArtistsMembers.
	
	`Alter Table XrefArtistsMembers ALTER RespParty`
	`SET DEFAULT 0`

Note

There is no MySQL code above for Example 2. A default value in MySQL has to be a constant; it cannot be a function or an expression. However, in MySQL you can make a field default to the current date and time by defining it with the Timestamp datatype.

Adding a Default Constraint with Create Table

As with primary key constraints, you can create default constraints with your Create Table code. Since this syntax does not allow you to name the constraint, the preferred method is to use Alter Table. In Access, defaults can be set up through the table design features of the graphical user interface, but not through the SQL query interface.

Adding a Default Constraint with Create Table	
	SQL Server, Oracle, MySQL

Syntax	`CREATE TABLE tablename (`
	`  Fieldname1 datatype NULL | NOT NULL PRIMARY KEY,`
	`  Fieldname2 datatype Default 0 NULL | NOT NULL`
	`)`

SQL Server (other databases vary only in datatypes)	1. Create a table called tblX with an integer ID field and integer anotherfield. Another field should have a default of 0.
	`Create Table tblX (`
	`  ID int Not Null,`
	`  anotherfield int Default 0 Not Null`
	`  )`

Setting Check Constraints

A check constraint requires that data match certain patterns or have certain values. If that sounds a little far reaching, it is because check constraints are wide open. Virtually anything that can go in a WHERE clause can be used in a check constraint. It can test against specific values. It can test against other columns. The only real limitation is that it cannot test against another table. You need a stored procedure to do that. So check constraints are great for assuring that your entries meet many kinds of business rules.

MySQL does not support check constraints. Microsoft Access does not support adding check constraints through the SQL query interface. Use the table design features of the graphical user interface.

Adding a Check Constraint with Alter Table

Use the syntax below to add a check constraint with Alter Table. Note that the expression to test goes inside parentheses. Write the expression to describe the data you want to include, not the data you want to exclude. If you want to test if any existing data would fail this test, write a SELECT statement using WHERE NOT followed by your expression.

Adding a Check Constraint with Alter Table	
SQL Server, Oracle	
Syntax	`ALTER TABLE tablename ADD CONSTRAINT constraintname CHECK (expression)`
Examples	1. Create a check constraint to require that Email in Members either be Null or include an @ sign. `Alter Table Members Add Constraint ck_members_email Check (email Like '%@%')`
	2. Create a check constraint to require that Gender in Members be either M or F. `Alter Table Members Add Constraint ck_members_gender Check (gender IN('M','F'))`
	3. Create a check constraint to require that Lengthseconds in Tracks be no more than 1200 seconds (20 minutes). `Alter Table Tracks Add Constraint ck_tracks_lengthseconds Check (lengthseconds<=1200)`

Adding a Check Constraint with Create Table

As with other constraints, the second syntax form below is preferred since it allows you to name the default constraint.

<table>
<tr><th colspan="2">Adding a Check Constraint with Create Table</th></tr>
<tr><th colspan="2">SQL Server, Oracle</th></tr>
<tr><td>Syntax</td><td><pre>CREATE TABLE tablename (
  Fieldname1 datatype NULL | NOT NULL PRIMARY KEY,
  Fieldname2 datatype
CHECK (expression) NULL | NOT NULL
)

CREATE TABLE tablename (
  Fieldname1 datatype NULL | NOT NULL,
  Fieldname2 datatype NULL | NOT NULL,
  CONSTRAINT constraintname CHECK (expression)
)</pre></td></tr>
<tr><td rowspan="2">SQL Server (Oracle varies only in datatypes)</td><td>1. Create a table called tblX with an integer ID field and integer anotherfield. Another field should have a check constraint to make sure its values are greater than zero.<pre>Create Table tblX (
  ID int Not Null,
  anotherfield int Check(anotherfield>0) Not Null
)</pre></td></tr>
<tr><td>2. Create a table called Contracts with the ArtistID from the Artists table and a ContractAmt currency field. Check ContractAmt entries to make sure they are greater than $100.<pre>Create Table tblContracts (
  ArtistID Integer Not Null,
  ContractAmt Smallmoney Not Null,
  Constraint ck_tblContracts_contractamt
Check(ContractAmt>100)
)</pre></td></tr>
</table>

Setting Foreign Key (Integrity) Constraints

We discussed earlier how primary keys are used in table relationships to relate tables to each other. But not every column involved in a table relationship is a primary key. Consider the Titles and Studios tables in the Lyric Music database. The primary key of Studios is StudioID. StudioID also exists in the Tables table, enabling the two tables to have a relationship that describes the studio at which each title was recorded. If TitleID is the primary key of Titles, what does that make StudioID in the Titles table? It makes it a foreign key. A foreign key is a column or set of columns in a table that relates to a primary key in another table. In other words, the foreign key sits at the opposite end of the table relationship from the primary key.

What foreign key constraints do in databases is very important. If we establish a foreign key relationship between the StudioID column of Titles and the StudioID column of Studios, then the database will require that every StudioID entered in Titles match an existing StudioID in Studios (or else be Null if nulls are allowed). This assures the integrity of the data so that no one can mistakenly enter that a title was recorded at StudioID 5 if, in fact, there is no StudioID 5.

The table whose primary key is involved in the relationship is called the parent table, while the table with the foreign key is called the child table. This makes sense when you realize that primary keys must be unique, but foreign keys in most cases do not. So just as a parent can have many children, a given primary key value in the parent table (StudioID 1 in the Studios table) can relate to many foreign key values in the child table (all the titles in the Titles table were recorded at StudioID 1). Another way to remember this is that the child depends on the parent.

Adding a Foreign Key Constraint with Alter Table

Since you are working with two tables in a foreign key, it is easy to get confused about which table you alter to create the foreign key constraint. The answer is the child table, the one (except in one-to-one relationships) that is not a primary key, the one that will get values from looking them up in the other table.

Foreign key constraints can be used in MySQL with InnoDB type tables with version 3.23.44 and higher. However, they can be set up only with Create Table, not with Alter Table.

<table>
<tr><th colspan="2">Adding a Foreign Key Constraint with Alter Table</th></tr>
<tr><th colspan="2">SQL Server, Oracle, Access</th></tr>
<tr><td>Syntax</td><td><pre>ALTER TABLE child_tablename
ADD CONSTRAINT constraintname
FOREIGN KEY (child_field1, child_field2)
REFERENCES parent_tablename (parent_field1,
parent_field2)</pre></td></tr>
<tr><td rowspan="2">Examples</td><td>1. Create a foreign key relationship to enforce that StudioID of the Titles table refers to StudioID of the Studios table.<pre>Alter Table Titles
Add Constraint fk_titles_studios
Foreign Key (StudioID)
References Studios (StudioID)</pre></td></tr>
<tr><td>2. Create a foreign key relationship between the Supervisor column of Salespeople and the SalesID column of Salespeople such that the Supervisor must be a valid SalesID.<pre>Alter Table Salespeople
Add Constraint fk_salespeople_salespeople
Foreign Key (Supervisor)
References Salespeople (SalesID)</pre></td></tr>
</table>

Note

Example 2 illustrates how to create a foreign key constraint from a foreign key in a table to the primary key of the same table. This parallels the discussion of Self Joins in Chapter 4.

Adding a Foreign Key Constraint with Create Table

You can create foreign key constraints with your Create Table code. Only one form of the syntax is shown because foreign keys often involve multiple columns.

Adding a Foreign Key Constraint with Create Table	
SQL Server, Oracle, MySQL, Access	

Syntax	`CREATE TABLE tablename (`
	`  Fieldname1 datatype NULL | NOT NULL,`
	`  Fieldname2 datatype NULL | NOT NULL,`
	`  CONSTRAINT constraintname`
	`FOREIGN KEY (child_field1, child_field2)`
	`REFERENCES parent_tablename (parent_field1,`
	`parent_field2)`
	`)`

SQL Server (other databases vary only in datatypes)	1. Create a table called Contracts with the ArtistID from the Artists table and a ContractDate field. Create a foreign key constraint between ArtistID and the ArtistID in the Artists table.
	
	`Create Table tblContracts (`
	`  ArtistID Integer Not Null,`
	`  ContractDate SmallDateTime Not Null,`
	`  Constraint fk_tblcontracts_artists`
	`Foreign Key (ArtistID)`
	`References Artists (ArtistID)`
	`)`

Cascading Updates and Deletes

Foreign key constraints do more than simply make sure all entries in the child table match the primary key in the parent table. They also constrain the parent table to an extent. The foreign key constraint will not allow someone to delete StudioID 1 in the parent Studios table if there are records for StudioID 1 in the child Titles table. If they were deleted that would leave child records without a parent; these are known as orphan records. Neither will the foreign key constraint allow someone to change StudioID 1 to StudioID 99, because that, also, would leave orphan StudioID 1 records in the Titles table.

There are multiple ways to handle these situations so that the parent records can be updated or deleted without leaving orphans. One way to handle these procedures is with triggers and stored procedures. The theory of these is discussed below, though writing them is beyond the scope of this book.

Some databases provide for ***cascading updates*** and ***cascading deletes***. A cascade update allows for an update in a parent table to cascade through related records in child tables. So, for instance, if you changed StudioID 1 in Studios to 99, the cascade update would change all references to Studio ID 1 in Titles to 99. A cascade delete operates similarly but with deletes, deleting all related child records as it deletes a parent record. Note that you wouldn't want cascade delete always turned on. If you deleted a member you would want the database to delete all records in XRefArtistsMembers that referred to that member. But if you deleted a studio, you would not want the database to delete all titles recorded at that studio. Because of foreign key constraints, you cannot delete a parent record and leave orphans or update the primary key of a parent record without updating the child records. So to have cascade update or cascade delete turned off will limit your ability to delete and update. Since that protects the integrity of your data, that's a good thing.

Cascade Updates and Deletes in Access

Microsoft Access handles cascade updates and deletes, but not through the SQL query interface. You can, however, use the relationships feature of the graphical user interface.

Cascade Updates and Deletes in SQL Server

SQL Server began supporting cascade updates and deletes with SQL Server 2000. Simply add On Delete Cascade and/or On Update Cascade to the end of the constraint clause.

Cascade Updates and Deletes in Oracle

Oracle supports cascade deletes with the inclusion of On Delete Cascade at the end of the constraint clause. Cascade updates can be handled with a trigger or stored procedure.

Cascade Updates and Deletes in MySQL

MySQL supports cascade deletes with the inclusion of On Delete Cascade at the end of the constraint clause.

Dropping Constraints

In Access, SQL Server, and Oracle you can drop constraints using the syntax below. In SQL Server you can leave a constraint in place, but disable it by replacing Drop with NoCheck. You can re-enable it by replacing NoCheck with Check.

Note

In MySQL you can drop only primary key constraints. The syntax is Alter Table tablename `DROP PRIMARY KEY.`

Dropping a Constraint	
	SQL Server, Oracle, MySQL, Access
Syntax	`ALTER TABLE tablename` `DROP Constraint constraintname`

Examples	1. Drop the fk_tblcontracts_artsists constraint on the tblContracts table.
	
	`Alter Table tblContracts`
	`Drop Constraint fk_tblcontracts_artists`

Working with Indexes

An ***index*** is used to speed up searches, sorts, and joins. A database index works much like an index in a book. Suppose you had a 2,000-page book on world history and wanted to look up the Spanish Armada. We'll assume you know nothing at all about the Spanish Armada, so the table of contents won't help you narrow down your search. Essentially you have just two options for finding your information. One way would be to start at page one and start reading until you got there. That "sequential" search method might take you weeks. So instead, you flip to the back of the book, find the index, and look under S. In moments you have the page number where you can read all about Queen Elizabeth, King Philip, and Sir Francis Drake.

The performance gains of a database index in a database with thousands of records can be just as dramatic. A complicated join with a WHERE clause and an ORDER BY clause can take minutes without the proper indexes and seconds with them. Best of all, you never have to tell SQL to use an index. If the proper index exists, then SQL will use it automatically.

Primary keys are by definition indexes. But you can create other indexes as well. How do you know what indexes to create? Here are some guidelines. Indexes should exist on all foreign key columns; if a foreign key uses more than multiple columns those columns should be set up together in an index. Indexes should exist on any non-foreign key columns used regularly to join tables. Indexes should exist on all columns regularly used in WHERE clauses. Indexes should exist on all columns or combinations of columns that are regularly used in ORDER BY clauses.

You might be thinking that if indexes are so great you should create them on every possible combination of columns that could ever by used in a WHERE or ORDER BY. But you would be wrong. The database system must maintain each index you create. Whenever the data in a table is changed, the indexes on that table must also be updated. Every so often the database must reorganize an index. When that happens, the delay can be significant.

One responsibility of database administrators is to "tune" a database by adjusting the indexes. It is a trade-off of one kind of performance against another. Some database systems provide tools for analyzing and tuning a database. For example, SQL Server comes with an Index Tuning Wizard that monitors SELECT statements being actually used in the database and then suggests what indexes would speed up performance.

There are many other aspects to indexes that database administrators need to concern themselves with, such as fill factors, statistics tracking, physical location of the indexes, and more. For our purposes, we will look at the basic syntax.

Creating an Index

Notice in the syntax below that indexes are not created with Alter Table or Create Table. Yet, though they are independent database objects, they are created with reference to a table and one or more columns in that table.

There is one other basic option that can be added to this syntax. You can place the word Unique between Create and Index to create an index that also acts as a unique constraint.

Creating an Index	
	SQL Server, Oracle, MySQL, Access
Syntax	`CREATE INDEX indexname` `ON tablename(fieldname1, fieldname2)`

Examples	1. Create an index on the SalesID column in Members.
	`Create Index ix_members_salesid`
	`On Members(SalesID)`

	2. Create a unique index on the Webaddress column in Artists.
	`Create Unique Index ix_artists_webaddress`
	`On Artists(webaddress)`

Dropping an Index

Dropping an Index is as easy as creating it. However, the syntax varies among our target databases.

Dropping an Index	
	SQL Server, Oracle, MySQL, Access

Syntax	`(SQL Server) DROP INDEX tablename.indexname`
	`(Oracle) DROP INDEX indexname`
	`(MySQL, Access) DROP INDEX indexname ON tablename`

SQL Server	1. Drop the ix_members_salesid index in Members. `Drop Index Members.ix_members_salesid`
Oracle	1. Drop the ix_members_salesid index in Members. `Drop Index ix_members_salesid`
MySQL, Access	1. Drop the ix_members_salesid index in Members. `Drop Index ix_members_salesid on Members`

Using Views

Of all the things we have dealt with in this chapter, views are about the easiest. If you can write a SELECT statement, you can write a ***view***. What is a view good for? When you create view, you create a virtual table. Users can select from a view just as they would select from a table. In fact, they wouldn't necessarily know they weren't working with a table. A view looks and acts just like a table, except that it doesn't really exist. It is constructed "on the fly" from the SELECT instructions inside the view. Views have three huge benefits to database users, programmers, and administrators:

- Views reduce complexity for end users and front-end programmers. How many end users or even front-end programmers can write a complex SELECT statement with joins, aggregates, subqueries, and more? Create a view for them, and all they have to know is SELECT *.
- Since views don't have to include all columns in a table, you can use them to hide sensitive data. Views can have their own security settings separate from the tables they select from, so a person who can select from a view would have to be given permission to select from the underlying table.
- Views can hide many of the differences between database systems. Your front-end programmer could write SELECT firstname+lastname from customers to get data from SQL Server. But if you migrate the database to Oracle, the programmer will

have to rewrite the query to be SELECT firstname||lastname from customers. In a large front-end application, those rewrites can be tedious and error prone. But use a view to do the concatenation behind the scenes, and, if you have to migrate, you just have to rewrite the view. The front-end code stays the same. The huge limitation to this is that MySQL doesn't yet support views.

Creating a View

Creating a view is extremely easy. You type Create View followed by the name you want to use for the view followed by As and the SELECT SQL. For instance, we could type:

```
Create View vwRespMembers
As
Select M.Firstname+' '+M.Lastname as Member, Homephone, Email,
S.Firstname+' '+S.Lastname as Salesperson
From Members M Inner Join Salespeople S on M.SalesID=S.SalesID
Inner Join XRefArtistsMembers X on M.MemberID=X.MemberID
Where RespParty=1
```

The join and concatenation code is for SQL Server, but the View syntax is the same in all our target database systems. Now that we have created the view, we can use it just as if it were a table.

```
Select *
From vwRespMembers
Order By Salesperson
```

```
Member              Homephone   Email                    Salesperson
------------------- ----------- ------------------------ -------------
Jose MacArthur      6331289393  jmac@dowop.com           Bob Bentley
Bonnie Taft         3721223292  taffygirl@signon.com     Bob Bentley
Roberto Goe         2771123943  NULL                     Bob Bentley
Terry Irving        5411252093  NULL                     Clint Sanchez
Brian Ranier        6231842933  NULL                     Clint Sanchez
Marcellin Lambert   8331929302  mlambert@corkscrew.com   Clint Sanchez
Roberto Alvarez     7651552983  ral@mightyhost1.com      Lisa Williams
Warren Boyer        8221722883  wbman@uptime.net         Lisa Williams
William Morrow      9981722928  wmorrow@wmorrow.com      Lisa Williams
Bryce Sanders       6441824283  bs@cookery.com           Lisa Williams
Louis Holiday       1451223838  NULL                     Lisa Williams
```

Notice that we can specify an Order By on one of the calculated rows in the view. It is just as if the view is a table.

Creating a View	
SQL Server, Oracle, Access (see note)	
Syntax	`Create View viewname SQL_Select_statement`

Examples	1. Create a view of just the Artistname, Webaddress, and Leadsource columns of Artists for just those Artists with a Webaddress.
	`Create View vwArtistWebs As`
	`Select Artistname, Webaddress, Leadsource`
	`From Artists`
	`Where Webaddress is not null`

Note

You cannot create views in Microsoft Access through the SQL Query interface. However, you can create and save the query and then use it as a view. This accomplishes essentially the same thing. In addition, if you are using Access through the Jet OLE DB provider and an ADO connection, you can use Create View syntax, and it will create a view. The view is not visible as a saved query, but it does exist.

Dropping a View

The syntax for dropping a view is what you would expect.

Dropping a View	
SQL Server, Oracle, Access	
Syntax	`DROP VIEW viewname`
Examples	1. Drop the view vwArtistWebs. `Drop View vwArtistWebs`

Stored Procedures and Triggers

Tables, constraints, indexes, and views are not the only database objects you can create. Some database systems also support ***stored procedures*** and ***triggers***. With stored procedures and triggers you move programming code from the front-end application to the back-end database. That is often helpful for several reasons:

- It simplifies front-end programming. Instead of issuing commands to update several tables, the front-end program can call the stored procedure and let it handle the details.
- It allows database programmers rather than application programmers to control and monitor complex data relationships. Database programmers are often more aware of the database and of ways to optimize performance.
- It can simplify data migration. Just as views can hide differences in databases, so can stored procedures and triggers. If you move the database from Oracle to SQL Server (or the other way), the stored procedure will have to be changed but the front-end call to it might not have to change at all.
- Back-end programming generally runs faster than front-end programming. With a series of front-end commands, the application and the database have to communicate back and forth several times. With a single call to a stored procedure, the front-end application can start the database server running an entire series of commands. This will often result in significant performance gains, especially over slower wide-area networking lines.

A stored procedure is a set of SQL commands stored inside the database and executed on the database server. Stored procedures can have input and output parameters, allowing the front-end program to specify the record or records that need to be affected by the stored procedure and allow the stored procedure to report back what it has done.

A trigger is a stored procedure that is automatically run when a particular event occurs. Triggers are attached to the INSERT, UPDATE, and DELETE events of tables and operate based on the changed data. For instance, a trigger can be used to implement cascading updates and deletes (though with several caveats and special considerations).

SQL Server and Oracle support both stored procedures and triggers. Programming them is beyond the scope of this book. They essentially combine SQL with procedural programming techniques and variables.

MySQL and Access do not support either stored procedures or triggers. However, Access programmers can write VBA (Visual Basic) subroutines that execute a series of SQL statements. These subroutines can be attached to form events or be called specifically. MySQL is considering supporting stored procedures and possibly triggers in future versions.

Scripts

What is a *script* and how do you make it? Let's answer the second question first. You make a script simply by saving a set of SQL commands to a text file. That also answers the first question.

A script is simply a text file full of SQL commands. Why would you want to make a script? For one thing, after working through the last two chapters of changing data and table structures, wouldn't it be nice to start over again with the Lyric Music database as it was? You could if all the data definition and insert commands were saved in a script.

A script is also useful for duplicating a database structure from one site to another. Often database programmers create and test a database on a development server and then replicate the structure using scripts on the production server. By using scripts you can be sure that the exact same commands are run in the exact same order on both servers. Because scripts are just text files, they can be easily transferred via e-mail. In addition, they can be edited in any text editor.

Scripts are not just for data definition. Complex SELECT queries can be tested against a development server and saved in a script for later use against the production server. If a large update has to be performed, it is wise to test it against a development server and then save the code in a script for use against the production server.

Using Scripts with SQL Server

In SQL Server's Query Analyzer you save SQL instructions to a script simply by selecting File | Save from the menu. Make sure you first click into the upper pane so that you save your code and not the results. By default the file is saved with a .SQL extension. To load a saved script, select File | Open from the menu. You can also use copy and paste to move instructions in and out.

There is one other issue related to multiple statements that applies just to SQL Server scripts. In Oracle you know that each SQL command must have a semi-colon (;) at the end of the line to execute. When the semi-colon is typed followed by Enter, the SQL command is immediately executed unless it is part of a transaction. This is not the case with SQL Server. In SQL Server the semi-colon is optional, and multiple SQL commands can be entered into Query Analyzer and run together as a batch. They are run one at a time in the order given but executed by the database server together. This can cause some anomalies. For instance, If you have a Create Table statement on one line and an Alter Table statement for the same table on the next line, the Alter Table statement will error out. Why? Because the two statements are executed by the database together and so, technically, the table hasn't yet been created when the Alter Table statement is run.

The solution is the SQL Server Go statement. Go separates your script into individual batches run sequentially. Go must be placed on a line by itself; lines above the GO will be fully executed prior to the lines below the Go. So, for example, you would place a Go between Create Table and Alter Table, and everything would run just fine.

As a rule all Create statements, whether for tables, views, stored procedures, or anything else, should be followed by a Go to be run as a separate batch.

Using Scripts with Oracle

In Oracle's SQL Plus, load and run a script by typing @ followed by the path and name of the script file to run. For example, to run a script file called test.sql stored in the root directory of the c drive, you would type: `@c:\test.sql`

You can create the script file in any text editor, such as Notepad. SQL Plus includes options for doing this. Select Edit | Editor | Invoke Editor.

Using Scripts with MySQL

MySQL can run scripts at a command prompt. Once at a command prompt you will probably need to change to the directory in which your MySQL programs are installed. Under Windows that is normally done with `cd\mysql\bin`, then type `mysql database_name < path_and_script_name`

For example, to run a script file called test.sql stored in the root directory of the c drive against the lyric database, you would type: `mysql lyric < c:\test.sql`

You can create the script file in any text editor, such as Notepad. In addition, some third-party MySQL front-end programs allow you to save and load scripts from a graphical user interface.

Using Scripts with Access

The Access Query interface has no capability to process multiple SQL statements. However, Access VBA programmers can implement scripts using either DAO or ADO connectivity to the database. Both allow VBA programs to execute an SQL statement against the database.

Chapter Summary

SQL offers powerful commands and structures for implementing a database structure. Constraints are any kind of restriction put upon what can be entered into a table. Primary key constraints enforce uniqueness among records. Unique constraints can require that non-primary key columns hold unique values. Default constraints automatically enter values to columns if no value was supplied by the user's INSERT command. Check constraints can perform many other kinds of data checking. Foreign key constraints maintain the integrity of the data by requiring that values in the foreign key child columns match values in a parent table. Another important database object is the index, which is used to speed up searches, sorts, and joins.

Indexes are powerful performance tools, but if not set wisely, indexes can actually decrease performance. Views are simply saved queries. Views can shield users from the complexity of SQL and the database structure. Views can also solve certain security and data migration issues. Stored procedures and triggers are advanced database objects that move programming right into the database. These powerful tools can simplify database access to users, provide more control, and increase performance.

The data definition language for all these objects, as well as other kinds of SQL, can be saved in scripts. Scripts are simply text files that contain SQL commands. Using scripts allows you to replicate database objects on multiple servers or to repeat past commands.

Key Terms

cascade delete
cascade update
check constraint
constraint
Data Definition Language (DDL)
default constraint
domain constraint
Drop
entity constraint
foreign key constraint
Globally Unique Identifier (GUID)
identity column
index
primary key constraint
referential integrity constraints
script
sequence
stored procedure
trigger
unique constraint
view

Review Questions

1. In the Lyric Music database, in the relationship between Tracks and Titles, which is the parent and which is the child?
2. Which two kinds of constraints we have looked at can be classified as domain constraints?
3. List three uses for views.
4. What is a sequence?
5. In the Lyric Music database, name a parent-child relationship in which a cascade delete would be useful and a parent-child relationship in which a cascade delete would not be good idea.
6. Using good naming conventions, what would be a good name for a default constraint on the Country column of the Members table?
7. List four advantages of using database back-end programming, such as stored procedures and triggers.
8. What is the difference between a primary key constraint and a unique constraint?
9. Which of our four target databases support stored procedures and triggers?
10. What are the advantages of using scripts?

Exercises

1. Write and save a script that does the following for the Contracts table as shown below:
    a. Create the table, setting up each column with the appropriate datatypes.
    b. Change OrderID to be an identity column or, in the case of Oracle, use a sequence.
    c. Make OrderID the primary key.
    d. Create foreign key constraints to Artists and Salespeople (Can be done only with Access, SQL Server, or Oracle).
    e. Create a default constraint on ContractType to default to "Management" (Can be done only with SQL Server, Oracle, or MySQL).
    f. Create an index on ExpirationDate, an index on ArtistID, and an index on SalesID.
    g. Populate the table with the data shown below:

OrderID	ArtistID	ContractType	ContractDate	ExpirationDate	ContractPrice	SalesID
1	1	Management	10/15/2002	10/15/2003	$400	1
2	15	Management	12/5/2002	12/5/2003	$400	1
3	10	E-Commerce	11/18/2002	11/18/2003	$150	3
4	1	E-Commerce	11/25/2002	11/25/2003	$150	2
5	5	E-Commerce	12/14/2002	12/14/2003	$150	3
6	2	Management	10/23/2002	10/23/2003	$400	3
7	17	Management	11/5/2002	11/5/2003	$400	2

2. The ContractPrice in the table above should be looked up from a ContractType table. Write and save a script that does the following:
    a. Create a ContractType table with ContractType and ContractPrice columns, setting up each with datatypes matching those in the Contracts table.
    b. Make ContractType the primary key.
    c. Create a foreign key constraint from Contracts (Can be done only with Access, SQL Server, or Oracle).
    d. Populate the table using a SELECT statement from the Contracts table.
3. Write and save a script to modify the Contracts and ContractType tables in the following ways:
    a. Add a TypeID column to ContractType that is set up as an identity or to use a sequence.
    b. Drop the original primary key for ContractType and make TypeID the primary key in the ContractType table.

c. Populate the TypeID column to match the ContractType in each row.
d. Add a TypeID column to Contracts as a foreign key field (Can be done only with Access, SQL Server, or Oracle).
e. Drop the original foreign key constraint between the two tables and create one based on TypeID (Can be done only with Access, SQL Server, or Oracle).
f. Drop the ContractType column in Contracts.

Additional References

MySQL – Auto_Increment
http://www.mysql.com/doc/en/example-AUTO_INCREMENT.html

AutoNumber and Identity functionality in Oracle
http://searchdatabase.techtarget.com/tip/1,289483,sid13_gci850770,00.html

MySQL Manual – Foreign Keys (registration required)
http://www.mysql.com/doc/en/ANSI_diff_Foreign_Keys.html

MSDN – Cascading Referential Integrity Constraints
http://msdn.microsoft.com/library/default.asp?url=/library/en-us/createdb/cm_8_des_04_92ib.asp

Experts Eschange – Cascade Update
http://www.experts-exchange.com/Databases/Oracle/Q_10167188.html

MSDN – Indexes
http://msdn.microsoft.com/library/default.asp?url=/library/en-us/createdb/cm_8_des_05_30s5.asp

Hot-Oracle – Views
http://hot-oracle.com/articles.html?articleId=17

Database Security

Chapter Overview

This chapter will explore the principles and implementation of security in a database. Security keeps hackers out of your database and protects the privacy of your customers and employees. Users should have all the privileges to the database that they need to do their jobs, and nothing beyond that. We will discuss security concepts of users, roles, privileges, and database objects. Then we will see how those concepts can be applied in each of our four target databases. This will include how to create users and roles, how to grant and revoke privileges, and how to perform necessary housekeeping chores, such as changing passwords and dropping old users. Finally, we will discuss password and role strategy.

Chapter Objectives

In this chapter, we will:

- Study basic security concepts of users, roles, privileges, and database objects
- Create users and roles/groups
- Grant and revoke privileges for users and groups
- Learn about share-level vs. user-level security in Access
- Learn about SQL Server versus Windows NT Authentication for SQL Server
- Understand the concepts of Grant, Revoke, and Deny
- Understand the concept of database object ownership and identification
- Understand the use of Oracle synonyms
- Understand sound password and role strategies

Basic Security Concepts

Whenever more than one person can access a database, security becomes relevant. A corporate database may contain sensitive information, such as employee pay rates or customer social security numbers that should be screened from various ***users***. You may want to allow some users to be able to view some information, but not make changes to it, for example, in a student grades database. For a database open to the Internet, such as an e-commerce database, security becomes an even more important issue.

Fortunately, SQL and each of our target databases provide powerful tools for controlling security. We will first discuss general security concepts and then see how those concepts are implemented in each database system.

Users

The first key to database security is to be able to identify users. Only when you know which user is which can you control the access of each user. Each of our database systems uses a ***login*** procedure (though Access masks it unless security is specifically turned on). The login procedure asks for a username and a ***password***. Passwords, then, provide one step in establishing security.

Privileges

Users are given (directly or indirectly) ***privileges*** to do various things in a database. What kinds of things? Here is a list of the basic user privileges.

- Login. Unless a user login is created or enabled for a user, he or she lacks that initial but crucial right.
- Access to a specific database. We will see that users need to be granted basic access privileges to a database before they can do anything else in that database.
- SELECT. This allows a user to "read" data from a table or view.
- INSERT. This allows a user to create new data in a table or through a view. Note that this is distinct from SELECT. You can allow data entry clerks to enter data without being able to see data they or someone else has created in the past.
- UPDATE. This allows a user to change existing data in a table or through a view. Note that this is distinct from INSERT or SELECT. Generally, a user with UPDATE privileges also needs SELECT privileges so he or she can see what needs to be changed. If that is the case you will need to specifically grant both UPDATE and SELECT privileges.
- DELETE. This allows a user to delete rows from a table or through a view.
- REFERENCES. This privilege is more difficult to understand. It is related to tables with foreign key constraints. Those constraints require that INSERTs and

UPDATEs to the child table "refer" to the parent table to make sure the data entered matches an existing value in the parent table. A user lacking SELECT privileges in the parent table would not be able to INSERT or UPDATE into the child table. That is where REFERENCES comes in. A user with REFERENCES privileges to the child table would be able to access the parent through the foreign key constraint and thus complete an UPDATE or INSERT in the child (provided the user also had UPDATE or INSERT privileges to the child table).

- EXECUTE. This applies only to stored procedures, allowing the user the right to execute (or run) the stored procedure.

Database Objects

All of the privileges discussed above can be granted, denied, or revoked for any table, any view, and any stored procedure in a database. Each of these tables, views, and stored procedures are called database objects. Note that each database object has its own security settings independent of every other database object. So, for instance, you can give a user SELECT privileges to a view but not give that user SELECT privileges to the table underlying that view. Thus, you could hide sensitive columns, such as pay rates, from certain groups of users.

Roles

Suppose you had a corporate database with 50 tables, 75 views, and 25 stored procedures. This gives you a total of 150 database objects. Assume that your organization had 1000 users. Each user is given a login and access to the database. But then you get to the privileges for the individual database objects. The 125 tables and views each have five settings (SELECT, INSERT, UPDATE, DELETE, and REFERENCES), so that's 625 settings per user, or a total of 625,000 settings. EXECUTE permissions for the 25 stored procedures for 1,000 users adds another 25,000 settings. We have a total of 650,000 individual security settings to set up.

Clearly that is a mind-numbing amount of tedious work. The tool used to cut down on this work is called database ***roles***. Roles are similar to user ***groups*** in network security. If we can group the 1000 users into eight groups and assign privileges to the groups, then we have just the 625 table and view settings plus the 25 stored procedure settings times 8 for a total of 5200 security settings. That is still a big task, but not nearly as big as 650,000 settings to manage. The relationship of users to groups to privileges is illustrated in the drawing below. The users are placed inside roles so that they can be handled as a group. The role groups then are assigned various privileges to the various database objects. Of course, individual users can also be assigned privileges. But that can get confusing quickly. The best practice is to use roles.

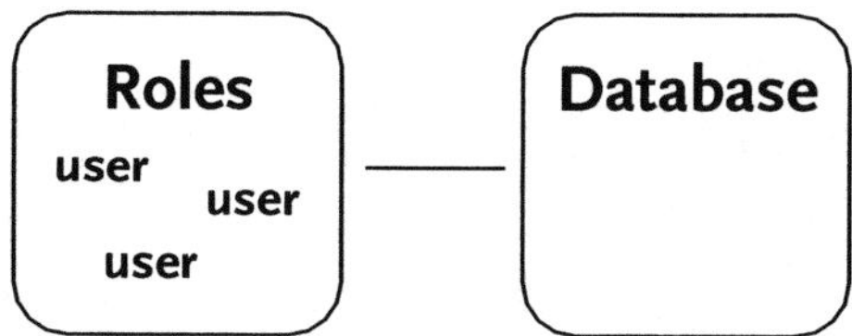

Can a user be placed in more than one role? Yes, and that gives the role tool much more power. Suppose you assign Role X a certain set of privileges and assign Role Y a different certain set of privileges. If you assign a user to both Role X and Role Y, that user would acquire privileges from both roles. In effect, that creates a virtual third role.

By creating roles carefully, you can make a few roles do a lot of work. At the end of the chapter we will discuss role-creation strategies.

Security Implementation in Access

Share-Level vs. User-Level Security

Access offers two levels of security. The basic share-level security is appropriate for small workgroups where everyone should either have full rights or no rights at all. With share-level security you create a case-sensitive database password. Each time the database is launched, users are asked for the password. To create this password, do the following:

- Launch Access
- From the menu select File | Open
- Browse to the folder where your database is located and highlight it
- Click on the drop-down list beside the Open icon and choose Open Exclusive
- From the menu select Tools | Security | Set Database Password

Share-level security offers no way to grant partial rights to users. If they can get in at all, they can do anything, including delete tables and other database objects. However, VBA (Visual Basic) programmers can manipulate the menus and windows that are available to provide further security. ***User-level security*** provides a more sophisticated security system. It allows you to create users and roles and give them various privileges. It is also much more complicated. The rest of our discussion on Access security will focus on user-level security.

The Admin User and the Workgroup Information File

Actually, Access always uses user accounts. When someone launches a non-secured database, they are in fact logging in as the default Admin user with no password. Therefore, the first step to establishing user-level security is to give the Admin user a password, forcing users to explicitly log in.

Setting up the Admin password can be a little tricky. The list of users, passwords, and user groups is stored in a special workgroup information file. By default, all Access applications use the workgroup information file system.mdw stored in the Windows directory. So without taking special precautions, creating an Admin password would affect every Access database on your PC. A separate workgroup information file for your database needs to be created and used whenever the database is launched.

One way to create a separate workgroup information file is simply to find system.mdw and copy it. The new workgroup information file can be placed anywhere on the hard drive. It is often a good idea to give it the same name as the database, but with a .mdw extension. How you make sure you use this workgroup information file whenever the database is launched depends on how you access the data.

If you access the database through an ADO connection, you can declare the workgroup information file as part of the connection properties. This is a textbook on SQL programming not ADO programming, so we will leave the explanation at that other than to include some sample code. This is ASP code taken from the execute_sql_secure.asp file on the CD:

```
Set objConn=Server.CreateObject("ADODB.Connection")
accessdb="lyric2k.mdb"
accessmdw="lyric.mdw"
With objConn
   .Provider="Microsoft.Jet.OLEDB.4.0;"
   .Properties("Jet OLEDB:System database") =
server.mappath(accessmdw)
   .Open "Data Source=" & server.mappath(accessdb) & ";" & "User Id="
& request.form("user") & ";Password=" & request.form("password") &
";"
End With
```

If you are writing an Access front-end program, you can create a shortcut that calls the MSAccess program, the database, and the workgroup information file. A shortcut like this, called "Lyric2K Secure Shortcut," is included on the CD that comes with this book. It has the following target property, which could be modified to work with any database and workgroup information file stored in any directory:

```
"C:\Program Files\Microsoft Office\Office\MSACCESS.EXE" "C:\Documents
and Settings\GR\My Documents\SQL Textbook\Lyric2K Secure.mdb" /wrkgrp
"C:\Documents and Settings\GR\My Documents\SQL Textbook\lyric.mdw"
```

With such a shortcut you can then open the database and set the Admin password without affecting all the other databases on your computer that you wish to leave unsecured. Of course, this still leaves the possibility of users bypassing your workgroup information file and accessing the database as they always did. The solution to that is to strip all rights from the Admin account so that they cannot access anything as that user. You will create another user account with administrative rights so you can still manipulate whatever you want.

Two Interfaces to Manage Access Security

Microsoft Access provides a graphical user interface for adding users and groups and setting database object privileges. It is also possible to issue SQL commands to accomplish the same thing, provided you issue the commands through an ADO/OLE DB interface. The SQL commands are more flexible, since they can be issued against a remote database over the Internet or wide area networking connection. This discussion will focus on the SQL commands but provide menu instructions to the graphical user interface.

These SQL commands can be tested provided you have access to a Microsoft web server (IIS or PWS). Copy the following files from the CD to a web site folder:

- Lyric2K Secure.mdb
- lyric.mdw
- execute_sql_secure.asp
- SQLSecureTest.htm

Make sure these files are not set to read-only. Run SQLSecureTest.htm through the web server. You will be prompted for an SQL command, a user name, and a password. The password for the Admin user is sql. We will set up other users and groups as we progress through the discussion. Then you can user the user name and password for those users to check the privileges.

Note

These statements cannot be run in the Access SQL query interface. They can be executed only through the Jet OLE DB provider and ADO.

Adding Users

Once you have user-level security established through a workgroup information file and are logged in, you are ready to start creating your users. The basic syntax is just Create User followed by the user name and password. Optionally you can add a ***personal identifier***, or ***PID***.

A PID is an alphanumeric value from 4 to 20 characters long. Access (or more precisely, the Jet database engine behind Access) will combine the PID with the user name to form a unique key value known as a ***security identifier***, or ***SID***. The SID is the value that Jet uses internally to identify and work with the user account, though you can simply use the user name. Specifying a PID allows you to recreate an identical account if the workgroup file becomes damaged, or if you need to move the account into another workgroup file. Once an account and its corresponding SID are created, you can never change or alter the PID value used to create it. For the best security, use PID values with a combination of numbers and both upper- and lowercase numbers. You can use the same PID for each user, but for best security you should use different PIDs for each user.

Adding a User	
	Access
Syntax	`CREATE USER UserName Password PID`
Examples	1. Create user Tom with a password of xyz11 and a PID of GR02db83. `CREATE USER Tom xyz11 GR02db83`
	2. Create user Mary with a password of abc12 and no PID. `CREATE USER Mary abc12`

In the Access graphical user interface, create users by selecting from the menu Tools | Security | User and Group Accounts and clicking on the Users tab. In the graphical user interface, users will be set up without passwords. Log in as that user and click on Change Logon Password to set or change the password.

Adding Groups

Access uses the networking term “groups” instead of the database term “roles,” but they work the same. By placing users into groups and assigning rights to the groups, you can greatly reduce the complexity of your security management. The basic syntax is just Create Group followed by the group name. As with users, optionally you can add a personal identifier, or PID.

Adding a Group	
	Access
Syntax	`CREATE GROUP GroupName`
Examples	1. Create a user group 'marketing' with a PID of MP80qhg. `CREATE Group marketing MP80qhg`
	2. Create user group 'accounting' with no PID. `CREATE Group accounting`

In the Access graphical user interface, create groups by selecting from the menu Tools | Security | User and Group Accounts and clicking on the Groups tab.

Assigning Users to Groups

After creating the users and groups, the next step is to add the users to the groups. The syntax is simply Add User, followed by the user name, followed by To, followed by the group name. You can add multiple users to a group with one statement by listing each user name separated by commas.

Adding Users to Groups	
	Access
Syntax	`ADD USER UserName | UserName, UserName To GroupName`
Examples	1. Add Tom to the marketing group. `Add User Tom To marketing`
	2. Add both Tom and Mary to the accounting group. `Add User Tom, Mary to accounting`
	3. Add both Tom and Mary to the default users group. `Add User Tom, Mary to users`

In the Access graphical user interface, add users to groups by selecting from the menu Tools | Security | User and Group Accounts. Select the user from the drop-down menu and establish that user's groups using the Group Membership section.

Setting Database Object Privileges

Access allows you to assign any or all of a set of rights for any individual database object to any user or group. You can mix and match these rights as needed for the security you want. *GRANT* is used to give privileges. *REVOKE* is used to disallow privileges. Or you can grant one or more of the privileges shown below. Multiple privileges can be assigned in a single command by listing them, separated by commas.

Privilege	Applies To	Description
SELECT	Tables, Objects, Containers	Allows user to read data
DELETE	Tables, Objects, Containers	Allows user to delete data
INSERT	Tables, Objects, Containers	Allows user to add new rows
UPDATE	Tables, Objects, Containers	Allows user to update data
DROP	Tables, Objects, Containers	Allows user to remove a specified database object
SELECTSECURITY	Tables, Objects, Containers	Allows user to view permissions for a database object
UPDATESECURITY	Tables, Objects, Containers	Allows user to change permissions for a database object
UPDATEIDENTITY	Tables	Allows user to change auto-increment values
CREATE	Tables, Objects, Containers	Allows user to create a database object
SELECTSCHEMA	Tables, Objects, Containers	Allows user to view the design of a database object
SCHEMA	Tables, Objects, Containers	Allows user to modify the design of a database object
UPDATEOWNER	Tables, Objects, Containers	Allows user to change the owner of a database object
ALL PRIVILEGES	All	Allows user all permissions on a database object
CREATEDB	Database	Allows user to create a new database
EXCLUSIVECONNECT	Database	Allows user to open a database in exclusive mode
CONNECT	Database	Allows user to open a database
ADMINDB	Database	Allows user to administer a database

Follow the list of permissions with ON and one of the following key words specifying the type of object: Table (for a table), Object (for a form, query, report, macro, view, or procedure), or Container. Container is a special Access concept that applies to the various types of database objects, such as tables, forms, and reports. Privileges set for a container object will apply to any new database objects of that type that are later created.

Follow the type with the name of the table, query, form, etc. (or name of the type of object in the case of Container). Follow this with TO and the name of the group or user to which you are granting the permission. To revoke privileges, replace the GRANT with REVOKE and the TO with FROM.

Assigning Privileges to Database Objects	
	Access
Syntax	`GRANT|REVOKE Privileges` `On ObjectType ObjectName To|From UserName|GroupName`
Examples	1. Grant SELECT rights for the Members table to the marketing group. `Grant Select On Table Members to marketing`

	2. Grant SELECT, INSERT, UPDATE, and DELETE rights for the Genre table to the user Tom.
	`Grant Select,Insert,Update,Delete`
	`On Table Genre to Tom`

	3. Grant to the marketing group SELECT rights for all tables that will ever be created. `Grant Select on Container Tables to marketing`

	4. Revoke all privileges for the Salespeople table to marketing.
	`Revoke All Privileges`
	`On Table Salespeople from marketing`

	5. Revoke the Delete rights for the Genre table previously given to Tom. `Revoke Delete On Table Genre from Tom`

In the Access graphical user interface, add users to groups by selecting from the menu Tools | Security | User and Group Permissions. Select the user or group whose permissions you want to set, select the object, then check the permission boxes at the bottom.

Note

If you are using an Access front-end program, you need to use the graphical user interface to set user and group privileges. Although users and groups can be set up from one interface and used in the other, privileges set up though an ADO connection are not accessible through an Access front-end program.

User and Group Housekeeping

The following commands allow you to change user passwords, remove users from groups, and drop users and groups.

Changing a Password	
Access	
Syntax	`ALTER USER UserName PASSWORD NewPassword OldPassword`
Examples	1. Change the password for the user Tom from xyz11 to abc23. `Alter User Tom Password abc23 xyz11`

In the Access graphical user interface, users can change their own passwords by logging in, selecting from the menu Tools | Security | User and Group Accounts and clicking on the Change Logon Password tab.

Removing a User from a Group	
Access	
Syntax	`DROP USER UserName FROM GroupName`
Examples	1. Drop the user Tom to the marketing group. `Drop User Tom From marketing`

In the Access graphical user interface, remove users from groups by selecting from the menu Tools | Security | User and Group Accounts. Select the user from the drop-down menu and change that user's groups using the Group Membership section.

Removing a Group	
Access	
Syntax	`DROP GROUP GroupName`
Examples	1. Drop the marketing group. `Drop Group marketing`

In the Access graphical user interface, remove groups by selecting from the menu Tools | Security | User and Group Accounts. Click on the Groups tab, select the group from the drop down menu, and click Delete.

Removing a User	
Access	
Syntax	`DROP USER UserName`
Examples	1. Drop the user Tom. `Drop User Tom`

In the Access graphical user interface, remove groups by selecting from the menu Tools | Security | User and Group Accounts. Click on the user's tab, select the user from the drop-down menu, and click Delete.

Security Implementation in SQL Server

SQL Server versus Windows NT Authentication

SQL Server has users, roles, and all the rights selected above. SQL Server also adds one important concept, which is ***Windows NT Authentication.*** With SQL Server, you have the option of either setting up SQL Server logins or just using the Windows NT/2000 logins on your network. Of course, that assumes you are using a Windows NT/2000 server for network authentication. Which kind of authentication should you choose?

Using Windows NT Authentication, or integrated security, works best for an in-house client-server application or intranet. That way users just have one login; when they log onto the network they gain rights to the SQL Server database. This scheme is also somewhat easier on the database administrator, who doesn't have to create separate logins and create passwords. However, the database administrator does have to specifically grant access for each NT login. This is much like creating a login, but it doesn't involve setting an initial password so you don't save huge amounts of work. The requirement to grant access for each NT login does give you the ability to not grant access for any NT login, which allows you to only let in your database the NT users you want to let in your database.

Using SQL Server logins works best for database-driven Internet sites where users will not have an NT/2000 network login. This independent scheme also works in small peer-to-peer networks not using Windows NT/2000 logins. A third situation would be organizations that use just a very few NT/2000 logins, giving everyone the same basic network rights, but wanting to be more selective about who can do what inside the database. On a local area network, using SQL Server logins generally means that users have to login twice: one for the network and once again for the database. That can be a hassle. Also, while Windows provides an applet for users to change their network password, you will have to write the front-end and back-end code to allow users to change their SQL Server password.

Actually, the choice to use SQL Server logins includes the option of also using Windows NT Authentication, so you can mix and match. This could cover situations in which a database can be accessed both over a network and the Internet. Network access to the database can be handled with Windows NT/2000 logins, while Internet access is handled with SQL Server logins.

The security choice is made at the server, not the database, level. In SQL Server's Enterprise Manager, you can right-click on the server icon and select Properties. The choices on the Security tab are shown below:

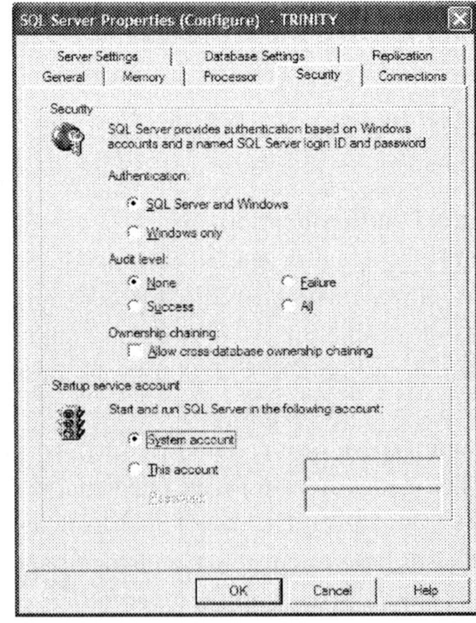

Creating Logins and Allowing Initial Access

Once you have selected which kind of login you want to use, you have to either create the SQL Server logins or allow access to Windows NT/2000 logins. That can also be done in Enterprise Manager. But in this book we will concentrate how to do it through SQL, a technique that allows you to build the settings and save them in a script file.

Whether you use SQL Server logins or Windows NT/2000 logins, setting up a user is a two-step process before you ever get to granting rights to database objects.

- Create the login (in the case of using SQL Server logins) or grant SQL Server access to an NT login (In the case of Windows NT/2000 logins).
- Allow the login to access one or more databases. This doesn't give the login rights to any database objects just to the database.

Executing the built-in sp_addlogin procedure creates an SQL Server login. Up to six parameters are passed into this procedure.

- LoginName is simply the user name for the login. It isn't strictly required, but you should surround the Loginname with quotation marks.
- Password is the initial password for that user to use. The password should be entered with quotation marks surrounding it.
- DefaultDB is the default database for that user—the starting database for that user. If this is left unspecified, it will default to the Master database, which is really a database of all your other databases. You do not want people working inside the Master database, so always specify a default database. It isn't strictly required, but you should surround the DefaultDB with quotation marks.
- DefaultLanguage is the default language for this user. Normally, you can leave this blank and let SQL Server use the default language on that server.
- SID stands for system identifier. It is a number the system uses to distinguish users. You can leave it blank and let the system generate an SID for you. If you supply it, you must make sure that each user's SID is different. Are there any good reasons to take on that responsibility and specify your own SIDs? There are a few. Specifying a SID can be handy when you are restoring a database from backups on a different server, but generally you can let the system generate its own SIDs.
- EncryptOption is an encryption option. Leave this blank to have the login name and password stored in an encrypted format. This makes it more difficult for hackers to steal your logins. You can specify skip_encryption to store the logins unencrypted, but that is not recommended.

Adding a Login	
SQL Server	
Syntax	`EXEC sp_addlogin LoginName, Password, DefaultDB, DefaultLanguage, SID, EncryptOption`
Examples	1. Create a login for user Tom with a password of xyz11 and defaulting to the lyric database. `Exec sp_addlogin 'Tom', 'xyz11', 'lyric'`

If instead you want to grant access to a Windows NT/2000 login, you would use the built-in sp_grantlogin procedure. This has only one parameter—the name of the NT login. However, the login has to be expressed in domain\login format. So a login of Tom for the ABC domain would be called ABC\Tom. This is surrounded by quotation marks.

Granting Access to a Windows NT/2000 Login	
SQL Server	
Syntax	`EXEC sp_grantlogin Domain\LoginName`
Examples	1. Grant access to SQL Server to a login called Tom in the ABC domain. `Exec sp_grantlogin 'ABC\Tom'`

Either of the two above commands will add the login to the list of SQL Server users. But this does not give that login any access to any database, not even when you specify the default database with sp_addlogin. So there is always a second step of granting initial access rights: execute the built-in sp_grantdbaccess procedure. This has only one parameter—the name of the login being granted access, surrounded by quotes. The login is granted access to the database currently being used, so you need to precede the command with Use and the database name.

Granting Database Access to a Login	
	SQL Server
Syntax	`USE Databasename` `EXEC sp_grantdbaccess LoginName`

Examples	1. Grant login Tom initial access to the lyric database.
	`Use lyric`
	`Exec sp_grantdbaccess 'Tom'`

	2. Grant access to the lyric database to a login called Tom in the ABC domain.
	`Use lyric`
	`Exec sp_grantdbaccess 'ABC\Tom'`

Creating Roles and Assigning Users

Now that we have the user both in SQL Server and in the database, we can either give that user various rights to various database objects or we can assign that user to a role. Using roles is much preferred because it ultimately simplifies and streamlines your work.

Creating a Role	
	SQL Server
Syntax	`EXEC sp_addrole RoleName`
Examples	1. Create a new role called marketing. `Exec sp_addrole 'marketing'`

After adding a role, use sp_addrolemember to add login accounts to the role. When using the GRANT, DENY, or REVOKE statements to apply permissions to the role, members of the role inherit the permissions as if the permissions were applied directly to their accounts. You can add a login to more than one role by simply using more statements.

In addition to the user-defined roles discussed above, SQL Server has several fixed database roles. Logins can be assigned to these roles also, giving them special permissions. The fixed database roles are:

- db_owner—This role possesses all rights for the database.
- db_accessadmin—This role can assign permissions for all existing logins as well as add NT logins. It cannot create new SQL Server logins.

- db_datareader—This role can SELECT from all tables in the database.
- db_datawriter—This role can INSERT, UPDATE, and DELETE in all tables in the database.
- db_ddladmin—This role can add, modify, or drop objects in the database.
- db_securityadmin—This role cannot create new logins, but can assign logins to roles and set all permissions.
- db_backupoperator—This role can run a data backup
- db_denydatareader—This provides the equivalent of DENY SELECT on every table.
- db_denydatawriter—This provides a DENY on INSERT, UPDATE, and DELETE on every table.

Adding a Login to a Role	
	SQL Server
Syntax	`EXEC sp_addrolemember RoleName, LoginName	Domain\LoginName`
Examples	1. Add the SQL Server login Tom to the marketing role. `Exec sp_addrolemember 'marketing','Tom'`
	2. Add the login Tom in the ABC domain to the marketing role. `Exec sp_addrolemember 'marketing','ABC\Tom'`
	3. Add the login Tom to the db_owner fixed database role. `Exec sp_addrolemember db_owner, Tom`

Note

SQL Server also has fixed server roles that provide equivalent power to the fixed database roles, but on the server level (i.e., they work on all databases). This goes beyond the scope of this book, but you might want to know they are there.

Granting, Denying, and Revoking Privileges to Databases Objects

SQL Server allows you to assign any or all of a set of rights for any individual database object to any login or role. You can mix and match these rights as needed for the security you want. GRANT is used to give privileges. Normally, the privileges a user gains from one role are added to the privileges a user gains from any other roles that user is a member of. DENY is used to specifically deny privileges, even if the login has gotten those privileges from another role. So a user in both the accounting role (which had been granted SELECT rights to a table) and the sales role (which had been denied SELECT rights to that table) would not gain access to the table. The DENY would trump the GRANT. REVOKE is used to counteract a previous GRANT or DENY.

All privileges can be granted, or you can grant one or more of the standard privileges (SELECT, INSERT, UPDATE, DELETE, REFERENCES, EXECUTE) discussed earlier in the chapter under Basic Security Concepts. In addition, you can grant any of the following special privileges: CREATE DATABASE, CREATE DEFAULT, CREATE PROCEDURE, CREATE RULE, CREATE TABLE, CREATE VIEW, BACKUP DATABASE, and BACKUP LOG. If granting multiple privileges, separate them with commas.

Follow the list of privileges with ON and the database object for which you are granting privileges. Notice that you can even grant or not grant privileges to the column level. Follow this with TO and the name of the role or login to which you are granting the privilege. Do not place the database object or the role/login inside quotes.

The WITH GRANT OPTION and AS arguments are not often used in a corporate setting, though they do have their place in Internet databases. WITH GRANT OPTION allows you to grant the right to grant rights to a particular login. This can lead you, as the database administrator, to lose control of who has what rights, which is why it is not often used in a corporate setting. However, in Internet databases offered by hosting companies to their clients, it is common to turn over granting rights to the client. The AS argument is used with GRANT when WITH GRANT OPTION has been given to a role. A member of that role can then grant privileges to someone else, provided that member uses AS followed by the role name. Related to this is a CASCADE argument that can be used with DENY to deny rights to a login or role, plus all others that login or role has granted rights to. Finally, REVOKE can use either CASCADE or AS.

<table>
<tr><th colspan="2">Assigning Privileges to Database Objects</th></tr>
<tr><th colspan="2">SQL Server</th></tr>
<tr><td>Syntax</td><td><pre>GRANT|DENY|REVOKE All|Privileges ON
  TableName|ViewName|StoredProcedureName|
  TableName(Field1,Field2)|ViewName(Field1,Field2) To
  LoginName|RoleName
  WITH GRANT OPTION
  AS Rolename</pre></td></tr>
<tr><td>Examples</td><td>1. Grant SELECT rights for the Members table to the marketing role
<code>Grant Select On Members to marketing.</code></td></tr>
<tr><td></td><td>2. Grant SELECT, INSERT, UPDATE, and DELETE rights for the Genre table to the login Tom.
<code>Grant Select,Insert,Update,Delete On Genre to Tom</code></td></tr>
<tr><td></td><td>3. Grant UPDATE rights for the RespParty column of the XRefArtistsMembers table to marketing.
<code>Grant Update On XRefArtistsMembers(respparty)
to marketing</code></td></tr>
<tr><td></td><td>4. Deny all privileges for the Salespeople table to marketing.
<code>Deny All On Salespeople to marketing</code></td></tr>
<tr><td></td><td>5. Revoke the SELECT rights for the Members table previously given to the marketing role.
<code>Revoke Select On Members to marketing</code></td></tr>
</table>

Database Object Ownership and Identification

Throughout the previous chapters of this book, you have created your own tables and views and have been the only person to use them. When you begin sharing access to database objects, the concept of ownership and the identification of database objects come into play.

Whenever a table, view, or stored procedure is created in a SQL Server database, it is identified by the name of the person who created it. So if login Tom created the Artists table, SQL Server would know it as Tom.Artists. Tom might never realize this. He could select from and update to Artists all day just using the name Artists. SQL Server would know he means Tom.Artists. This, in fact, is how you have worked with database objects in previous chapters.

However, if Tom gives privilege to login Mary to select records, she would have to refer to the table as Tom.Artists. Otherwise, SQL Server would report that the table did not exist. There is one huge exception to this rule. There is one login who initially creates the database. It could be the master SQL Server SA (System Administrator) login, or it could be another login that has been granted the right to create a database. The database accords this login a special title, dbo (database owner). The database objects created by dbo can be accessed by any other user simply with the name of the database object. In other words, if dbo creates Artists, then Tom, Mary, and everyone else can refer to Artists simply as Artists, not dbo.Artists.

In a real world situation, then, it is a good idea for all tables to be created by dbo. It eliminates much potential confusion. But the ownership/naming rules can actually be useful in some situations. For instance, several students could have tables named the same in the same database and yet keep them separate.

Login and Role Housekeeping

With the above commands you can set up a sophisticated security system in SQL Server. But things never stay the same, so you will probably need the following housekeeping commands to change passwords, remove logins from roles, and drop logins and roles:

Changing a Password	
	SQL Server
Syntax	`EXEC sp_password OldPassword, NewPassword, LoginName`
Examples	1. Change the password for the login Tom from xyz11 to abc23. `Exec sp_password 'xyz11','abc23','Tom'`

Removing a Login from a Role	
	SQL Server
Syntax	`EXEC sp_droprolemember Rolename, LoginName | Domain\LoginName`
Examples	1. Drop the SQL Server login Tom to the marketing role. `Exec sp_droprolemember 'marketing','Tom'`

Removing a Role	
SQL Server	
Syntax	`EXEC sp_droprole Rolename`
Examples	1. Drop the marketing role. `Exec sp_droprole 'marketing'`

Removing a SQL Server Login	
SQL Server	
Syntax	`EXEC sp_droplogin LoginName`
Examples	1. Drop the login Tom. `Exec sp_droplogin 'Tom'`

Revoking Access to a Windows NT/2000 Login	
SQL Server	
Syntax	`EXEC sp_revokedbaccess Domain\LoginName`
Examples	1. Revoke access to the login Tom from the ABC domain. `Exec sp_revokedbaccess 'ABC\Tom'`

Security Implementation in Oracle

Oracle supports users, roles, and all the standard SQL privileges. Oracle security can be created either through SQL commands or through the graphical user interface of the Oracle Enterprise Security Manager or the Oracle Enterprise Manager Console. In this book we will focus on how to do it through SQL, since that technique allows you to build the settings and save them in a script file.

Adding Users and Allowing Initial Access

There are two ways to create a user in Oracle. One way is with the CREATE USER command. The other way is to create the user at the same time you grant the user specific privileges. The first way is preferred since the second way does not allow you to use roles.

The syntax of the CREATE USER command is simply CREATE USER, followed by the user name, followed by the words Identified By, followed by the initial password you want to use for that user. Passwords cannot begin with a number.

Adding a User	
Oracle	
Syntax	`CREATE USER UserName Identified By Password`
Examples	1. Create user Tom with a password of xyz11. `Create User Tom Identified By xyz11;`
	2. Create user Mary with a password of abc23. `Create User Mary Identified By abc23;`

Once the user has been created, it needs to be allowed the right to connect to the database. This doesn't give the user rights to any database objects, just to the database.

Granting Connect Rights to a User	
Oracle	
Syntax	`GRANT CONNECT to UserName`
Examples	1. Grant connect rights to user Tom. `Grant Connect to Tom`

Note

Instead of granting connect rights to users, you can assign the users to roles and grant connect rights to the roles. It accomplishes the same thing with fewer commands.

Creating Roles and Assigning Users

Now that we have the user created, we can either give that user various rights to various database objects or we can assign that user to a role. Using roles is much preferred because it ultimately simplifies and streamlines your work.

Note

If you did not grant connect rights to users as discussed above, you need to grant connect rights to the roles.

Creating a Role	
Oracle	
Syntax	`CREATE ROLE RoleName`
Examples	1. Create a new role called marketing. `Create Role marketing;`
	2. Create a new role called accounting and grant it connect rights. `Create Role accounting;Grant Connect to accounting;`

With both roles and users created, you can then assign the users to roles. You can assign multiple roles to a user with one statement by listing all roles separated by commas.

Adding a User to a Role	
Oracle	
Syntax	`GRANT RoleName To UserName`
Examples	1. Add user Tom to the marketing role. `Grant marketing to Tom;`
	2. Add the user Mary to both the accounting and marketing roles. `Grant accounting, marketing to Mary;`

Granting and Revoking Rights to Databases Objects

Oracle allows you to assign any or all of a set of rights for any individual database object to any user or role. You can mix and match these rights as needed for the security you want. GRANT is used to give privileges. REVOKE is used to counteract a previous GRANT.

All privileges can be granted (which gives the user every privilege except the GRANT OPTION discussed below). Or you can grant one or more of the standard privileges (SELECT, INSERT, UPDATE, DELETE, REFERENCES, EXECUTE) discussed earlier in the chapter under Basic Security Concepts. Oracle allows setting INDEX and ALTER privileges. INDEX allows a user to create an index on the table. ALTER allows the user to alter the table structure. INSERT, REFERENCES, and UPDATE can also be applied to just certain columns by following the privilege with a list of columns in parentheses, separated by commas.

Follow the list of privileges with ON and the database object for which you are granting privileges. Follow this with TO and the name of the role or users to which you are granting the privilege. Multiple roles or users can be assigned privileges with a single command by listing the roles or users separated by commas.

The WITH GRANT OPTION is not often used in a corporate setting, though it does have its place in Internet databases. WITH GRANT OPTION allows you to grant the right to grant rights to a particular user or role. This can lead to you, as the database administrator, to lose control of who has what rights, which is why it is not often used in a corporate setting. However, in Internet databases offered by hosting companies to their clients, it is common to turn over granting rights to the client.

When revoking rights, replace the GRANT with REVOKE and the TO with FROM. You can only revoke rights that have been granted.

Assigning Privileges to Database Objects	
	Oracle

Syntax	`GRANT|REVOKE Privileges(Field1,Field2) ON`
	`TableName|ViewName|StoredProcedureName`
	`To|From UserName|RoleName`
	`WITH GRANT OPTION`

Examples	1. Grant Select rights for the Members table to the marketing role. `Grant Select On Members to marketing;`
	2. Grant Select, Insert, Update, and Delete rights for the Genre table to the user Tom. `Grant Select,Insert,Update,Delete On Genre to Tom;`

	3. Grant Update rights for the RespParty column of the XRefArtistsMembers table to marketing.
	`Grant Update On XRefArtistsMembers(respparty)`
	`to marketing;`

	4. Revoke the Select rights for the Members table previously given to the marketing role. `Revoke Select On Members from marketing;`

In addition to the above arguments, you can also create users "on-the-fly" with the GRANT command. Follow the user name with Identified By and a password. The problem with this is that it essentially eliminates the use of roles.

Database Object Ownership and Identification

As mentioned before, throughout the previous chapters of this book you have created your own tables and views and been the only person to use them. When you begin sharing access to database objects, the concept of ownership and the identification of database objects come into play.

Whenever a table, view, or stored procedure is created in an Oracle database, it is identified by the name of the person who created it. So if user Tom created the Artists table, it would be known to Oracle as Tom.Artists. Tom might never realize this. He could select from and update to Artists all day just using the name Artists. Oracle would know he means Tom.Artists. This, in fact, is how you have worked with database objects in previous chapters.

However, if Tom gives privilege to user Mary to select records, she would have to refer to the table as Tom.Artists. Otherwise, Oracle would report that the table did not exist. If working with remote databases, the naming scheme gets more complex. In that case you follow the name of the database object with an @ sign and the name of the database server, as in Tom.Artists@MyServer.

These ownership/naming rules can actually be useful in some situations. For instance, several students could have tables named the same in the same database and yet keep them separate.

You can streamline the table-naming syntax by using a ***synonym***. A synonym is simply an alternate name for a database object. A synonym is similar to an alias with one major difference. An alias exists only for the life of the SQL command that uses it. A synonym is permanent until you drop it. A private synonym can be used only by the user who created it. A public synonym can be used by anyone. Typically, the owner of a table or view would create a public synonym for other users. Or a user of someone else's table would create a private synonym for his or her own use. Create a public synonym by including the word Public in the command; leave it out to create a private synonym.

Creating a Synonym	
Oracle	
Syntax	`CREATE Public Synonym SynonymName for Object`
Examples	1. Create a public synonym lyric_tracks for the Tracks table. `Create Public Synonym lyric_tracks for Tracks;`
	2. Create a private synonym ltracks for the system Tracks table. `Create Synonym ltracks for system.Tracks;`

Note

If you later want to drop a synonym, replace CREATE with DROP.

User and Role Housekeeping

The following commands allow you to change user passwords, remove users from groups, and drop users and groups.

Changing a Password	
Oracle	
Syntax	`ALTER USER UserName Identified BY NewPassword`
Examples	1. Change the password for user Tom to abc23. `Alter User Tom Identified by abc23;`

Removing a User from a Role	
Oracle	
Syntax	`REVOKE RoleName FROM UserName`
Examples	1. Drop the user Tom to the marketing role. `Revoke marketing From Tom`

Removing a Role	
Oracle	
Syntax	`DROP ROLE RoleName`
Examples	1. Drop the marketing group. `Drop Role marketing`

Removing a User	
Oracle	
Syntax	`DROP USER UserName`
Examples	1. Drop the user Tom. `Drop User Tom`

If the user was granted WITH GRANT OPTION rights, then to drop the user you must add CASCADE to the end of the command.

Security Implementation in MySQL

Unlike our other target databases, MySQL does not support roles. This can make it more difficult to use in a large corporate setting. However, for small organizations and most web sites, the lack of roles does not cause a lot of problems.

The master user account in any MySQL database is called root. The root user has all rights, including deleting the entire database. Therefore, the root user should rarely be used and should have a complex password. For day-to-day use, you should create other users with fewer rights. You can add users to a MySQL database in either of two ways. One way is to directly manipulate the MySQL grant tables. The preferred method, which we will discuss here, is by using GRANT statements. GRANT statements are more concise and less error-prone.

Creating Users and Granting Rights

In MySQL, users are created as part of the right-granting process. You simply grant rights to a user name. If that user does not already exist, it is created. That adds more complexity to the GRANT statement, but allows you to do more with fewer statements.

ALL privileges can be granted (which gives the user every privilege except the GRANT OPTION discussed below). Or you can grant one or more of the standard privileges (SELECT, INSERT, UPDATE, DELETE) discussed earlier in the chapter under Basic Security Concepts. You cannot currently grant EXECUTE or REFERENCES privileges because MySQL does not currently support stored procedures or foreign key constraints. If granting multiple rights, separate them by commas.

In addition, you can grant any of the special privileges shown below. Many of these privileges are very powerful. Since they will be included when granting ALL, you should rarely grant ALL privileges.

Privilege	Description
ALTER	Allows use of ALTER TABLE
CREATE	Allows use of CREATE TABLE
CREATE TEMPORARY TABLES	Allows use of CREATE TEMPORARY TABLE
DROP	Allows use of DROP TABLE
FILE	Allows use of SELECT ... INTO OUTFILE and LOAD DATA INFILE
INDEX	Allows use of CREATE INDEX and DROP INDEX
LOCK TABLES	Allows use of LOCK TABLES on tables for which one has the SELECT privilege
PROCESS	Allows use of SHOW FULL PROCESSLIST
RELOAD	Allows use of FLUSH
REPLICATION CLIENT	Allows user to ask where the slaves/masters are
REPLICATION SLAVE	Needed for the replication slaves (to read binlogs from master).
SHOW DATABASES	Allows user to show all databases
SHUTDOWN	Allows use of mysqladmin shutdown
SUPER	Allows user to connect even if max_connections is reached and execute administrative commands
USAGE	Synonym for no privileges

The options for naming database objects are: (1) a single table, (2) all tables using the name of the database followed by a period and *, and (3) a list of columns in a particular table with the column names separated by commas and the entire list enclosed in parentheses prior to the ON TableName. You cannot currently set privileges for views and stored procedures because MySQL does not currently support views and stored procedures.

Notice that multiple users can be granted rights in one statement; just place a comma between each UserName. When specifying the UserName follow it by an @ sign and the database host name. The IDENTIFIED BY password options only have to be included the first time a user is named and created.

The WITH GRANT OPTION grants the right to grant rights to the user. This is not uncommon in Internet databases offered by hosting companies to their clients. The root user at the hosting company will create the database and the master user for that database with granting rights. However, if you are the master user of that database, you would rarely use this option, as it can lead to your losing control of who has what rights. Notice that you can also limit the number of queries, updates, and connections a user can have.

In addition to these options, GRANT also has options for requiring an encrypted connection to the database, such as SSL or X509. These are beyond the scope of this book. See the Additional References at the end of the chapter for more information.

Creating Users and Granting Privileges to Database Objects	
	MySQL

Syntax	`GRANT PRIVILEGES Optional_Column_List`
	`ON TableName | DatabaseName.*`
	`TO 'UserName'@'HostName' IDENTIFIED BY 'password',`
	`'UserName'@'HostName' IDENTIFIED BY 'password', ...`
	`WITH GRANT OPTION | MAX_QUERIES_PER_HOUR # |`
	` MAX_UPDATES_PER_HOUR # | MAX_CONNECTIONS_PER_HOUR #`

Examples	1. Grant SELECT rights for the Members table of the lyric database hosted on localhost to a user named Tom with the password 'xyz11'.
	`Grant Select On Members to tom@localhost`
	`Identified by 'xyz11'`

	2. Grant SELECT, INSERT, UPDATE, and DELETE rights for the Genre table to the user Tom, which already exists.
	`Grant Select,Insert,Update,Delete`
	`On Genre to 'tom'@'localhost'`

	3. Grant UPDATE rights for the RespParty column of the XRefArtistsMembers table to the user Tom, which already exists.
	`Grant Update (RespParty)`
	`On XRefArtistsMembers to 'tom'@'localhost'`

	4. Create users Bob (password great01) and Doug (password white02). Give both Select and Insert access to all tables in the lyric database hosted on localhost.
	`Grant Select, Insert On lyric.* to bob@localhost`
	`Identified by 'great01',doug@localhost`
	`Identified by 'white02'`

Revoking Rights

The syntax for revoking rights is simpler since you are only listing what you are taking away. The list of privileges is the same. The specification of the database object is the same when specifying the UserName followed by an @ sign and the database host name.

Each previously granted privilege must be specifically revoked. For instance, in the examples above, we granted Tom SELECT rights to Members and SELECT, INSERT, UPDATE and DELETE rights to Genre. Could we then revoke All on lyric.* and remove all these rights? No. Revoking All on lyric.* would only work if All privileges had been previously granted. Otherwise, the GRANT and REVOKE would not match. If after granting Tom the above privileges we then granted All on lyric.*, what would revoking All on lyric.* do? It would only revoke the All privilege and leave the other privileges in tact. Because of this, it is a good idea to store all GRANT statements in scripts and examine them carefully if you ever have to revoke privileges.

Revoking Privileges to Database Objects	
	MySQL

Syntax	`REVOKE PRIVILEGES Optional_Column_List`
	`ON TableName | DatabaseName.*`
	`  FROM 'UserName','UserName',...`

Examples	1. Revoke the DELETE right for the Genre table granted to user Tom. The database is hosted on localhost. `Revoke Delete On Genre From tom@localhost`
	2. Revoke all rights granted to user Bob in the lyric database hosted on localhost. `Revoke Select, Insert On lyric.* From bob@localhost`

Changing Passwords

When specifying the UserName following by an @ sign and the database host name.

Changing User Passwords	
MySQL	
Syntax	`SET PASSWORD FOR UserName=PASSWORD('password')`
Examples	1. Change the password for user Doug on the localhost to gwn11. `SET PASSWORD FOR doug@localhost=PASSWORD('gwn11')`

Removing Users

To completely remove a user and all the user's privileges, you need to directly manipulate the user and privilege tables, as shown in the syntax below. The UserName and the HostName are both surrounded by quotes.

Removing a User and All Privileges	
MySQL	

Syntax	`DELETE FROM mysql.user`
	`WHERE Host='HostName' AND User='UserName';`
	`DELETE FROM mysql.db`
	`WHERE Host='HostName' AND User='UserName';`
	`DELETE FROM mysql.tables_priv`
	`WHERE Host='HostName' AND User='UserName';`
	`DELETE FROM mysql.columns_priv`
	`WHERE Host='HostName' AND User='UserName';`
	`Flush Privileges;`

Examples	1. Completely remove user Bob and all of Bob's privileges from the localhost.
	`DELETE FROM mysql.user`
	`WHERE Host='localhost' AND User='bob';`
	`DELETE FROM mysql.db`
	`WHERE Host='localhost' AND User='bob';`
	`DELETE FROM mysql.tables_priv`
	`WHERE Host='localhost' AND User='bob';`
	`DELETE FROM mysql.columns_priv`
	`WHERE Host='localhost' AND User='bob';`
	`Flush Privileges;`

Password and Role Strategies

One User per Person, One Person per User

The rule of thumb for database access as well as network access is that each person should have his or her own login. Often organizations are tempted to save some time at setup by using generic logins for everyone or at least large groups of people. There are some situations in which this may be appropriate. But with generic logins you lose the ability to audit the activity of any one employee. With generic logins there is also the temptation to assign more privileges to the generic login than some of the users of that login should have. This can, in some cases, lead to disastrous results. The bottom line is that if roles/groups can be implemented (and they can with Access, Oracle, and SQL Server), then it is not that much more work to create separate logins for each person.

The situation is a little different with database-driven web sites. On many web sites, users do not log in. The web pages simply access the database using a login that is the same for all users. There is nothing wrong with that. But the login used by the web pages should not be the master user for the database (admin in Access, root in MySQL, sa in SQL Server, system in Oracle). Yes, your web programming has security features built in. But how secure is it? If a hacker could find a way to access your source files on the web server, he or she would then have full access to your database. It is better to set up a separate login with only the rights a web user needs and expose that to the Internet. Keep your master user password a secret only to you.

Similarly for in-house databases, users should not be regularly logging in with the master user. Even if you have two people with database administrator rights, they should each have their own login rather than logging in with the master user. Again, this gives you the ability to audit the activity of each employee. But a better reason is that if people regularly use the master user, you will make the password for it something easy to type and remember and therefore easier to hack. Better practice is to use a very difficult password for the master user and set up other logins with similar rights for daily use.

Password Structure

Here are some rules of thumb for the makeup of the passwords:

- Passwords should not be English words. A standard hacker technique is to "throw a dictionary" at a login.
- Passwords should not be birthdays, social security numbers, names of spouses, children, pets, or other easily discoverable pieces of information. Remember this: No English word is a good password.
- Passwords can be unusual combinations of words (dog-chair).

- Passwords can be words and letters mixed with numbers and/or punctuation marks. This does not have to make them difficult to remember (33penguins, 123sesame, etc.).
- Passwords should be at least four characters in length. Again, the goal is to get a password that would be difficult for a hacker to decrypt. The more characters the better. But once passwords get beyond seven or eight characters, your users will complain. Worse, if you require passwords they cannot remember, they will respond by writing them down on notes near their computer. This makes them public knowledge for other employees, custodians, and visitors.

Password Expiration

Some database systems allow you to set an expiration period on passwords. In general, it is a very good idea to have passwords expire. Users will share their login information with other users. They may want to delegate a task to another person who doesn't have the privileges to do it. They may accidentally type their password in the user name text box where it will be displayed to a passerby. Periodically forcing a change in passwords clears these past sins from the table.

That being said, having passwords expire too often may actually cause a decrease in the quality of security. Users faced with coming up with a new password every 30 days may respond with passwords like March and April. They are also more likely to write down the password, making the password public. So set an expiration period short enough to deal with issues of shared or stolen passwords and long enough to avoid user issues. That is probably at least sixty days but no longer than one year.

Login Controls

What should you do if a user enters a bad user name and password combination? Obviously, you will tell them of the failure. Will you give them additional chances? How many? Some database systems allow you to set those parameters. Generally the number of attempts is set at from three to five. If the user fails that many times, the system can disable the account for a specified period of time. Another alternative is to simply close the application, allowing them to restart it and try again. This second option is much easier on hackers, but it is also much easier on users with faulty memories and poor typing skills. It depends on a corporate choice in favor of security versus ease of use.

Role Strategies

The degree to which using database roles (or Access groups) really facilitates your security and eases the task of setting up that security depends a lot upon the role scheme you develop. Here are some tips:

- **Have as few roles as possible.** Remember that the purpose of roles is to keep you from having to set up individual privileges for each of your users. So the fewer roles you have, the less work you have to do and the simpler will be management.
- **Pattern roles around job functions.** Generally, people who work in the same department will have the same access needs for the data. Accounting people need to enter deposits. Salespeople need to select prospects. In planning your roles begin with the various job functions. Then look for exceptions
- **Use multiple roles with incremental privileges for users with unique needs.** Suppose you have set up a salesperson role with full rights to prospects, but only reference rights to the salesperson table so they can select their own ID for the prospects. The supervisor of the salespeople is also a salesperson with essentially the same access needs. However, the supervisor also needs full access to the salesperson table for setting commissions. One way to handle that is to assign the supervisor to the salesperson role and also to a sales supervision role that has only the additional rights the supervisor needs beyond what he or she gets as a salesperson. This greatly simplifies the process of setting the rights for the sales supervision role because you only have to set up the incremental privileges. It also makes it easier to change salesperson privileges later because you only have to change privileges in that one role.

Chapter Summary

Security is an issue on any database that has more than one user. To protect the integrity and privacy of the data you must institute a security scheme that allows legitimate users to do everything they need to do while screening out everyone else. Each of our four database systems allows for security using some variation of the following concepts. Each person is a user or login to the database. To avoid having to set database privileges for each user individually, Oracle, SQL Server, and Access allow you to create roles or groups, assign users with similar access needs to a role or group, and then grant the necessary privileges to the role or group. The privileges that can be granted or revoked for users and roles vary somewhat among the various database systems, but generally they include SELECT, INSERT, DELETE, UPDATE, REFERENCES, and EXECUTE. The first four allow users to issue the SQL commands of the same name. REFERENCES allows users to make sure that the data being entered to a child table matches a value in the parent table, even if the user lacks SELECT rights to the parent table. EXECUTE allows a user to run a stored procedure. Each of these privileges can be assigned to each user or role for each database object (table, view, etc.). In addition to the task of setting up privileges, database administrators need to consider their password and role strategy. Requiring good passwords is a must, and they should expire from time to time. However, requiring long and frequently changing passwords can cause users to rebel, defeating your security scheme.

Key Terms

GRANT
group
login
password
personal identifier (PID)
privilege
REVOKE
role
(security identifier) SID
share-level security
synonym
user
user-level security
Windows NT Authentication

Review Questions

1. How does the use of roles or groups simplify the job of setting up security for a database?
2. What does the REFERENCES privilege do?
3. If using SQL Server, what are the advantages of using SQL Server authentication? What are the advantages of using Windows NT authentication?
4. What does the WITH GRANT OPTION do in the GRANT syntax? When might you want to use it?
5. What is an Oracle synonym and why is it helpful?
6. If a table called Employees was created by user Greg, how would other users on the same server refer to it in Oracle and SQL Server?
7. Why should the master login for a database (admin in Access, root in MySQL, sa in SQL Server, system in Oracle) not be used on a regular basis by anyone?
8. What is wrong with each of the following passwords: driveway, Jeremy, p@ssword?
9. What are the trade-offs to keep in mind when selecting a password expiration period?
10. Which of the four target databases allows privileges to be granted for individual columns of a table?

Exercises

1. Write and save a script that implements the following security scheme for the Lyric Music database:
   a. Create the following roles: Admin, Sales Production. If using MySQL, skip this step.
   b. Create the following users with good passwords and (unless using MySQL) assign them to roles as shown below:

User	Role
Bob	Sales
Lisa	Sales
Clint	Sales
Scott	Sales, Admin
Sayyid	Production
Abbey	Production
Ramy	Admin

   c. Grant the following privileges to the roles. If using MySQL, grant them to the appropriate users:

Table	Sales	Production	Admin
Artists	SIUD	SIUD	SIUD
Members	SIUD	SIUD	SIUD
XRefArtistsMembers	SIUD	SIUD	SIUD
Titles	S	SIUD	SIUD
Tracks	S	SIUD	SIUD
Genre	S	S	SIUD
Salespeople	NP	NP	SIUD
Studios S	SIU	SIUD	
S=Select, I=Insert, U=Update, D=Delete, NP=No privileges			

2. Given the above security scheme, Abbey has quit her job, and Nadine has been hired to take her place. Write a script that removes Abbey as a user and adds Nadine with the same rights that Abbey previously had.
3. Given the above security scheme, write a script to change each user's password to a new password. Make sure you use good passwords.

Additional References

Advanced Microsoft Jet SQL for Access 2000
: **http://msdn.microsoft.com/library/default.asp?url=/library/en-us/dnacc2k/html/acadvsql.asp**

Free MS Access Tutorial – Security
: **http://www.moretools.com/lessons/access_security.htm**

Administering SQL Server – Managing Security
: **http://msdn.microsoft.com/library/default.asp?url=/library/en-us/olapdmad/agsecurityroles_3n77.asp**

Oracle 9i Database Security Overview for Application Developers
: **http://rainbow.mimuw.edu.pl/oracle9i/appdev.901/a88876/adgsec01.htm#1005653**

MySQL User Account Management
: **http://www.mysql.com/doc/en/User_Account_Management.html**

MySQL – Using Secure Connections
: **http://www.mysql.com/doc/en/Secure_connections.html**

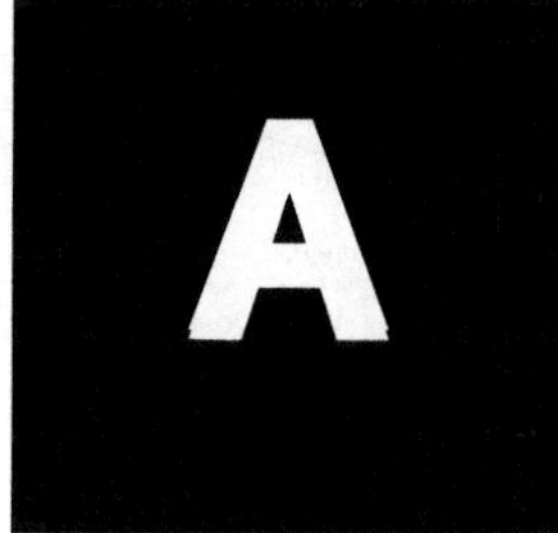

Appendix: The Lyric Music Database

Lyric Music

Lyric Music is an e-commerce company that provides web services to music artists. Among its services are offering mp3 and Real Audio files for download, selling CDs, and developing promotional materials for artists.

Lyric Music Data

A database can be described in more than one way. One technique is to simply list the rows and columns of each table. These are shown below.

Artists

The Artists table holds information about each artist. An artist could be a band or group. It could also be a solo artist.

ArtistID	ArtistName	City	Region	Country	WebAddress	EntryDate	LeadSource
1	The Neurotics	Peterson	NC	USA	www.theneurotics .com	5/14/2003	Directmail
2	Louis Holiday	Clinton	IL	USA		6/3/2003	Directmail
3	Word	Anderson	IN	USA		6/8/2003	Email
5	Sonata	Alexandria	VA	USA	www.classical.com /sonata	6/8/2003	Ad
10	The Bullets	Alverez	TX	USA		8/10/2003	Email
14	Jose MacArthur	Santa Rosa	CA	USA	www.josemacarthur .com	8/17/2003	Ad
15	Confused	Tybee Island	GA	USA		9/14/2003	Directmail
17	The Kicks	New Rochelle	NY	USA		12/3/2003	Ad
16	Today	London	ONT	Canada	www.today.com	10/7/2003	Email
18	21 West Elm	Alamaba	VT	USA	www.21westelm.com	2/5/2003	Ad
11	Highlander	Columbus	OH	USA		8/10/2002	Email

Members

The Members table holds information about the individuals who are members of each artist group. See the table on the facing page.

MemberID	First Name	LastName	Address	City	Region	PostalCode	Country	HomePhone	WorkPhone	EMail	Gender	Birthday	SalesID
10	Roberto	Alvarez	Rt 1	Anderson	IN	46019	USA	7651552983	7651628837	ral@mightyhostl.com	M	1/18/1968	2
31	Jose	MacArthur	51444 Vine	Santa Rosa	CA	99999	USA	6331289393		jmac@dowop.com	M	6/24/1978	1
13	Mary	Chrisman	1772 East 117th	Fishers	IN	46123	USA	3171820387		mjc17@daviscorp.com	F	3/1/1973	1
15	Warren	Boyer	167 Alamo Dr	Alverez	TX	75601	USA	8221722883		wbman@uptime.net	M	4/19/1969	2
32	Doug	Finney	2020 Dubois	Savannah	GA	30003	USA	9821222929		fennyd@bitspeed.com	M	8/4/1963	3
19	Terry	Irving	18a 7th St	Tybee Island	GA	30004	USA	5411252093			M	6/22/1959	3
21	Michelle	Henderson	201 Bonaventure	Savannah	GA	30005	USA	8221928273			F	3/15/1964	2
34	William	Morrow	PO Box 1882	New Rochelle	NY	10014	USA	9981722928		wmorrow@wmorrow.com	M	3/17/1965	2
29	Frank	Payne	5412 Clinton	New Rochelle	NY	10014	USA	9981737464			M	1/17/1960	1
35	Aiden	Franks	167 East 38th	Alverez	TX	75601	USA	8321729283	8321723833	kosmo@ispl.com	M	9/2/1983	2
3	Bryce	Sanders	PO Box 1292	Peterson	NC	27104	USA	6441824283		bs@cookery.com	M	6/11/1966	2
14	Carol	Wanner	787 Airport Rd	Alverez	TX	75601	USA	6831223544			F	11/8/1978	3
33	Brian	Ranier	23 Gregory Lane	London	ONT	M6Y 2Y7	Canada	6231842533			M	10/19/1957	3
7	Marcellin	Lambert	142 Sample Rd	Alexandria	VA	20102	USA	8331929302		mlambert@corkscrew.com	M	11/14/1959	3
8	Caroline	Kale	1515 Stone Church Rd	Allen	VA	20321	USA	7321223742			F	5/30/1956	3
9	Kerry	Fernandez	15 Midway	Lynchberg	VA	21223	USA	2211229384	2211223939		M	1/16/1962	1
26	Tony	Wong	115 Maple St	McKensie	ONT	M8H 3T1	Canada	3311692832	3311692822	twong@tamilla.org	M	11/1/1955	2
18	Bonnie	Taft	RR4	Alamaba	VT	05303	USA	3721223292		taffygirl@signon.com	F	9/21/1960	1
20	Louis	Holiday	15 Davis Ct	Clinton	IL	63882	USA	1451223838			M	7/27/1969	2
22	Bobby	Crum	RR2	Pine	VT	05412	USA	1831828211			M	6/10/1965	3
28	Vic	Cleaver	100 Maple	Reston	VT	05544	USA	8111839292			M	2/10/1957	2
30	Roberto	Goe	14 Gray Rd	Columbus	OH	48110	USA	2771123943			M	9/12/1967	1
36	Davis	Goodman	2020 Country Rd	Columbus	OH	48318	USA	2771152832	2771128833	goody@irvingnet.com	M	10/27/1980	2

XrefArtistsMembers

An artist (band) may have several members. But also a member may be part of more than one artist group. For instance Band X may have four members, one of whom also works as a solo artist. A cross-reference (xref) table is needed to maintain this complex relationship between artists and members. XrefArtistsMembers is that table. Its primary key is a combination of MemberID and ArtistID, so it can match any artist with any member and vice-versa. The RespParty is a Yes/No field that identifies which of each artist's members is the person responsible for paying bills and receiving official correspondence from Lyric Music.

MemberID	ArtistID	RespParty
20	2	1
31	14	1
3	1	1
10	3	1
13	3	0
7	5	1
8	5	0
9	5	0
32	15	0
19	15	1
21	15	0
34	17	1
29	17	0
15	10	1
35	10	0
14	10	0
33	16	1
26	16	0
18	18	1
28	18	0
22	18	0
30	11	1
36	11	0

Titles

The Titles table tracks information on each CD title produced by each artist. ArtistID is a foreign key that relates this table to Artists.

TitleID	ArtistID	Title	StudioID	UPC	Genre
1	1	Meet the Neurotics	1	2727366627	alternative
3	15	Smell the Glove	2	1283772282	metal
4	10	Time Flies	3	1882344222	alternative
5	1	Neurotic Sequel	1	2828830202	alternative
6	5	Sonatas	2	3999320021	classical
7	2	Louis at the Keys	3	3838227111	jazz

Tracks

Each CD title can have multiple tracks. The primary key of this table is the combination of TitleID and TrackNum. The mp3 and RealAud fields are Yes/No fields that indicate whether that track is available in mp3 or Real Audio formats.

TitleID	TrackNum	TrackTitle	LengthSeconds	MP3	RealAud
1	1	Hottie	233	1	1
1	2	Goodtime March	293	1	1
1	3	TV Day	305	1	1
1	4	Call Me an Idiot	315	1	1
1	5	25	402	1	1
1	6	Palm	322	1	1
1	7	Front Door	192	1	1
1	8	Where's the Rain	175	1	1
3	1	Fat Cheeks	352	1	1
3	2	Rocky and Natasha	283	1	1
3	3	Dweeb	273	1	1
3	4	Funky Town	252	1	1
3	5	Shoes	182	1	1
3	6	Time In - In Time	129	1	1
3	7	Wooden Man	314	0	0

TitleID	TrackNum	TrackTitle	LengthSeconds	MP3	RealAud
3	8	UPS	97	0	0
3	9	Empty	182	0	0
3	10	Burrito	65	0	0
4	1	Bob's Dream	185	1	1
4	2	My Wizard	233	1	1
4	3	Third's Folly	352	1	1
4	4	Leather	185	1	1
4	5	Hot Cars Cool Nights	192	1	1
4	6	Music in You	204	1	1
4	7	Don't Care About Time	221	1	1
4	8	Kiss	218	1	1
4	9	Pizza Box	183	1	1
4	10	Goodbye	240	1	1
5	1	Song 1	285	1	1
5	2	Song 2	272	1	1
5	3	Song 3	299	1	1
5	4	Song 4	201	1	1
5	5	Song 5	198	1	0
5	6	Song 6	254	1	0
5	7	Song 7	303	1	1
5	8	Song 8	230	1	0
5	9	Song 8 and 1/2	45	1	0
6	1	Violin Sonata No. 1 in D Major	511	1	1
6	2	Violin Sonata No. 2 in A Major	438	1	1
6	3	Violin Sonata No. 4 in E Minor	821	1	0
6	4	Piano Sonata No. 1	493	1	0
6	5	Clarinet Sonata in E Flat	399	1	0
7	1	I Don't Know	201	1	0
7	2	What's the Day	332	1	0
7	3	Sirius	287	1	0
7	4	Hamburger Blues	292	1	0
7	5	Road Trip	314	1	0
7	6	Meeting You	321	1	1
7	7	Improv 34	441	1	1
7	8	Hey	288	1	1

Genre

Each title is classified according to its genre. The Genre table is a simple look-up table that lists the valid genres.

Genre
alternative
rap
pop
R&B
jazz
classical
metal

Salespeople

The Salespeople table tracks information on the salespeople who work with each member and studio.

SalesID	FirstName	LastName	Initials	Base	Supervisor
1	Bob	Bentley	bbb	$100.00	4
2	Lisa	Williams	lmw	$300.00	4
3	Clint	Sanchez	cls	$100.00	1
4	Scott	Bull	sjb		

Studios

The Studios table holds information about the studios that produce each CD title.

StudioID	StudioName	Address	City	Region	PostalCode	Country
1	MakeTrax	3000 S St Rd 9	Anderson	IN	46012	USA
2	Lone Star Recording	PO Box 221	Davis	TX	76382	USA
3	Pacific Rim	681 PCH	Santa Theresa	CA	99320	USA

More columns

StudioID	WebAddress	Contact	EMail	Phone	SalesID
1	www.maketrax.com	Gardner Roberts	groberts@maketrax.com	7651223000	3
2	www.lsrecords.com	Manuel Austin	ma@lonestarrec.com	8821993748	2
3	www.pacrim.org	Harry Lee	harry@pcrim.org	3811110033	2

Lyric Music Database Design

Another way to describe a database is with its fields, datatypes, and relationships. The following diagram does that. Here are a few notes on the meaning of the various parts of the diagram:

- Each table is shown in a box.
- The field or fields that make up the primary key are shown at the top of each box between the table name and the rest of the fields and in bold.
- The datatypes are shown for each field using generic datatypes. Char indicates a text field with the maximum number of characters in parentheses. Intenter and Smallint are numeric datatypes. Currency holds money values. Datetime holds a date and/or a time value. Boolean is a Yes/No field.
- The foreign keys are marked with FK in the far left column and shown in bold.
- The relationships between the tables are marked with lines. The symbols on the end of each line indicate the nature of the relationship. Two slashes across the end of the line indicate the "one" or parent side of a one-to-many relationship. A circle and crow's foot at the end of the line indicates the "many" or child side of a one-to-many relationship. You might notice that some lines are solid and some are dashed. The solid line indicates that the primary key of the parent table is part of the primary key of the child table.

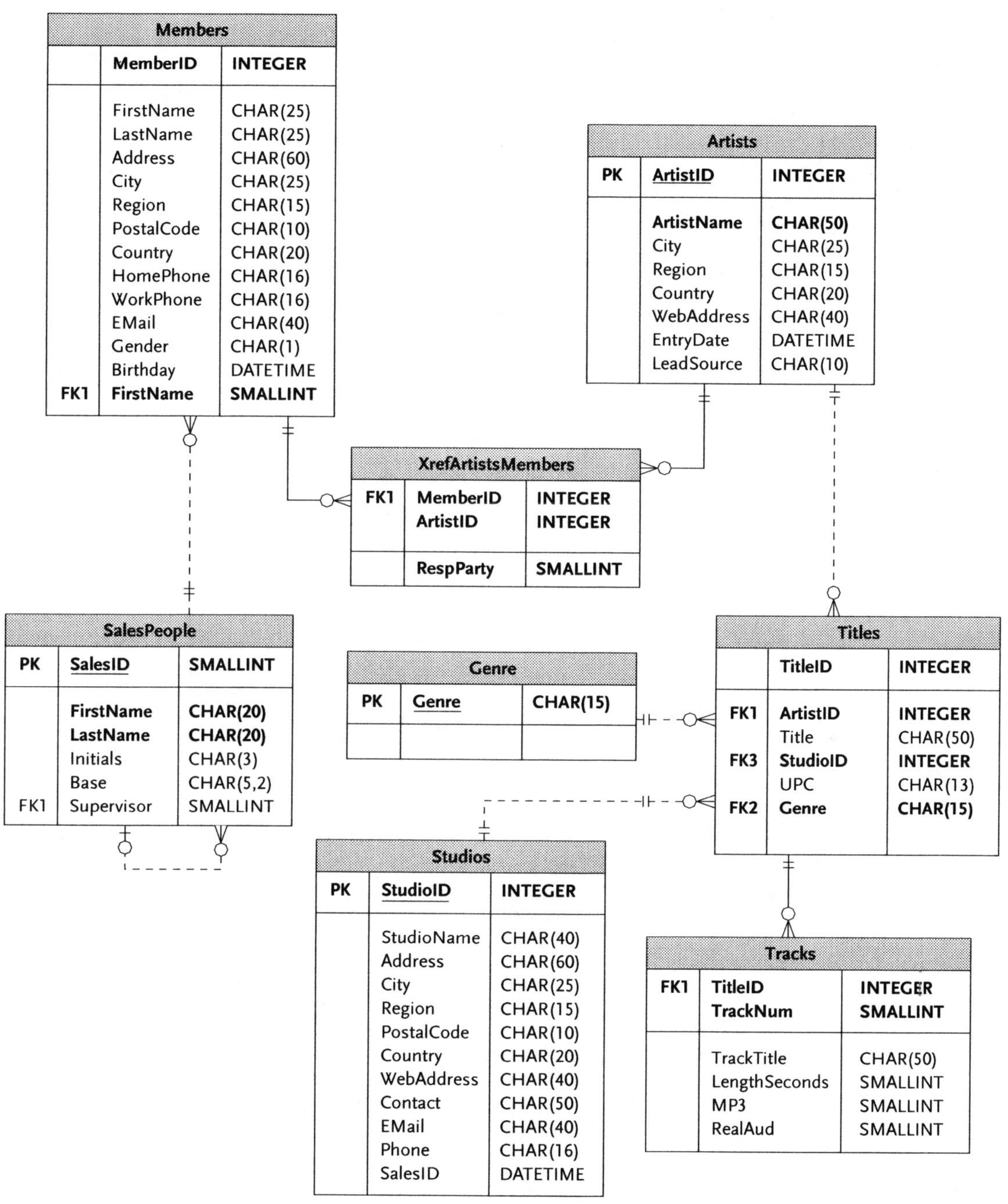
Members
MemberID INTEGER
FirstName CHAR(25)
LastName CHAR(25)
Address CHAR(60)
City CHAR(25)
Region CHAR(15)
PostalCode CHAR(10)
Country CHAR(20)
HomePhone CHAR(16)
WorkPhone CHAR(16)
EMail CHAR(40)
Gender CHAR(1)
Birthday DATETIME
FK1 FirstName SMALLINT
Artists
PK ArtistID INTEGER
ArtistName CHAR(50)
City CHAR(25)
Region CHAR(15)
Country CHAR(20)
WebAddress CHAR(40)
EntryDate DATETIME
LeadSource CHAR(10)
XrefArtistsMembers
FK1 MemberID INTEGER
ArtistID INTEGER
RespParty SMALLINT
SalesPeople
PK SalesID SMALLINT
FirstName CHAR(20)
LastName CHAR(20)
Initials CHAR(3)
Base CHAR(5,2)
FK1 Supervisor SMALLINT
Genre
PK Genre CHAR(15)
Titles
TitleID INTEGER
FK1 ArtistID INTEGER
Title CHAR(50)
FK3 StudioID INTEGER
UPC CHAR(13)
FK2 Genre CHAR(15)
Studios
PK StudioID INTEGER
StudioName CHAR(40)
Address CHAR(60)
City CHAR(25)
Region CHAR(15)
PostalCode CHAR(10)
Country CHAR(20)
WebAddress CHAR(40)
Contact CHAR(50)
EMail CHAR(40)
Phone CHAR(16)
SalesID DATETIME
Tracks
FK1 TitleID INTEGER
TrackNum SMALLINT
TrackTitle CHAR(50)
LengthSeconds SMALLINT
MP3 SMALLINT
RealAud SMALLINT

Appendix: Datatypes

Access Datatypes

Numeric

Three Access datatypes have different (and conflicting) names depending on whether you refer to them in SQL or in the Access graphical user interface. This can be confusing. For what it's worth, the SQL names are equivalent to the names used in SQL Server.

DataType	Nature of Data	Size
Byte	Whole numbers in the range of 0 - 255.	1 byte
Integer (SmallInt in SQL)	Whole numbers in the range of +/- 32767.	2 bytes
Long Integer (Int in SQL)	Whole numbers in the range of +/- 2,147,483,647.	4 bytes
Autonumber (Counter in SQL)	An auto-generating value equivalent to a long integer.	4 bytes
Single	Stores numbers with seven digits of precision ranging from-3.402823E38 to-1.401298E-45 for negative values and from1.401298E-45 to 3.402823E38 for positive values.	4 bytes
Double	Stores numbers with 15 digits of precision ranging from-1.79769313486231E308 to-4.94065645841247E-324 for negative values and from 1.79769313486231E308 to 4.94065645841247E-324 for positive values.	8 bytes
Decimal	Stores numbers with 28 digits of precision.	12 bytes
Currency	Currency values accurate to 15 digits on the left side of the decimal and to four digits on the right side.	8 bytes

Date/Time

DataType	Nature of Data	Size
DateTime	Date and time values for the years 100 through 9999.	8 bytes

Text

DataType	Nature of Data	Size
Text(x)	Alpha-numeric characters up to 255 characters in length. Specify number of characters as X.	1 byte per character
Memo	Alpha-numeric characters up to 65,535 characters in length.	Variable

Special

DataType	Nature of Data	Size
Yes/No	Yes/No, True/False values. True is coded as -1. False is coded as 0.	1 byte
OLE Object	A sound, graphic, or other binary object, including Microsoft Excel spreadsheets and Microsoft Word documents that are linked to or embedded in a Microsoft Access table.	Up to 1 gigabyte
Hyperlink	Alpha-numeric characters stored and used as a click-able hyperlink address. A hyperlink can include the text to display, the address and subaddress to link to, and a screen tip.	Variable

SQL Server DataTypes

Numeric

DataType	Nature of Data	Size
Bit	0 or 1 (Y/N).	1 byte
TinyInt	Whole numbers in the range of 0 - 255.	1 byte
SmallInt	Whole numbers in the range of -32768 to +32767.	2 bytes
Int	Whole numbers in the range of -2,147,483,648 to +2,147,483,647.	4 bytes
BigInt	Whole numbers in the range of -9223372036854775808 to +9223372036854775807.	8 bytes

Decimal (x,y)	Fixed precision xx.xxx
	Specify:
	x = total # digits
	y = # digits right of decimal point.
		Precision: Bytes
		1–9: 5
		10–19: 9
		20–28: 13
		29–38: 17

SmallMoney	Currency +/- 214,748.3647.	4 bytes
Money	Currency +/- 263 precision to four digits.	8 bytes
Float (or Real)	Approximate numerics Specify total number of digits in bits.	Varies

Date/Time

DataType	Nature of Data	Size
DateTime	Dates from 1/1/1753 through 12/31/ 9999 with accuracy to 1/100ths of a second.	8 bytes
SmallDateTime	Dates from 1/1/1900 through 6/6/2079 with accuracy to one minute.	4 bytes

Text

Unicode is a standard for representing characters as integers. Unlike ASCII, which uses eight bits for each character, Unicode uses 16 bits, which means that it can represent more than 65,000 unique characters. This is a bit of overkill for English and Western-European languages, but it is necessary for some other languages, such as Greek, Chinese, and Japanese. Many analysts believe that as the software industry becomes increasingly global, Unicode will eventually supplant ASCII as the standard character-coding format.

ASCII DataType	Unicode DataType	Nature of Data	Size
Char(X)	NChar(X)	Fixed-length. Values shorter than the set length are padded with spaces. Specify length up to 8000 for Char or up to 4000 for NChar as X.	Length
VarChar(X)	NvarChar(X)	Variable-length. No padding. Specify length up to 8000 for Char or up to 4000 for NvarChar as X.	Length
Text	NText	Variable-length up to 2,147,483,647 characters for Text or up to1,073,741,823 characters for Ntext. Allocated in 8K pages. Could store entire web pages.	Length

Special

DataType	Nature of Data	Size
Timestamp	Special value guaranteed unique within a given database. Value set by SQL Server each time a record is changed. Used to test for updates.	8 bytes
UniqueIdentifier	Special Globally Unique Identifier (GUID). Used as primary key in distributed or replicated databases.	16 bytes
Binary (X)	Fixed-length binary data, such as sound, picture, etc. up to 8,000 bytes. Specify number of bytes as X.	Varies
VarBinary (X)	Variable-length binary data. Specify number of bytes as X.	Varies
Image	Variable-length binary data up to 2,147,483,647 bytes.	Varies

MySQL DataTypes

Numeric

Some MySQL numeric datatypes can be either signed or unsigned. Signed means that they carry a positive or negative sign and so can include negative numbers. Unsigned means they can be only positive numbers. Signed is the default setting. You declare a field to be unsigned by declaring the datatype followed by the word "Unsigned."

MySQL integer (whole number) datatypes can optionally take a width specification shown as (w) below. The width specification is used to left-pad the display of values whose width is less than the width specified for the column. It does not constrain the range of values that can be stored in the column, nor the number of digits that will be displayed for values whose width exceeds the specification.

DataType	Nature of Data	Size
TinyInt(w)	Whole numbers in the range of +/- 127 if signed or 0-255 if unsigned.	1 btye
SmallInt(w)	Whole numbers in the range of +/- 32767 if signed or 0-65536 if unsigned.	2 btyes
MediumInt(w)	Whole numbers in the range of +/- 8,388,608 if signed or 0-16,777,216 if unsigned.	3 btyes
Int(w)	Whole numbers in the range of +/- 2,147,483,647. If unsigned, in the range of 0 to 4,294,967,295.	4 bytes
BigInt(w)	Whole numbers in the range of +/- 9,223,372,036,854,775,808. If unsigned, in the range of 0 to 18,446,744,073,709,551,616.	8 bytes

Float(x,y)	Floating point decimal number with a maximum of 24 digits of accuracy. Fixed precision xx.xxx. Specify:
	x = total # digits
	y = # digits right of decimal point
	Float cannot be unsigned. Float is rounded, so money values are better represented by the Decimal datatype.
		4 bytes

Real (or Double)	Double-precision floating point number, with a range of -1.7976931348623157E+308 to 1.7976931348623157E+308.	8 bytes

Decimal(x,y) or Numeric(x,y)	Numbers stored as strings to preserve the decimal point. Best for currency. Fixed precision xx.xxx. Specify:
	x = total # digits
	y = # digits right of decimal point.
		Varies

Date/Time

DataType	Nature of Data	Size
Date	Dates stored in the format: YYYY-MM-DD. Dates can range from 1000-01-01 to 9999-12-31.	3 bytes
Time	A time in HH:MM:SS format in the range of -838:59:59 to 838:59:59.	3 bytes
DateTime	This is a date and time combination, and it stores data in a yyyy-mm-dd-hh:mm:ss format. The allowed range is from 1000-01-01 00:00:00 to 9999-12-31 23:59:59.	8 bytes
Year	Stores a year value in either 'YYYY' or 'YY' format. Two-digit years are assumed to lie between 1970 and 2069, inclusive. Four-digit years can range from 1901 to 2155.	1 byte

Text

DataType	Nature of Data	Size
Char(x)	Fixed-length. Values shorter than the set length are padded with spaces. Specify length up to 255 as X.	length
VarChar(x)	Variable-length. No padding. Specify length up to 255 as X.	length
TinyBlob	A binary field (case-sensitive) with a maximum length of 255 characters.	length+1
TinyText	A text field (case-insensitive) with a maximum length of 255 characters.	length+1
Blob	A binary field (case-sensitive) with a maximum length of 65,535 characters.	length+2
Text	A text field (case-insensitive) with a maximum length of 65,535 characters.	length+2
MediumBlob	A binary field (case-sensitive) with a maximum length of 16 MB characters.	length+3
MediumText	A text field (case-insensitive) with a maximum length of 16 MB characters.	length+3
LongBlob	A binary field (case-sensitive) with a maximum length of 64 MB characters.	length+4
LongText	A text field (case-insensitive) with a maximum length of 64 MB characters.	length+4
Enum	A character string that can take only one of two values. Usually only takes up one byte of space.	1 byte
Set	A character string that can take one of up to 65 specified values.	1-8 bytes

Special

DataType	Nature of Data	Size
Timestamp	Automatically updates every time the row is modified, using the format: yyyymmddhhmmss.	4 bytes

Oracle DataTypes

Numeric

DataType	Nature of Data
Bit or YesNo	0 or 1 (Y/N).
Byte	Whole numbers in the range of 0 - 255.
SmallInt	Whole numbers in the range of +/- 32767.
Integer	Whole numbers in the range of +/- 2,147,483,647.

Number (x,y)	Specify:
	x = total # digits other than zeros (up to 38)
	y = # digits right of decimal point (up to 130).

Float	Floating point number.
Real	Floating point number.

Date/Time

DataType	Nature of Data
Date	Dates from 4712 BC to 9999 AC.
Timestamp(p)	

Text

Unicode is a standard for representing characters as integers. Unlike ASCII, which uses eight bits for each character, Unicode uses 16 bits, which means that it can represent more than 65,000 unique characters. This is a bit of overkill for English and Western-European languages, but it is necessary for some other languages, such as Greek, Chinese and Japanese. Many analysts believe that as the software industry becomes increasingly global, Unicode will eventually supplant ASCII as the standard character-coding format.

DataType	Nature of Data
Char(X)	Fixed-length. Stores ASCII characters. Values shorter than the set length are padded with spaces. Specify length up to 255 as X.
NChar(X)	Fixed-length. Stores Unicode characters. Specify length up to 255 as X.
VarChar2(X)	Variable-length. Stores ASCII characters. No padding. Specify length up to 255 for full access. Lengths from 256 to 4,000 are permissible but cannot be sorted, searched, or indexed.
NVarChar2(X)	Variable-length. Stores Unicode characters. No padding. Specify length up to 255 for full access. Lengths up to 4,000 depending on national character set.
Long	Variable-length up to two gigabtyes. Stores ASCII characters.
Clob	Variable-length up to four gigabtyes. Stores ASCII characters. Cannot be sorted, searched, or indexed.
Nclob	Same as Clob but for Unicode characters.

Special

DataType	Nature of Data
Timestamp(p)	Automatically fills in the current date and time. P is precision, the number of digits (0-9) in the fractional part of the second.
Blob	Binary data, such as images, video, or sound up to two gigabytes.
Raw(x)	Binary data, such as images, video, or sound up to 2000 bytes. Specify size as X.
LongRaw(x)	Binary data, such as images, video, or sound up to two gigabytes. Specify size as X.

Appendix: Principles of Database Design

Creating a database was once the domain of programmers and database administrators (DBA), but with modern database programs such as Access it is relatively easy for anyone to create one. However, creating a well designed database is another matter. With a well designed database it is easy to enter and update information and generally simple to create the queries needed to report the information. On the other hand, a poorly designed database is difficult to maintain, difficult to query, and difficult to modify.

The database design process is often accomplished using a technique called entity-relationship (ER) modeling. This technique uses entity-relationship diagrams (ERDs) to show the relationships among the various entities in a database. Entity-relationship modeling is a very complex topic that we won't be presenting in this book. Another complex topic in database design is the process of normalization. Normalization will be presented at a very high level later in this appendix.

Fortunately, good database design is not a mysterious science, but more of an art. In fact, it can be summarized in three basic steps:

1. Identify entities and attributes
2. Identify primary keys
3. Normalize the data structure

As with any art, becoming proficient at database design takes practice, so don't become discouraged by having to redesign your database multiple times. Let's get started by looking at each of the three basic steps in our design process.

Identifying Entities and Attributes

The database design process begins by identifying the things that we want to keep data about. Each individual thing is referred to as an entity, which is defined as a person, place, or thing for which a particular kind of data is kept. For instance, a student database might have an entity for student information, another entity for courses, and another entity for enrollment information. A general rule to help you get a handle on entities is that in a relational database there is generally one table for each entity.

Recognizing which entities you need in a database is a skill that develops with practice. Nevertheless, some tips can help get you started. In database design you have one entity for each data topic. In the example above, you can see that student information is different from course information, so there is one entity for student and one for course information. Often when you start detailing the specific pieces of information that need to be stored, those data "topics" naturally emerge. Another tip is to ask yourself what is the purpose of the database. The purpose generally points to one entity. For instance, a database designed to track employees will almost always have an employee entity. A parts inventory database will certainly have a parts entity.

Once you have determined the entities in a database, it's time to identify the data elements that are going to be kept about each entity. These data elements are called attributes. Each attribute corresponds to the fields or columns in a relational database table.

Attributes describe some characteristic of an entity. For instance, an Employee entity could have attributes of Name, Address, Wage, etc. All of the things that would describe a real employee also describe an employee entity, and so could be attributes. To determine the attributes of an entity you need to understand the data. One way to begin to understand the data is to obtain information from the current system, which could be a sample form that is used for data collection. Each blank on the form is likely to be an attribute. Go through each and ask yourself which entity it describes. If it doesn't describe any of the entities, then perhaps you need to add another entity.

In cases where you don't have forms to look at, you can ask the users of the system to just list on paper the things they want to track in the database. Then go through that list as if it were a form.

When you get stuck, ask the users. They probably won't speak in terms of attributes and entities, but they know the data and can explain it to you. For instance, suppose you are looking at a form with a phone number field on it. You can ask a user, "Whose phone number is that?" If they say it is the employee's phone number, then it is an attribute of the employee entity. If they say it is the department's phone number, then it is an attribute of the department entity.

This discussion makes the process sound easier than it actually is. Discovering the attributes for an entity is a trial-and-error process that takes practice. But with practice, it is a skill that can be mastered.

Identifying Primary Keys

If our database had an employee entity there would no doubt be many employees that would be recorded. Each employee would have his or her own information for Name, Address, Wage, Dept ID, Employee ID, and any other attribute that might describe this employee. Each collection of these attributes for an employee is called a record. In a relational database, each record appears as one row in the table. What happens when more than one person has the same name? There needs to be some way of uniquely identifying each row in the table. This is accomplished with a primary key.

A primary key is a group of one or more attributes that uniquely identifies each row from the others in the table. Suppose one employee is given a raise. It will be necessary to find the record for that employee and enter the new wage. To make sure that the raise is applied to the correct record, there needs to some way to distinguish that employee's record from the many other records. That is the job of the primary key.

Consider the list of attributes for the Employee entity (Name, Address, Wage, Dept ID, Employee ID). Would any of them be unique among all employees? "Name" might be a reasonable candidate. But you know it is fairly common for two people to have the same name, so name won't work as a primary key. Address would not work; two employees could share an apartment or house. There will probably be many employees in the same department or earning the same wage, so those attributes won't work either. But no two will have the same employee identification number. Many times an employee's Social Security number is used as an employee ID because no two citizens or legal aliens have the same number. Therefore it is unique and could serve as a primary key.

Sometimes it takes a combination of attributes to make a primary key. Consider the following:

ID	Project	Hours
12105	1893	40
12106	1893	20
12106	1921	20
12107	2072	15
12107	1893	25

Figure C.1. Employees Projects Table

This table tracks which projects are worked on by which employees. The Emp ID (Employee ID) can't serve as the primary key. There are multiple records for some employees due to the fact that they work on multiple projects. Similarly, the Project can't be a primary key, because some projects have more than one employee working on them. But the combination of Emp ID and

Project is unique. For instance, there is only one record for employee 12106's work on project 1893. Therefore, Emp ID and Project can serve together as the primary key.

Primary keys can also help you discover the entities you need and the attributes for those entities. For instance, if you were working from a sample sales order form and you saw a blank for Order ID, you could reasonably start with the assumption that Order ID would be a primary key. From that you could also assume that there should be an Order entity. Then you could look at each of the other blanks on the sample form and ask yourself if it describes something about the order. If so, it is probably an attribute of the Order entity. If it doesn't, you need other entities.

As you go through the process of identifying entities, attributes, and primary keys keep in mind that you can discover attributes from entities, and you can discover entities from attributes. The most important thing is to keep asking questions of the users until you understand the data.

Normalizing the Data Structure

Now that you know what tables are needed and the required attributes for each, the next step is normalization. Normalization is a process used to organize data, thereby eliminating data redundancy and inconsistency. Databases that are not normalized can be difficult to maintain, difficult to query, difficult to modify, and produce inaccurate results.

Normalization is based on the concept of normal forms defined by Dr. E.F. Codd. Normal form is a set of constraints applied to relational database tables and are referred to as first normal form (1NF) through fifth normal form (5NF). In most applications it is only necessary to normalize the database to 3NF, and it is rare to go beyond that level. Let's explore the definition and application of the normal forms.

First Normal Form (1NF)

First normal form (1NF) is the most basic and requires that there be no repeating groups. A repeating group is defined as a column that has multiple occurrences of data. This means that an attribute can have only one value for a particular instance of an entity. To bring a table into 1NF compliance, it is necessary to eliminate repeating groups. Consider the table shown in Figure C.2. This table tracks the various projects that each employee works on along with the number of hours each employee is assigned to that project.

ID	Project 1	Hours 1	Project 2	Hours 2
12105	1893	40		
12106	1893	20	2072	20
12107	2072	15	1893	25

Figure C.2. Employees Project Table

Notice that Project and Hours repeat (Project 1 & Hours 1, Project 2 & Hours 2). This can cause problems. Suppose you wanted to create a query to calculate the number of hours being worked on project 1893. The query would have to test for 1893 in both the Project 1 field and the Project 2 field. And it would have to add up the hours in Hours 1 and Hours 2. It would be quite a task to design that query correctly.

Another problem with this design is that it is not very flexible. What if an employee was assigned to a third project? The table would have to be redesigned before that information could be entered.

For these reasons, you should eliminate repeating fields and repeating groups of fields. How do you do that? There are two ways. Sometimes you can just restructure the table. Figure C.3 shows the Employees Project table restructured to eliminate the repeating fields. In this design, each employee can have multiple rows and can be assigned to any number of projects. Of course, this means that ID cannot be the primary key of the revised table. The primary key would have to be ID and Project used together.

ID	Project	Hours
12105	1893	40
12106	1893	20
12106	1921	20
12107	2072	15
12107	1893	25

Figure C.3. Employees Project Table

In this new design it would be quite easy to create a query to calculate the number of hours being worked on project 1893. You would test for 1893 in the Project field and add up the Hours field.

For other tables, the best way to eliminate repeating groups of fields is to split the table into two or more tables. An example of this is shown in Figures C.4, C.5, and C.6. Figure C.4 shows the original table with the repeating group of Item, Qty, and Price. Those repeating fields are eliminated in Figures C.5 and C.6 by splitting the table into two separate tables. The reason these tables are split is to establish primary keys that work. We'll talk more about that in the sections that follow.

PO#	Date	Supplier	Item 1	Qty 1	Price 1	Item 2	Qty 2	Price 2
1101	2/1/04	Acme	Widgets	5	$1	Things	10	$5
1102	2/2/04	Ace	Things	5	$5			
1103	2/3/04	Acme	Widgets	20	$1	Things	5	$5

Figure C.4. Purchase Order Table

PO#	Date	Supplier
1101	2/1/04	Acme
1102	2/2/04	Ace
1103	2/3/04	Acme

Figure C.5. Revised Purchase Order Table

PO#	Item	Qty	Price
1101	Widgets	5	$1
1101	Things	10	$5
1102	Things	5	$5
1103	Widgets	20	$1
1103	Things	5	$5

Figure C.6. Purchase Order Details Table

Second Normal Form (2NF)

Second normal form (2NF) requires that a relational table be in 1NF and every non-primary key attribute be fully dependent on the entire primary key, not just part of the composite key. This dependency is referred to as a functional dependency. The 2NF only applies to tables that have a composite primary key. To bring a table into 2NF compliance, it is necessary to remove the partial dependencies.

Earlier we said that attributes describe some characteristic of an entity. Since the primary key, in effect, represents the entity as its unique identifier, we can also say that each non-key attribute should describe or depend on or be related to the primary key.

Consider the table shown in Figure C.7. It is an expanded version of the Employees Projects table shown earlier. The primary key is a combination of the employee's ID and Project. Each non-key field must relate to all parts of the primary key. So every other field in the table should be describable in terms of both of these key fields.

ID	Project	Hours	Project Start	Project End
12105	1893	40	4/1/2004	10/15/2004
12106	1893	20	4/1/2004	10/15/2004
12106	1921	20	5/1/2004	11/01/2004
12107	2072	15	5/1/2004	11/01/2004
12107	1893	25	4/1/2004	10/15/2004

Figure C.7. Employees Projects Table

In examining the non-key fields we see that the Hours field checks out. The Hours field holds the number of hours Employee 12105 worked on Project 1893. The Hours data can only be described in terms of both fields of the primary key. But in the Project Start field we see that 4/1/2004 is the starting date of project 1893. Since the data in Project Start can be described using only one part of the primary key, that indicates a problem. The same problem applies to Project End.

What do you do to correct the problem? You take the fields that are not related to both parts of the primary key and move them off into a separate table. Also, copy to that table (but don't remove from the original table) the part of the primary key that those fields do relate to. Figure C.8 shows the revised Employees Projects table. Figure C.9 shows the new table consisting of Project Start, Project End, and Project (the part of the primary key that the other two fields did relate to). Now if a Project End date changes, we only need to edit it in one place.

ID	Project	Hours
12105	1893	40
12106	1893	20
12106	1921	20
12107	2072	15
12107	1893	25

Figure C.8. Employees Projects Table

Project	Project Start	Project End
1893	4/1/2004	10/15/2004
1921	5/1/2004	11/01/2004

Figure C.9. Projects Table

The Project field is now present in both tables. It is the primary key of the Projects table, because it is the field that Project Start and Project End related to. It is part of the primary key in the Employees Projects table. In the Employee Projects table, it also serves as a foreign key to the Project Table. Foreign keys are attributes or groups of attributes in one entity that relate to the primary key of another entity.

Third Normal Form (3NF)

In order for tables to comply with third normal form it is necessary that they be in second normal form and eliminate transitive dependencies. A transitive dependency occurs when an attribute depends on another non-key attribute.

Every table should have a primary key. That primary key can be a single field, as in the Purchase Order Details table shown in Figure C.6, or a combination of fields, as in the revised Employees Projects table shown in Figure C.8. Every non-key field (a field that is not part of the primary key) must describe or be related to the primary key and all parts of the primary key.

The table in Figure C.10 has Project as the primary key.

Project	Project Name	Manager	Phone
1893	Install wireless network	Fernandez	895
2072	Install Oracle server	Owen	726
3810	Lyric Music Systems data design	Fernandez	895
3825	Lyric Music System stored procedures	Hawes	154
3855	Lyric Music System user interface design	Fernandez	895
3920	Lyric Music System prototype	Owen	726
4055	Lyric Music System documentation	Weinstein	763
4239	Lyric Music System construction	Benson	638

Figure C.10. Projects Table

As with 2NF, you can determine whether each of the non-key fields describe or are related to the primary key by simply explaining to yourself what the data in each field is. For instance, you might explain the data in the Name field by saying, "'Install wireless network' is the name of project 1893." Notice that we had to use the primary key field to describe the Name field. That means that Name is related to the primary key. Let's do the same thing for the Manager field. Fernandez is the manager of project 1893. Manager also must be related to the primary key. For Phone we would say that 895 is the phone number for Fernandez. Notice that this explanation of Phone said nothing about project 1893. Therefore, Phone does not describe or relate to the primary key. Therefore, the "Projects" table contains a transitive dependency relationship because the attribute "Phone" depends on the non-key attribute "Manager."

This problem can lead to all kinds of headaches in working with this table. What if Fernandez changes her phone number? Since Fernandez manages multiple projects, that change has to be made multiple times. What if you wanted a simple list of all managers and their phone numbers? Fernandez and Owen would be listed more than once.

How do you solve that problem? The transitive dependency is eliminated by removing the attributes that are dependent on the non-key attribute to a separate table. This is accomplished by creating a "Project Managers Table" table as shown below in Figure C.12.

You start the process by taking the field that is not related to the primary key (Phone in this case) and moving it off into a separate table. Generally that field will describe or relate to some other field (in this case, Manager). If it does, you also copy that field to the new table (but don't remove from the original table) and make it the primary key. The reason you copy instead of move it is so that it can serve as a foreign key in the original table. This has been done in this example in Figures C.11 and C.12.

Project	Project Name	Manager
1893	Install wireless network	Fernandez
2072	Install Oracle server	Owen
3810	Lyric Music Systems data design	Fernandez
3825	Lyric Music System stored procedures	Hawes
3855	Lyric Music System user interface design	Fernandez
3920	Lyric Music System prototype	Owen
4055	Lyric Music System documentation	Weinstein
4239	Lyric Music System construction	Benson

Figure C.11. Projects Table

Manager	Phone
Fernandez	895
Owen	726
Hawes	154
Weinstein	763
Benson	638

Figure C.12. Project Managers Table

Figure C.11 shows Phone removed from the Projects Table. Figure C.12 shows Phone moved to a new table along with Manager. Manager is the primary key of the new Project Managers table. Manager in the Projects table becomes a foreign key, a field in one table that relates to the primary key in another table.

Now each field in each table is related to its primary key. In addition, if Fernandez's phone number changes, only one record needs to be updated. To run a list of all project managers, you only need to list the records in the Project Managers table.

As you can see from Figures C.11 and C.12, two tables that are related always share a field in common.

Specifically the primary key of one table becomes a foreign key in the other table. A common mistake of beginning data designers when relating two tables is to copy the primary key from the wrong table. For instance, one could arrange the fields as shown below with the primary key of Projects as a foreign key in Managers.

Projects Table

Project	Name

Managers Table

Manager	Phone	Project

How do you know which way to orient the primary key-foreign key relationship? The answer is in the nature of the relationship. Most relationships are one-to-many, meaning that one record in one of the tables can relate to many records in the other table. In Figures C.11 and C.12, you can see from the data that one manager can manage many projects. The table on the "one side" of the relationship is called the Parent while the table on the "many side" of the relationship is called the Child (because one parent can have many children). Now here is the rule of thumb for setting up your foreign key relationships between tables: The primary key of the parent becomes a foreign key in the child. You see that in practice in Figures C.11 and C.12. The primary key of the Managers parent table, Manager, becomes a foreign key in the Projects child table. Follow that rule, and it will guide you through setting up most table relationships.

Appendix: SQL Reserved Words

The first SQL standard (called SQL89) was released in 1989. The SQL specification has since been twice revised with SQL92 (in 1992) and SQL99 (in 1999). Most DBMSs meet SQL89 standards, and many meet SQL92 standards. So to a large extent, SQL written for one DBMS will work in another DBMS with few or no changes. However, every DBMS vendor wants to differentiate its product on the market with more powerful features. This also includes the use of reserved words. In addition, the SQL standard does not define some things that programmers often want to do with data, thus leaving a gap in functionality that each vendor must fill. Finally, for whatever reason, DBMS vendors often digress from the SQL standard in both minor and major ways.

Reserved words have a specific meaning in the SQL language and cannot be changed or altered. This means that these words are restricted in how the can be used and must only appear in certain contexts.

Problems using SQL are usually encountered by developers trying to create tables with columns named using SQL reserved words. Debugging these types of problems can be very challenging because there are so many reserved words in the SQL standard. To make matters worse each database—Access, SQL Server, Oracle, and MySQL—has its own reserved words to meet their particular implementation needs.

So every implementation of SQL is at least a little different. Throughout this book, we have stayed as close to ANSI-SQL as possible and note differences among the various DBMS products. The reserved words listed below are the reserved words for SQL92 and SQL99 standards, and each database implementation presented in this book.

SQL92 Standard Reserved Words

ABSOLUTE	ACTION	ADD	ALL
ALLOCATE	ALTER	AND	ANY
ARE	AS	ASC	ASSERTION
AT	AUTHORIZATION	AVG	BEGIN
BETWEEN	BIT	BIT_LENGTH	BOTH
BY	CALL	CASCADED	CASE
CAST	CATOLOG	CHAR	CHAR_LENGTH
CHECK	CLOSE	COALESCE	COLLATION
COLUMN	COMMIT	CONDITION	CONNECT
CONNECTION	CONSTRAINT	CONSTRAINTS	CONTAINS
CONTINUE	CONVERT	CORRESPONDING	COUNT
CREATE	CROSS	CURRENT	CURRENT_DATE
CURRENT_TIME	CURRENT_TIMESTAMP	CURRENT_USER	CURSOR
DATE	DAY DEALLOCATE	DEC	DECIMAL
DECLARE	DEFAULT	DEFERABLE	DEFERED
DELETE	DESC	DESCRIBE	DESCRIPTOR
DETERMINISTIC	DIAGNOSTICS	DISCONNECT	DISTINCT
DO	DOMAIN	DOUBLE	DROP
ELSE	ELSEIF	END	ESCAPE
EXCEPT	EXCEPTION	EXEC	EXECUTE
EXISTS	EXIT	EXTERNAL	EXTRACT
FALSE	FETCH	FIRST	FLOAT
FOR	FOREIGN	FOUND	FROM
FULL	FUNCTION	GET	GLOBAL
GO	GOTO	GRANT	GROUP
HANDLER	HAVING	HOUR	IDENTITY
IF	IMMEDIATE	IN	INDICATOR
INITIALLY	INNER	INOUT	INPUT
INSENSITIVE	INSERT	INT	INTEGER
INTERSECT	INTERVAL	INTO	IS
ISOLATION	JOIN	KEY	LANGUAGE
LAST	LEADING	LEAVE	LEFT
LEVEL	LIKE	LOCAL	LOOP
LOWER	MATCH	MAX	MIN
MINUTE	MODULE	MONTH	NAMES
NATIONAL	NATURAL	NCHAR	NEXT
NO	NOT	NULL	NULLIF
NUMERIC	OCTET_LENGTH	OF	ON
ONLY	OPEN	OPTION	OR
ORDER	OUT	OUTER	OUTPUT
OVERLAPS	PAD	PARAMETER	PARTIAL
PATH	POSITION	PRECISION	PREPARE
PRESERVE	PRIMARY	PRIOR	PRIVILEGES
PROCEDURE	PUBLIC	READ	REAL
REFERENCES	RELATIVE	REPEAT	RESIGNAL
RESTRICT	RETURN	RETURNS	REVOKE

RIGHT
ROLLBACK
ROUTINE
ROWS
SCHEMA
SCROLL
SECOND
SECTION
SELECT
SESSION
SESSION_USER
SET
SIGNAL
SIZE
SMALLINT
SOME
SPACE
SPECIFIC
SQL
SQLCODE
SQLERROR
SQLEXCEPTION
SQLSTATE
SQLWARNING
SUBSTRING
SUM
SYSTEM_USER
TABLE
TEMPORARY
THEN
TIME
TIMESTAMP
TIMEZONE_HOUR
TIMEZONE_MINUTE
TO
TRAILING
TRANSACTION
TRANSLATE
TRANSLATION
TRIM
TRUE
UNDO
UNION
UNIQUE
UNKNOWN
UNTIL
UPDATE
UPPER
USAGE
USER
USING
VALUE
VALUES
VARCHAR
VARYING
VIEW
WHEN
WHENEVER
WHERE
WHILE
WITH
WORK
WRITE
YEAR
ZONE

SQL99 Standard Reserved Words

ABSOLUTE
ACTION
ADD
ADMIN
AFTER
AGGREGATE
ALIAS
ALL
ALLOCATE
ALTER
AND
ANY
ARE
ARRAY
AS
ASC
ASSERTION
AT
AUTHORIZATION
BEFORE
BEGIN
BINARY
BIT
BLOB
BOOLEAN
BOTH
BREADTH
BY
CALL
CASCADE
CASCADED
CASE
CAST
CATALOG
CHAR
CHARACTER
CHECK
CLASS
CLOB
CLOSE
COLLATE
COLLATION
COLUMN
COMMIT
COMPLETION
CONNECT
CONNECTION
CONSTRAINT
CONSTRAINTS
CONSTRUCTOR
CONTAINS
CONTINUE
CORRESPONDING
CREATE
CROSS
CUBE
CURRENT
CURRENT_DATE
CURRENT_PATH
CURRENT_ROLE
CURRENT_TIME
CURRENT_TIMESTAMP
CURRENT_USER
CURSOR
CYCLE
DATA
DATALINK
DATE
DAY
DEALLOCATE
DEC
DECIMAL
DECLARE
DEFAULT
DEFERRABLE
DELETE
DEPTH
DEREF
DESC
DESCRIPTION
DIAGNOSTICS
DICTIONARY
DISCONNECT
DO
DOMAIN
DOUBLE
DROP
END-EXEC
EQUALS
ESCAPE
EXCEPT
EXCEPTION
EXECUTE
EXIT
EXPAND
EXPANDING
FALSE
FIRST
FLOAT
FOR
FOREIGN
FREE
FROM
FUNCTION
GENERAL
GET
GLOBAL
GOTO

GROUP GROUPING HANDLER HASH
HOUR IDENTITY IF IGNORE
IMMEDIATE IN INDICATOR INITIALIZE
INITIALLY INNER INOUT INPUT
INSERT INT INTEGER INTERSECT
INTERVAL INTO IS ISOLATION
ITERATE JOIN KEY LANGUAGE
LARGE LAST LATERAL LEADING
LEAVE LEFT LESS LEVEL
LIKE LIMIT LOCAL LOCALTIME
LOCALTIME-STAMP LOCATOR LOOP MATCH
MEETS MINUTE MODIFIES MODIFY
MODULE MONTH NAMES NATIONAL
NATURAL NCHAR NCLOB NEW
NEXT NO NONE NORMALIZE
NOT NULL NUMERIC OBJECT
OF OFF OLD ON
ONLY OPEN OPERATION OPTION
OR ORDER ORDINALITY OUT
OUTER OUTPUT PAD PARAMETER
PARAMETERS PARTIAL PATH PERIOD
POSTFIX PRECEDES PRECISION PREFIX
PREORDER PREPARE PRESERVE PRIMARY
PRIOR PRIVILEGES PROCEDURE PUBLIC
READ READS REAL RECURSIVE
REDO REF REFERENCES REFERENCING
RELATIVE REPEAT RESIGNAL RESTRICT
RESULT RETURN RETURNS REVOKE
RIGHT ROLE ROLLBACK ROLLUP
ROUTINE ROW ROWS SAVEPOINT
SCHEMA SCROLL SEARCH SECOND
SELECTION SELECT SEQUENCE SESSION
SESSION_USER SET SETS SIGNAL
SIZE SMALLINT SPECIFIC SPECIFICTYPE
SQL SQLEXCEPTION SQLSTATE SQLWARNING
START STATE STATIC STRUCTURE
SUCCEEDS SUM SYSTEM_USER TABLE
TEMPORARY TERMINATE THAN THEN
TIME TIMESTAMP TIMEZONE_HOUR TIMEZONE_MINUTE
TO TRAILING TRANSACTION TRANSLATION
TREAT TRIGGER TRUE UNDER
UNDO UNION UNIQUE UNKNOWN
UNTIL UPDATE USAGE USER
USING VALUE VALUES VARIABLE

Microsoft SQL Server 2000 Reserved Words

ADD	ALL	ALTER	AND
ANY	AS	ASC	AUTHORIZATION
BACKUP	BEGIN	BETWEEN	BREAK
BROWSE	BULK	BY	CASCADE
CASE	CHECK	CHECKPOINT	CLOSE
CLUSTERED	COALESCE	COLLATE	COLUMN
COMMIT	COMPUTE	CONSTRAINT	CONTAINS
CONTAINSTABLE	CONTINUE	CONVERT	CREATE
CROSS	CURRENT	CURRENT_DATE	CURRENT_TIME
CURRENT_TIMESTAMP	CURRENT_USER	CURSOR	DATABASE
DBCC	DEALLOCATE	DECLARE	DEFAULT
DELETE	DENY	DESC	DISK
DISTINCT	DISTRIBUTED	DOUBLE	DROP
DUMMY	DUMP	ELSE	END
ERRLVL	ESCAPE	EXCEPT	EXEC
EXECUTE	EXISTS	EXIT	FETCH
FILE	FILLFACTOR	FOR	FOREIGN
FREETEXT	FREETEXTTABLE	FROM	FULL
FUNCTION	GOTO	GRANT	GROUP
HAVING	HOLDBACK	IDENTITY	IDENTITY_INSERT
IDENTITYCOL	IF	IN	INDEX
INNER	INSERT	INTERSECT	INTO
IS JOIN	KEY	KILL	LEFT
LIKE	LINENO	LOAD	NATIONAL
NOCHECK	NONCLUSTERED	NOT	NULL
NULLIF	OF	OFF	OFFSETS
ON	OPEN	OPENDATASOURCE	OPENQUERY
OPENROWSET	OPENXML	OPTION	OR
ORDER	OUTER	OVER	PERCENT
PLAN	PRECISION	PRIMARY	PRINT
PROC	PROCEDURE	PUBLIC	RAISERROR
READ	READTEXT	RECONFIGURE	REFERENCES
REPLICATION	RESTORE	RESTRICT	RETURN
REVOKE	RIGHT	ROLLBACK	ROWCOUNT
ROWGUIDCOL	RULE	SAVE	SCHEMA
SELECT	SESSION_USER	SET	SETUSER
SHUTDOWN	SOME	STATISTICS	SYSTEM_USER
TABLE	TEXTSIZE	THEN	TO
TOP	TRAN	TRANSACTION	TRIGGER
TRUNCATE	TSEQUAL	UNION	UNIQUE
UPDATE	UPDATETEXT	USE	USER
VALUES	VARYING	VIEW	WAITFOR
WHEN	WHERE	WHILE	WITH
WRITETEXT			

Oracle Reserved Words

ACCESS
ADD
ALL
ALTER
AND
ANY
AS
ASC
AUDIT
BETWEEN
BY
CHAR
CHECK
CLUSTER
COLUMN
COMMIT
COMPRESS
CONNECT
CREATE
CURRENT
DATE
DECIMAL
DEFAULT
DELETE
DESC
DISTINCT
DROP
ELSE
EXCLUSIVE
EXISTS
FILE
FLOAT
FOR
FROM
GRANT
GROUP
HAVING
IDENTIFIED
IMMEDIATE
IN
INCREMENT
INDEX
INITIAL
INSERT
INTEGER
INTERSECT
INTO
IS
LEVEL
LIKE
LOCK
LONG
MAXEXTENTS
MINUS
MLSLABEL
MODE
MODIFY
NOAUDIT
NOCOMPESS
NOT
NOWAIT
NULL
NUMBER
OF
OFFLINE
ON
ONLINE
OPTION
OR
ORDER
PCTFREE
PRIOR
PRIVILEGES
PUBLIC
RAW
RENAME
RESOURCE
REVOKE
ROW
ROWID
ROWNUM
ROWS
SELECT
SESSION
SET
SHARE
SIZE
SMALLINT
START
SUCCESSFUL
SYNONYM
SYSDATE
TABLE
THEN
TO
TRIGGER
UID
UNION
UNIQUE
UPDATE
USER
VALIDATE
VALUES
VARCHAR
VARCHAR2
VIEW
WHENEVER
WHERE
WITH

Microsoft Access 2002/2003 Reserved Words

ADD
ALL
ALPHANUMERIC
ALTER
AND
ANY
APPLICATION
AS
ASC
ASSISTANT
AUTOINCREMENT
AVG
BETWEEN
BINARY
BIT
BOOLEAN
BY
CHAR
CHARACTER
COLUMN
COMPATDATABASE
CONSTRAINT
CONTAINER
COUNT
COUNTER
CREATE
CREATEDATABASE
CREATEFIELD
CREATEGROUP
CREATEINDEX
CREATEOBJECT
CREATEPROPERTY
CREATERELATION
CREATETABLEDEF
CREATEUSER
CREATEWORKSPACE
CURRENCY
CURRENTUSER
DATABASE
DATE
DATETIME
DELETE
DESC
DESCRIPTION
DISALLOW
DISTINCT
DISTINCTROW
DOCUMENT
DOUBLE
DROP
ECHO
ELSE
END
EQV
ERROR
EXISTS
EXIT
FALSE
FIELD
FIELDS
FILLCACHE
FLOAT
FLOAT4

FLOAT8
FOREIGN
FORM
FORMS
FROM
FULL
FUNCTION
GENERAL
GETOBJECT
GETOPTION
GOTOPAGE
GROUP
GROUP BY
GUID
HAVING
IDLE
IEEEDOUBLE
IEEESINGLE
IF
IGNORE
IMP
INDEX
INDEXES
INNER
INSERT
INSERTTEXT
INT
INTEGER
INTEGER1
INTEGER2
INTEGER4
INTO
IS
JOIN
KEY
LASTMODIFIED
LEFT
LEVEL
LIKE
LOGICAL
LOGICAL1
LONG
LONGBINARY
LONGTEXT
MACRO
MATCH
MAX
MIN
MOD
MEMO
MODULE
MONEY
MOVE
NAME
NEWPASSWORD
NO
NOT
NULL
NUMBER
NUMERIC
OBJECT
OLEOBJECT
OFF
ON
OPENRECORDSET
OPTION
OR
ORDER
OUTER
OWNERACCESS
PARAMETER
PARAMETERS
PARTIAL
PERCENT
PIVOT
PRIMARY
PROCEDURE
PROPERTY
QUERIES
QUERY
QUIT
REAL
RECALC
RECORDSET
REFERENCES
REFRESH
REFRESHLINK
REGISTERDATABASE
RELATION
REPAINT
REPAIRDATABASE
REPORT
REPORTS
REQUERY
RIGHT
SCREEN
SECTION
SELECT
SET
SETFOCUS
SETOPTION
SHORT
SINGLE
SMALLINT
SOME
SQL
STDEV
STDEVP
STRING
SUM
TABLE
TABLEDEF
TABLEDEFS
TABLEID
TEXT
TIME
TIMESTAMP
TOP
TRANSFORM
TRUE
TYPE
UNION
UNIQUE
UPDATE
VALUE
VALUES
VAR
VARP
VARBINARY
VARCHAR
WHERE
WITH
WORKSPACE
XOR
YEAR
YES
YESNO

MySQL Reserved Words

ACTION
ADD
AGGREGATE
ALL
ALTER
AFTER
AND
AS
ASC
AVG
AVG_ROW_LENGTH
AUTO_INCREMENT
BETWEEN
BIGINT
BIT
BINARY
BLOB
BOOL
BOTH
BY
CASCADE
CASE
CHAR
CHARACTER
CHANGE
CHECK
CHECKSUM
COLUMN
COLUMNS
COMMENT
CONSTRAINT
CREATE
CROSS
CURRENT_DATE
CURRENT_TIME
CURRENT_TIMESTAMP
DATA
DATABASE
DATABASES
DATE

DATETIME
DAY
DAY_HOUR
DAY_MINUTE
DAY_SECOND
DAYOFMONTH
DAYOFWEEK
DAYOF YEAR
DEC
DECIMAL
DEFAULT
DELAYED
DELAY_KEY_WRITE
DELETE
DESC
DESCRIBE
DISTINCT
DISTINCTROW
DOUBLE
DROP
END
ELSE
ESCAPE
ESCAPED
ENCLOSED
ENUM
EXPLAIN
EXISTS
FIELDS
FILE
FIRST
FLOAT
FLOAT4
FLOAT8
FLUSH
FOREIGN
FROM
FOR
FULL
FUNCTION
GLOBAL
GRANT
GRANTS
GROUP
HAVING
HEAP
HIGH_PRIORITY
HOUR
HOUR_MINUTE
HOUR_SECOND
HOSTS
IDENTIFIED
IGNORE
IN
INDEX
INFILE
INNER
INSERT
INSERT_ID
INT
INTEGER
INTERVAL
INT1
INT2
INT3
INT4
INT8
INTO
IF
IS
ISAM
JOIN
KEY
KEYS
KILL
LAST_INSERT_ID
LEADING
LEFT
LENGTH
LIKE
LINES
LIMIT
LOAD
LOCAL
LOCK
LOGS
LONG
LONGBLOB
LONGTEXT
LOW_PRIORITY
MAX
MAX_ROWS
MATCH
MEDIUMBLOB
MEDIUMTEXT
MEDIUMINT
MIDDLEINT
MID_ROWS
MINUTE
MINUTE_SECOND
MODIFY
MONTH
MONTHNAME
MYISAM
NATURAL
NUMERIC
NO
NOT
NULL
ON
OPTIMIZE
OPTION
OPTIONALLY
OR
ORDER
OUTER
OUTFILE
PACK_KEYS
PARTIAL
PASSWORD
PRECISION
PRIMARY
PROCEDURE
PROCESS
PROCESSLIST
PRIVILEGES
READ
REAL
REFERENCES
RELOAD
REGEXP
RENAME
REPLACE
RESTRICT
RETURNS
REVOKE
RLIKE
ROW
ROWS
SECOND
SELECT
SET
SHOW
SHUTDOWN
SMALLINT
SONAME
SQL_BIG_TABLES
SQL_BIG_SELECT
SQL_SMALL_RESULT
SQL_BIG_RESULT
SQL_WARNINGS
STRAIGHT_JOIN
STARTING
STATUS
STRING
TABLE
TABLES
TEMPORARY
TERMINATED
TEXT
THEN
TIME
TIMESTAMP
TINYBLOB
TINYTEXT
TINYINT
TRAILING
TO
TYPE
USE
USING
UNIQUE
UNLOCK
UNSIGNED
UPDATE
USAGE
VALUES
VARCHAR
VARIABLES
VARYING
VARBINARY
WITH
WRITE
WHEN
WHERE
YEAR
YEAR_MONTH
ZEROFILL

Index